AMERIKARMA

Good Things Come to Those Who Can't Wait

Sarah Ivens

ALSO BY THE AUTHOR:

A Modern Girl's Guide to the Perfect Single Life

A Modern Girl's Guide to Getting Organized

A Modern Girl's Guide to Networking

The Bride's Guide to Unique Weddings

A Modern Girl's Guide to Dynamic Dating

A Modern Girl's Guide to Etiquette

A Modern Girl's Guide to Getting Hitched

No Regrets: 101 Fabulous Things to Do Before You're Too Old, Married or Pregnant

For Peter, who is with us always

AMERIKARMA

Good Things Come to Those Who Can't Wait

Sarah Ivens is the founding editor in chief of OK! magazine in America. Her writing has been featured in Marie Claire, Brides, YOU, GQ, Cosmopolitan, Glamour, Hello!, CNN and The Daily Mail. She writes a baby blog for the Mail Online, the world's most popular news website. A born and bred Londoner who has made her home in Los Angeles, via New York City and Louisville, Kentucky, she is a bestselling author in her native UK.

ACKNOWLEDGEMENTS

This emotional journey into writing down my story started as a creative culminating project for my Masters in Literature at the University of Louisville in Kentucky. Thanks go to my classmates who listened to me read and offered such useful critiques and to my professor, Paul Griner, for being so encouraging, fun and helpful. Thank you also to Mathew Biberman and Suzette Henke for their kind words, Claire Misata for her excitement and Charlotte Robertson for believing. Thanks also go to Jack Phillips for his wonderfully vibrant and happy illustrations. Most thanks of course have to go to the people whose lives, as they weaved in and out of mine, are captured here. I've had to edit, condense and ignore certain conversations and events for pace and space, and of course, everything in here is seen through my often hormonal, sometimes comical, always subjective lens, but the affection I have for my family and friends is hopefully beyond question when put in black and white. This book could not have been written without the love of many people – but following the theme of my story so far, I'd like to give a special mention to Peter, Russell and William Moffett, and Keith, James and William Ivens.

CONTENTS

1

Putting It Out There

'It's a funny thing about life. If you refuse to settle for anything less than the best, that's what it will give you.'

Somerset Maugham

'We have a proposition for you. We want you to move to New York, to launch an American version of the magazine,' my editorial director tells me with the whimsical smile of an Edwardian benefactor. I stare back at him, mouth open, for what feels like hours, before turning my contemplative gaze out of his office window and down to The Thames. He misunderstands my delay in responding and adds, 'you'll be the editor in chief of course.'

New York? Editor in Chief? New York? I was currently the deputy editor of the Number One weekly celebrity magazine in Britain, OK!, and had never voiced a desire to take the top job, let alone across the Pond. I was happy with my lot – press trips, free shampoo and the occasional discount card at a department store. I loved being a journalist, a career I'd first set my sights on at the age of 11 and had pursued ever since. And I loved London. I was a born and bred Londoner. I lit up like a Christmas tree when Chas 'n' Dave played on the radio.

'Tell me more…' is all I can eventually muster in response.

The rest of our conversation – well, one-sided list of benefits and demands - goes something like this:'Your salary will be $200,000 a year. That's about $800,000 less than your contemporaries in New York will be on but you're only 29 years old and not very fancy, so it'll be enough for you. And we won't give you a bonus, any benefits or a pension. You know how we like to do things here. But if it goes well, you'll do well. Not financially but we'll invite you to speak at our annual conference perhaps. Prove yourself and we'll prove we're grateful.' He fingers his beard like a modern-day Fagin.

'Er…' My mind races to keep up with these exciting and horrifically scary offers.

'There won't be a relocation allowance or private healthcare. We won't pay for you to ship your belongings out. And there certainly isn't a company apartment or car to make your move easier. But we will pay for flights back to London if we need you to explain yourself in a board meeting,' he wiggled one of his over-sized, banana-shaped fingers in my face. 'We have sorted out a nice office on Fifth Avenue. Well, it will be nice once you've found someone – cheap – to paint it and lay the carpets. And you've got rid of the rats and unblocked the toilets.'

What an offer.

'What do you think?' He was desperate for my answer.

Being a natural blonde with a sense of adventure and a healthy dose of imposter syndrome, this all sounded marvelous. How soon could I sign?

'Yes. I'll do it. Thanks. Cool.'

'Good. We knew you'd say yes. We have every faith in you.'

'Thanks, I won't let you down.'

'We know you won't. Oh and Ms Cool,' this was a nickname I'd earned for myself not from an impressive sense of style but my unprofessional overuse of the word in business meetings, 'you leave next Sunday. We won't launch the first issue for three months but you need to hire the entire team in New York, set up the Los

Angeles office, schmooze every publicist in America and attend weekly advertising, distribution, legal, finance, public relations and marketing meetings to set up a plan of action. And those toilets certainly won't unblock themselves.'

I wished he was joking but I'd worked for the company for a year and knew how they liked their staff to multi-task.

Two days later, I gather my university girlfriends to spread the news in my favorite Italian restaurant in a tree-lined Victorian high street not far from my terraced Edwardian house. We order three bottles of Chianti and too much garlic bread. 'I have something huge to tell you,' I divulge, unable to wait for the pasta main courses to arrive to share my shocking news.

'You're moving to New York,' they reply in unison.

'Yes! What? How did you know I wasn't becoming a vet or that I was pregnant or something?' I acknowledge their spot-on answer with a grumpy defeat usually reserved for my mother when our hormones clashed in traffic jams. They snigger at such outlandish suggestions as my becoming a vet or a mother.

'I haven't ever heard you talk about wanting to become a mum,' says Hayley. 'But you've always wanted to live in NYC.'

'Have I?''

'Yes. And you've always wanted to be an editor,' explains Jo.

'Have I?'

'Yes. We know you've been praying on your knees every night for a limo life on Wall Street,' jokes Catherine. I hadn't but I suppose the idea was always in the back of my mind.

'When are you going?' Excella cuts to the chase.

'On Sunday. This Sunday. I've rented a tiny yet ridiculously expensive apartment I found on the internet for a year and hired a humongous couch and a bed to fill it with. Everything else, I'll just squeeze into my suitcase or buy once I'm over there. How hard can it be? I've been to my dentist and doctor for check-ups, Marks & Spencer's for new knickers and my grandma's for my last slice of her apple pie in a while. I'm practically ready to go.'

My friends toast my future success with a bottle of chilled cava and bear hugs as we say goodbye until Christmas – when I'd promised my mum I'd return for a visit.

One thing that wasn't so ready to go was my husband. We'd been married for four years and had spent most of our twenties together, doggedly battling to earn more than the other and arguing every Saturday.

'Why do we do this?' I'd asked on one particular stormy afternoon, as we walked across Greenwich Park to our nearby home in Blackheath. 'Why do we fight every weekend when we should be relaxing? When it should be our favorite day of the week because we get to be with each other?'

'I think it's because we've been apart for five days and we've got into our own comfortable routines, then suddenly we're thrust into each other's presence for a solid 48 hours and it's too much', was his honest answer. He was impressively climbing the slippery ladder offered to him in the film business while I tried to carve a name for myself in journalism. The stress, time and ego-building our chosen industries supplied were not proving beneficial to a happy home life. And to think our relationship had all started out so promisingly. Well, at least, we'd persuaded ourselves it had.

My husband and I had met a year after we had both graduated, at a pub in Covent Garden. I was instantly impressed by his quick wit, fine brain and love for Broadway musicals. He wasn't my usual type but my spirit had just been broken by the epitome of my usual type (a tall, fair, sporty lad with bucket loads of swagger), so I stumbled, dragging my weeping heart and shattered confidence behind me, into his eager arms. And then, when 15 months later a ring was produced on a holiday to Italy, I loved the romance of it all – and the security, the comfort I felt that a man wanted me and wasn't going to leave. On flashing my modern diamond and white gold band in my glossy magazine office the following Monday, an older - and I assumed at the time, bitter – female colleague, Liz, made herself heard forcefully above the din of oohs and aahs. 'I might like Mars bars right now,' she philosophized. 'But in ten years time I might fancy switching to Dairy Milk. Why would someone restrict themselves to a lifetime of dull, routine sweetness in such a manner?'

I was furious at such condemnation. Now, six years on, if I could go back and talk to my 23 year old self I would use her metaphor and say a similar thing: sample the whole sweet shop, and try and live without chocolate for a while, then make your decision. 'Please don't get engaged on the rebound or under the age of 30,' I'd urge myself, furiously knocking on the glass wall of delusion I'd built around this fragile relationship. My younger self wouldn't have listened though. Because 23 year olds aren't good at listening to themselves. Or their parents.

'We don't understand why you want to get married,' my mum pleaded with me at an emergency family conference when we'd just announced our engagement. 'You have everything to live for – both of you do – so why do you want to trap yourselves so early on into a relationship that could run its course in a few years.'

'How dare you! I love him!' I barked back.

'But darling, listen to the warning bells in your head. Can you really not hear them? Do you really think this young man can make you happy forever? Do you really think he is a kind man who will put you first? Does he love you with all his heart?'

'I love him!' I wailed, dripping hot tears on to the vinyl tablecloth in the little café where the three of us were seated for this painful tete-a-tete. My caring step-father, who I had called dad since I was thirteen, had chosen a public place on mutual territory in the hope of avoiding such dramatics.

'Well, you do now...' he questioned me gently.

'Always!' I bellowed 'What do you know anyway?'

'Sadly too much,' he replied. '

'I knew the marriage to your father was wrong too', my mother agreed, reaching over to take my dad's hand and giving it a squeeze. I knew they both found it hard to talk about their previous marriages in front of each other. 'I heard all these bells in my head, these warning sirens going off, yet I just pushed them away.

'Well, I know what I'm doing,' I answered quietly, blowing my nose into a paper napkin. 'You can't judge me by your own mistakes. He is clever and witty and he's doing really well in his career. I'm going to the loo.'

As I flounced off I heard my dad say, 'he hasn't got enough life for Sarah though', with a sadness in his voice that made me lock myself in that café's toilet for a considerable amount of time and weep over what I was about to do.

The wedding went ahead of course and it was fabulous fun. I was strong-willed so the chat with my parents did little else than drive a slight wedge between us, which I tried to remedy by allowing them to invite whomever they wanted and to dictate many of the finer details: the car, the bridesmaids, the menu etc. My parents responded by kindly pushing their doubts to one side and getting in the spirit of things. I think everyone, all 400 guests and my parents, had a wonderful time. I spent more time worrying about the party aspect of it than the vows, which was a self-defense mechanism I should have probably paid closer attention to. I distinctly remember walking up the aisle and thinking to myself 'I don't have to do this for ever if it gets too bad. Starter marriages are acceptable these days. There won't be too much of a scandal.' This was a totally sick thought process for a young woman in an expensive, off-white duchesse satin dress to be having as she walks towards a vicar and her fiancé, I admit, but it was how I genuinely felt at that moment. When I reached the front, I said – out of nerves I imagine – 'Alright mate?' The second we stepped out of the church, on to the grass for the classic confetti shot, he pulled me towards him with a grimace. 'You said "alright mate"? That wasn't the appropriate thing to say!"

'You know if you ever leave me,' he told me, shortly after we'd returned from our honeymoon, a two week trip to Mauritius on which I'd had a panic attack and nightly recurring nightmares that I was being suffocated, 'everyone will take my side, I'll make sure of it.'

Consciously or not, this New York job offered me a chance to escape and I think that's why I said yes so quickly. Jumping on a plane and moving across an ocean gave me the opportunity to avoid the slow, heart-breaking mock-process of a trial separation, followed by the anal splitting of joint possessions that once provided a façade to a life as a happy couple. Four years of marriage in, we were both miserable. We thought we still loved each other, but I knew – and he would soon realize – that we would be happier without each other. I wasn't the perfect wife for him: I could be needy, immature, paranoid and selfish. So I did the most seemingly cowardly and cruel thing I have ever done in my life. I accepted a job in a different country and planned a life without him, without giving him the opportunity to win me back. Or even looking back. Emotionally, I'd checked out. I wanted to cut my losses and put the whole experience down to a mistake in my twenties. I didn't want to carry this weight any longer. I wasn't ready for children and I knew that would be the expected next step; and I really didn't want my heart to feel this cold forever. I wanted my Saturdays back. I wanted to be able to answer for myself and only myself for a while. I wanted to admit that I had failed (the minute I announced our split to friends and family that was my over-riding emotion: that I was a failure) and to move on and correct it. I had less than four months until my 30th birthday and I was, somewhat naively, determined to be happier by then. I decided, as I ordered my one-way plane ticket to JFK, that I'd rather be alone than lonely in this marriage. 'I'm sorry,' was all I could pathetically offer when I made my life-changing announcement in our just-renovated kitchen. I watched with a coldness and distance that I was shocked by, as if I was looking down on someone else's defining moment. 'You can't change my mind. I'm sorry,' I said matter-of-factly.

***

Ten days after accepting the position in New York, my parents drive me to Heathrow and wait with me as I check in. My dad twitches nervously and shuffles from side to side clutching his copy of *The Daily Mail* while my caring mother fusses and bothers, stroking my hair and begging me to eat properly and to avoid street gangs. She understands why I'm going though: she'd been to the city on numerous occasions and loved the shops, restaurants and atmosphere more and more after each visit. She still proudly went to keep fit with her gym kit in a Bloomingdale's bag. My dad couldn't comprehend it though. A homebody, he'd have preferred me to remain in London perusing Laura Ashley catalogues and coming for roast dinners every Sunday in Essex than moving 3,500 miles away. He'd watched Mean Streets and The Sopranos and to him New York City represented everything that was dirty, noisy and dangerous.

'Take care, darling,' my mother stifles a sob, then my dad grabs me in an awkward cuddle and pats me on the back.

'And do remember,' she adds, looking intently into my eyes, clinging on to my dad's arm. 'That you are not a failure. Your dad and I, and your brothers, and your grandma and aunties, *we* do not think you are a failure. We think you are brave and strong. You would have been a true failure if you'd allowed this situation to carry on. You would have been a true failure if you'd given up on your own life and your own happiness. We are proud of you, darling.'

They wave me through the departure gate then my dad wraps his arm around my mother's shoulders, giving her a comforting kiss on the cheek, as they make their way back to the short stay car park. I watch them go for longer than they watch me. I feel completely alone.

In a spasm of generosity that I would no doubt pay for in the near future, the company has allowed me to embark on this new adventure in business class. With a glass of champagne in one hand – who cares if it is served in a plastic beaker – and a menu of the lunchtime delights in the other, we swing over the green patchwork of my beloved country towards a life that I know nothing about, friends I have yet to meet, a city I don't understand and a magazine that does not exist. Shit. I did keep making these rash decisions without thinking them through. I was so desperate to run away; perhaps I hadn't looked sensibly at what I was running into.

2

If I Can Make It There, I'll Make It Anywhere

'Live all you can; it's a mistake not to. It doesn't so much matter what you do in
particular, so long as you have your life.'

Henry James

My first day in the Fifth Avenue office is unremarkable considering
I'd just left everything I'd ever known to take on the challenge of
launching a weekly magazine in the most vicious, competitive media
market in the world. My new headquarters is the entire second floor
of an impressive Art Deco building opposite the Public Library,
surrounded by Starbucks signs and harshly lit shops offering 3 'I
heart NY' t shirts for $10. I meet the doorman, Tony, a bearded
Brooklynite who can't understand a word I'm saying and then I
locate a Prêt A Manger, which thrills me as I was sure I'd have
missed their brie, basil and tomato baguettes as much as I'd have
missed my close family. And the London office calls. The bosses
have demanded I set up a video-cam on my desk, so they can check
I'm there and talk to me 'face to face' when needed. 'We want to be
sure you're not eating hot dogs on Coney Island,' my bearded boss
alerts me. 'We need you in the office, 24/7, hiring staff and getting
to know American celebrity culture inside and out. This is no joking
matter.' I don't know why he thought I'd be laughing. I was terrified.

A week into my new life in Manhattan, I'm still jet lagged. Know-it-
alls warn you this will happen, that you'll be waking up at 4.30am
day after day in NYC, and it's true. Living in a rabbit hutch of thin
white walls and cheap pine floors on Sixth Avenue doesn't help –
the car beeping, shouting and garbage trucks have driven me so mad

already that I could totally understand why New Yorkers have a reputation for being more crazy than Londoners or Parisians. A few well-travelled friends of mine warned me to not to live in Chelsea, to head for the quieter Upper East Side or The Village, or even the up and coming Williamsburg in Brooklyn, but of course I thought I knew best. Chelsea was within walking distance of work, very fashionable and very gay. This meant it was a totally safe place for a 29-year-old girl to live on her own. A little too safe perhaps. I didn't get admiring glances in my new neck of the woods, except on my first day, when a cowboy in hot pants stopped me in the rain to ask me where I'd got my Giles Deacon umbrella.

Far from being glamorous and sexy in fact, my first month in NYC involved 12 hour days in the office, too much pizza from Ray, the Italian stallion with a family business on my block (I'd decided not to cook: due to space constrictions, I'd converted the oven into a place to store my shoes), an insatiable addiction to Fruit Punch Snapple and an insane need to cover my apartment in photos of my friends and family back from home. The bare walls were soon covered in blue-tak smudges and smiling faces, drunk poses and sun burnt shoulders. This may sound miserable but on the whole my new life and attempt at singledom was easier than I'd imagined and I knew already I'd done the right thing; the nagging voices of my failure were slowly being drowned out by the constant groan of the angry, concrete animal I now called home and I was too busy during the day to miss anyone. The reality of being alone only whispered in my ears as I tried to get to sleep at night. It was in those dark hours, when I wasn't trying to launch a $100 million magazine that I cried myself to sleep, exhausted and scared, trying to ignore the huge question marks dangling from my ceiling. In a symbolic bid to feel more connected to my new life, by week three I'd taken to saying goodnight to the Empire State Building out of my bedroom window. It came to represent something bright, hopeful and constant to watch over me. Every few days it would change colors as if to remind me that nothing stays the same and that was a good thing. *Each chapter in our lives can be just as beautiful as the next, just*

17

different, it would remind me. *And some of the new chapters we have yet to write could send us soaring into the sky.*

***

British people like to imagine that Americans are the same as us. This is not true. We couldn't be more different. We loosely, I was discovering, share a language and a love of Prince Harry but that's about it. We love football. They don't understand it. Take That are our national treasures. They've never heard of them. We enjoy a simple cuppa. The Yanks aren't happy if they haven't got a double choc-chip mint skinny mocha-chino. On ice. To go. With sweetener.

A month into my new job in NYC, I had gathered about 400 resumes to sort through and with these the difference between our nations becomes all the clearer. I needed to hire writers, editors, graphic designers, copy editors, personal assistants and picture researchers. The magazine couldn't launch without a team of 50 media darlings signed and sealed immediately; and they had to be Americans, which meant I had to work out what they were rattling on about in their letters of application. For starters, there's no date of birth – it isn't acceptable in the US to ask how old someone is in case it puts you off employing them, and I'd been warned not to ask how old anyone is during the interviewing process. And there's no note of nationality either. That's considered politically incorrect. The biggest difference between US and UK job-seekers however is that from these CVs, you'd think I had the media equivalent of 400 Einstein-taught Picassos with Donald Trump's business acumen to select my team from. In the UK, people tend to underplay their successes – not mentioning netball captaincies, charity work or fluency in multiple languages. Here in NYC, everything was mentioned – and everything was the best, the biggest, the brightest… the bollocks basically. Unfortunately, there was a huge whiff of bullshit around most of it. I battled through the pile and set up a hellish timetable of interviews. Here are some examples of the gemstones I discover:

18

Interviewee 1: The Disillusioned Peroxide Princess

'I was an intern for the President, he adored me, but I decided to abandon politics in the end. I was too attractive, too blonde, and too curvy. I drove the men wild. It got totally inappropriate. Then I moved in to radio, but the producers wouldn't leave me alone, I was too attractive for radio. So I figure magazines are the best place for me. It's mostly women so it'll be hands off. Unless there are lesbians on staff of course...'

Interviewee 2: The Psychotic Jane Bond

'To earn regular money, I do picture research but secretly I'm in the FBI. I can't promise to work the full five days because I never know when I will be called upon to perform a secret mission for the government. They will fly me back to the office in a helicopter and drop me on the roof of your building once my work is completed though.'

Interviewee 3: The Stalker

'I love love love celebrities! I live them, I breathe them, I think like them... and the chance to work on a celebrity magazine - wow wow wow! It would be heaven. I could research them for you and cut out pictures and stick them up around the office and go backstage at concerts and tell them all about the magazine. Celebrities love me. And their parents love me too. I often meet them when I'm standing on doorsteps and in really cold weather some of the parents have offered me a hot drink after a few hours of waiting.'

Interviewee 4: The Brazilian

'Eh?' (He didn't speak English – but he was very, very handsome and came into the office in his motorbike leathers!)

Interviewee 5: The Neurotic Fashionista

'This season it's all about trees and green and life and feeling fresh in your clothes. And being thin. Really thin. But having curves too. And good skin. And not eating. And here are some mood boards I did on my bedroom floor last night. Don't you just worship at the shrine of John Galliano? I do. I kneeled down and prayed last night for him to inspire my mood boards for this job interview.'

I'd love to say I threw this mad bunch out of the building, but I was new in town and I had a lurking fear that all Americans were crazy so I couldn't do any better and I hired three out of the five mentioned above. (And it wasn't just because he drove a motorbike!) And a selection of others who I sensed had promise and/or good experience in celebrity weeklies. I had my team.

The last day of interviews lasted from 8am to 8pm and it was exhausting. Of course I'd have loved to go home for an early night with my tasty new lovers – Pizza and Snapple - but there was a burning issue at hand: I needed to make friends. I'd never had to make an effort before. I found friends at school, at university, at work… some of them I found in dive bars in the East end … and they'd always been on hand and happy to share a Bombay Sapphire and tonic with me when I needed it. In NYC, I had no one.

Willing this to change and for my Blackberry address book to expand with more than corrupt Hollywood agents and Chinese food delivery numbers, I head after work to the hottest hairdressing salon in Manhattan. Mathew is a fellow imported Brit, six months into his time in the Big Apple, who I'd heard about from journo friends back in England. 'Sweetie!' he wrestles me into a revolving chair and covers me in plush white towels. 'I believe a girl can never be too blonde, too British, or have too many deep conditioning treatments.' We proceed to bond over a champagne-fuelled chat about my split ends and his fashion designer ex-boyfriend who wouldn't commit and just used him for sex, and who then eventually stopped using him for sex, which was even worse. After two hours, I am Carolyn Besette Kennedy blonde ('You have to be! It's New York!') And perfectly layered. Mathew is miserable from all the talk of his ex, his asexual fashionista.

Sensing I have an opportunity to make my first friend, I suggest what he needs is a night out with the girls (i.e. me) and so we head to Soho House, a swanky private club where he is a member. 'It's a bit more *so-so* than *Soho* now,' he admits, as we sway along the dark corridors and into a sexily-lit elevator up to the pool deck, 'and the service is so slow, but it's still the only natural habitat for all us wet-behind-the-ears Britons on Manhattan Island, so you'll need to come here regularly to feel sane again.'

Soho House was everything a homesick, patriotic Brit Stateside could want. For a start, it had a snooker room where you could smoke. Yes, cigarettes – the scourge of New York for a few years – were happily lit and inhaled at this private members club. I looked forward to waking up the next morning, my throat sore and my hair stinking like an ashtray, as it had every weekend during my three glory years at Kent University in Canterbury, which was the last time I had felt as free and full of promise as I did now. Mathew and I celebrated finding each other by chaining four Marlboro lights in quick succession, swigging bright pink Cosmopolitans and scoring the snooker players bottoms out of ten as they bent over to take shots.

'Now let me give you the lowdown, gorgeous,' he taps my knee conspiratorially and leans in, as we take a seat on a red velvet chaise longue in a quiet corner. 'This place is murder! New York I mean. The straight men are arrogant, the straight women will try and destroy you and the gays may look pretty but they'll eat you alive. And you will love every minute of it.' I raise an eyebrow as I gulp down some alcohol in fear. 'Seriously, you will. For all the horror and the mayhem, there is no place like it in the world for pure, selfish fun and frolics. Just remember the following,' he raises his left hand and starts counting with his fingers. 'Never look up; everyone will assume you're a tourist. Avoid the L train in the evenings. Start tipping your doorman immediately. Do not go into

Irish bars. And make plans for every Sunday in advance. That's the day that kills you here, especially if you're single. You can go from Saturday night to Monday morning without speaking to anyone other than your local barista and dry cleaner. You could have been eaten by your own plughole and in New York no one would know.'

'Brunch at Pastis this Sunday then?' I suggest desperately. And thankfully he agrees.

Five cosmos and a misguided attempt at setting fire to a shot of drambuie and downing it in one later; I stumble out on to the shiny cobbles of the Meat Packing District. Sequined fashionistas try to balance on four inch stilettos as yellow taxis hurtle past them, playing dodge ball with tourists and street-meat vending carts. New Jersey glamour pusses attempt to remain calm as they are told to join the end of snake-like nightclub queues, while the bouncers immediately usher in rich silver foxes with hanger-thin teens dangling around their neck. It's all so wonderful and different from home, I admit to myself, as I kiss my one and only friend on each cheek and slump into a yellow bumper car. 'Someone saved my life tonight,' I warble along to the radio as we dart up the numbered streets to Chelsea, to my new home. 'And my savior is a gay hairdresser from Birmingham,' I squeal in delight, astonishing the snoozing doorman in my building's lobby as I sway up to the 25th floor, to my tiny, photo-papered apartment. I can't quite be bothered to get undressed or take off my makeup, so I just switch my Blackberry to vibrate and place it on the pillow next to my head. Dizzy from the cocktails and excitement, I forget to say good night to my old friend, the Empire State Building, who is winking at me through the rainy shadows on my windowpane. *What doesn't kill you makes your stronger*, I hear amongst the drizzle.

***

Amazingly, three months after my bombshell job offer back in London, the magazine comes out to a fanfare of criticism (from our competitors), excitement (from tabloid junkies and Anglophiles) and exhaustion (among the 50 staff I'd hired a short while previously) while my bosses back in Blighty just send me rude emails. But together, we'd pulled together a production schedule, a distribution network, a non-embarrassing amount of advertising pages and one hundred pages of adequate – if not world-changing – celebrity content. Jessica Simpson had done an exclusive photo shoot and interview for our first cover and she looked beautiful, even if her words were a little bland (something I had already become immune to amongst American starlets).

The day the first issue hits the newsstand also happens to be my 30th birthday, so instead of succumbing to a hot bath and an extra slice of pizza (which would have been my honest preference), I call in some favors from my new-found contacts and take over the fourth floor of Planet Hollywood which overlooks the bright lights of Times Square and is therefore to me, still uniquely and wonderfully New York. One of the owners is an English guy who loves to welcome any fellow Brit to NYC, so to celebrate my arrival he generously throws in an open bar, a hot and cold buffet and an 80s disco (at my special request) for my New York friends – who had now grown in number from one to about ten by this time – and my hard-working colleagues. There are also a few newspaper columnists and television crews in attendance. Apparently I am the youngest editor in chief in New York, and therefore one to watch. Not so much for my successes, as my failures, I would find out the next morning.

After a decadent night of grapevining to Duran Duran, feasting on two birthday cakes (one for me, one for the magazine) and wearing a joke t shirt gifted to me by a publicist that said So Happy I'm Thirty (which spelt SHIT! In huge letters across my boobs), I awake to my first brush with the infamous Page 6 column in the New York Post. I ring my mum in tears.

'It says that no one showed up, that the few people who did complained about the nasty buffet and terrible music, and that I'm pretending to be some Carrie Bradshaw character – without her fashion sense or writing ability.' I hyperventilate down the phone while my mother tries to soothe my fears.

'Well, darling, this sounds like someone is jealous to me,' which was her biased, stock response to anyone who criticized her only daughter. 'You're the youngest editor in New York, and you're British. People are bound to be annoyed you've gone over there and made a success of yourself. How many people came to your party?'

'There were about a hundred of us, and it was really fun. We all got tipsy, and danced, and ate, and celebrated pulling off quite a feat. It was fabulous. And no one had to pay for a drink! That was the best bit'

'See, there you go! And do you seriously think you are trying to be a Carrie Bradshaw, whoever she is?'

'No, that's the most ridiculous bit! I *can* be accused of forcing people on to the dance floor when a Wham! song comes on, but I cannot be accused of confusing my very British, editor, and 30 year old self with a 40 year old American fashionista who has the luxury of tinkering away at a dating column from her boujis apartment in Manolos all day. My bottom is too big for that!'

'Well ignore it then. Just cling on to what you told me last week when you were planning the party: how lucky you felt to have so many great new people in your new life; that you've been given a second chance; and the fact that a kind donor was offering to buy all the cocktails for everyone. Drinks are bloody expensive in that city! Enjoy it honey. No one can make you feel bad about yourself unless you allow them to.'

'Have you been reading self-help books again?' I joke, feeling better in a way only a nice chat with your mum can make you feel.

'Perhaps. Now, go get 'em. Keep making us proud over there.'

My divorce papers arrive a short while later, heralding the beginning of a new time when I would be the one reading self-help books. My doorman hands me the recorded delivery envelope and wishes me a good evening. Looking down at the official letter and the court stamp, my heart sinks into my stomach and for the first time in the whole process, I experience serious doubts. What had I done? He was a good man. We just weren't compatible. Would I now be alone forever? The date and venue of our wedding are typed across the decree absolute and the black and whiteness of it freezes my brain. Now what? Now I had got what I wanted – my freedom, for the price of a London home and a bad reputation amongst certain people who once cared for me - what should I do with it? I fold the paper and place it at the bottom on an IKEA box I was using to store my apartment lease and my employment contract, run a hot bath, plunge myself into the water and cry until my hands and feet turn into the wrinkled extremities of an 80 year old. 'What have I done? What will I do?' I repeat to myself, over and over, shivering as the steam dissipates and my alarm clock ticks steadily into the early hours of the morning.

By morning, my head is clearer. *I know what I'll do*, I thought to myself as I power-walked uptown through the sea of grey suits to the office in my Birkenstocks, cappuccino in one hand and lox bagel in the other. *I'll keep so busy I won't have to think about what I've done. And I will grab every opportunity that comes my way until I realize I made the right decision to come here. I'll travel America and try new things. I'll make the magazine a huge success and I'll nurture my team. I'll get drunk and dance on tables if I want to and sleep all weekend if I need to. And if living on my own in a foreign country with this scary job doesn't teach me who and what is important to me, I'll use some of this money I'm earning to have some experts winkle it out of me.*

***

The following few months in New York were spent doing just that and although I missed London and my friends and family, the painful daily longing for them was lessening and I felt alive and

25

needed and respected in a way I had never felt before. Running away had worked. On my first year anniversary of living there I queued to go up the Empire State Building with thousands of tourists and looked down on the crowded streets that I marched every day with a new sense of familiarity. This was my home, for the time being anyway. The magazine was starting to be a success. I had my Sundays covered most weeks. And my private yoga teacher said my muscle tone had improved massively. If Frank Sinatra was on the money, I had every right to be proud of myself.

3

The Golden Girl

'There are certain things we feel to be beautiful and good, and we must hunger after them.'

George Eliot

I glide into the twinkling ballroom feeling like Cinderella. Seriously, for the first time in my life I look like a princess. And it feels damn good. 'That dress is amazing,' my faithful colleague Jen tells me again, not that I need to hear it. I know it. Thanks to my position at the magazine and my Britishness, the hip new red carpet designers Marchesa have started donating me gowns to wear to all and every fabulous occasion. Two wonderful London girls who came to New York around the same time as me, we bonded over the ubiquitous Soho House cocktail list during our first year in the city and incredible, sequined, feathered, jewel colored gowns had been couriered in white bags straight to my office ever since. Tonight, I'm in a heavily beaded midnight blue gown... with a train! Yes, a train. Well, I was at Elton John's Oscar party in Beverly Hills. Even an Essex girl like me can class it up when it's absolutely required.

As I sweep (for that is all I can do in this floor-length number, sweep) into the party and am handed a crisp flute of Moet & Chandon, I feel like I'm entering a living, breathing Madame Tussards. A-listers are everywhere (embarrassingly wrestling each other for the free goody bags) and admiring the billions of dollars of bling dangling from everyone's ears and throats. I meet up with my LA partner-in-crime, Tara Reid, the party girl who is actually a total sweetheart and a good person to be around (until she has you looking for her phone in bushes. Seriously, I'd never been out with her and she hadn't lost her phone) and we go and chat to Victoria Beckham, who is polite but, quite rightly, disinterested.

The only downside to attending such fabulous Hollywood events was that I usually had to attend them with my big boss from London. We'd always got on quite well, which isn't actually a good reflection on my character, because he is a notoriously difficult, loose cannon of a man who made his money in porn and swore a lot. He'd given me this opportunity though (which, if he had been saner and less of a loose cannon wouldn't have happened, cause this job clearly shouldn't have been given to a 29 year old who'd never edited a magazine in America before) so I felt I owed him my hard work and attention... and would do my best not to complain as he puffed cigar smoke in my face, as he had once done continuously as we flew his private jet between LA and NYC a few months earlier, or started fights on my behalf in public places, or swore at me.

A year into our operation, we'd set up a swanky office near Rodeo Drive which I had to visit every couple of months for meetings and pep talks with the West Coast team. I refused to drive in LA so the CFO reluctantly agreed that I could stay at a hotel within walking distance of the West Coast Bureau. Luckily for me, and not so luckily for the budgets, the only hotel that fitted the bill was the Regent Beverly Wilshire: the Reg Bev Wil made famous in the Pretty Woman movie. It soon became my home from home and the suite they put me up in each time was twice the size of my minute NYC abode, and the bath tub four times as big as my office. It was during these stays that I felt more content in my new big, scary role. Not hard to imagine why, I'm sure. Being greeted by name in the marble lobby, and having little treats left on your pillow and flowers in your lounge every day, would make anyone happy. I'd host girl-power lunches in cabanas by the pool with important publicists, agents and celebrities, and head to hot spots like Nobu, Mr. Chow and Orso for early suppers with renowned photographers and television presenters. As my knowledge of LA and its movers and shakers grew, so did the magazine's reputation and success. It was a win-win. Even slipping a few steps down a gigantic glass staircase after a business lunch with my boss (where he told me to stop showing him up and calm down as I clung inelegantly to the banister), couldn't break my belief that my baby, the magazine, was growing up steadily and I was the captain of its smooth sailing. Two years after our shaky launch, we were the seventh biggest retail magazine in America with the most PR hits of any celebrity tabloid out there. My critics, and there were many, didn't want to admit it, but the magazine was doing well and I'd done a rather good job.

As the magazine grew, so did the invitations that poured into my Manhattan corner office or suite at the Regent Beverly Wilshire. I went to a few parties at the Playboy Mansion, once on an uncomfortably humid night when I had to pull a red silk Marchesa dress up to my knees to dip my toes in the sullied waters of Hugh Hefner's saucy water grotto.

'How many people do you think have had sex in here?' Jen grimaced, her face distorted even more by the flickering candles placed around the rock-carved den, on one summer visit.

'Gross. Don't. You'll put me off the canapés,' I said, heading towards the ice flume and Ryan Seacrest.

'Well, just make sure you don't get added to the long list tonight!' We both laughed. We should have been so lucky. While work was flourishing, our love lives were non-existent. Most of the women I knew in LA and New York, and back in London, were single. Some, like me, had just come out of tricky relationships while others hadn't ever had anyone special. Some loved being single, others hated it. Things would change, I knew I needed to get back in the saddle, but at that very moment I'd have resented sharing my plush, peaceful bed with anyone; especially any of the bizarrely tall and monotonous basketball players on offer at the Playboy Mansion. Hugh Hefner was the most interesting man there by a mile.

29

Hugh Hefner was a total sweetheart – as were his girlfriends at the time Holly, Kendra and Bridget – so I got to take my brother there on his 21st birthday. He bonded with Kendra, the youngest of Hugh's playthings, over sports and BBQ and declared me to be a fine, fine sister. I was constantly grateful for the unusual, crazy things I got to see and do and was thrilled when my friends and family came over the pond to share them with me. Taking my mum and dad to Vegas to see Celine Dion was a highlight. 'We're in the second row!' my mum squealed as we took our seats.

'Its $150, are you sure?' my dad checked after the show, when I took them to Tao, the hottest Asian Bistro on the strip and he eyed up the Kobe steak. 'Seriously, we've featured this place many, many times in the magazine and they said they'd love to treat us,' I assured him. 'They're famous for throwing celebrity birthday parties and we always run a photo or two.' As if to prove my point, after our decadent dinner of steak and sushi, we are ushered upstairs past the giant Buddha to Kevin Ferderline's birthday extravaganza. 'I don't like all this semi-naked women business,' my dad said uncomfortably, trying to avert his eyes from the topless ladies, posing decoratively in bathtubs full of rose petals. 'But it's interesting to see what Janet Jackson looks like in real life.' At 2am, it was me who was desperate to get back to the Bellagio and bed, not my 59 year old parents.

'We've had a great weekend, Sarah,' my mum pecked me on the cheek the afternoon after our Celine and steak parent-daughter bonding, before our separate flights homewards, choosing to spend our last hour together sipping Strawberry Daiquiri from a 2ft plastic Eiffel Tower in the faux-French bistro at the Paris Hotel. You could take two girls out of Essex but you could never take the Essex out of a girl.

The West Coast provided my most fabulous editrix moments for sure. Amongst the Palm trees and fake boobs, my job became the glamorous occupation others assumed it was. The reality of New York was long days, grim Subway journeys home, cockroaches and rats, and mean, highly-strung people who couldn't see that their jobs in tabloid media were quite unimportant in the grand scheme of things, so they didn't need to - and indeed shouldn't - act like they were the saviors of the free world. A few years in to my tenure, there were things I truly loved about New York (skating around the Rockefeller Christmas tree, burst sprinklers in the heat of summer, gorging on Crackerjack at the Yankee Stadium) and loved about my job when I was in the city. Backstage passes at Madison Square Garden to mingle with Barry Manilow and Roger Daltry after their shows, sitting front row next to a charming Kim Cattrall and a doll-likeTori Spelling during Fashion Week, flirting with Diddy at the Gansevoort Hotel, sitting next to Jennifer Aniston at one of her film premiers and being envious of her unbelievably shiny, smooth hair; being introduced to Jennifer Lopez at a fashion party and wishing I hadn't worn heels, because at nearly 6 foot, I already made this exquisite superstar look like a Latino oompa-loompa... stylish and stunning, yet still an oompa-loompa.

But I found New York to be a hard place to stay bright and cheerful. Los Angeles – with its close proximity to the ocean and constant sunshine – suited me more and my most mwah-mwah moments definitely happened out West. Amusing the fervently Anglo-loving Britney Spears with my 'awesome accent' on a shoot high up in the Hollywood Hills; impersonating London cabbies in a spontaneous comedy skit designed to amuse a bored looking George Clooney at a Golden Globes party; getting covered in kisses by supermodel Janice Dickinson, who insisted I had lovely boobs; swaying with Sharon Stone 10 feet from Elton John as he performed Tiny Dancer on the piano; watching The Eagles make a rare performance while Dustin Hoffman clapped at the next table.

Uncomfortable moments and embarrassing situations kept my feet on the ground during all my visits to Hollywood. I slipped over on the dance floor of Teddy's nightclub one night and couldn't get up without the help of two burly bodyguards thanks to a foolishly tight dress. Another time, I went to grab a pedicure at a swanky

Westwood spa and the therapist painfully inhaled when I took my Uggs off and insisted on wearing a face mask for my entire treatment. My oldest friend Claire came to visit from London around Halloween one year and I took her to Universal Studios where I proceeded to jump out of my skin at the surprise appearance of an actor dressed as a mummy in the haunted house, leaping unintentionally over the 'keep off' barrier and landing on a pile of skulls and bones, where I remained until security pulled me out. Another time I attended a charity event wearing a dress that, when I was snapped under a weird florescent light, had an incongruous looking stain on the crutch than looked Monica Lewinsky-esque. No, I could never believe my own hype – although it would have been quite possible if I'd been blessed with an abundance of self-confidence. Yes, I was told I was wonderful, and clever, and pretty on constant rotation but I was always aware people were talking to my status and position not to the real me. The real me was rather boring. A few years into my American life, I still liked early nights, cups of tea and biscuits and secretly re-reading Sweet Valley High books in bed.

The truth was I was knackered. A star seemed to plan her wedding or divorce announcement for any weekend I had mentally decided to relax for a bit. One weekend when I had a friend in town, Brad and Angelina decided to auction Shiloh's baby photos and I ended up being locked in a room in the downtown Getty offices overnight with my picture editor. Another weekend when a colleague and I decided to escape the cold and head to Puerto Rico for a couple of night, Demi Moore and Ashton Kutcher got married, we won the photo exclusive, and we were forced to spend the weekend in our hotel's business centre waiting for contracts to be signed and faxed. One weekend just before Christmas was spent panicking that our mega-expensive exclusive – an interview and shoot with a newly pregnant, unmarried and 16 year old Jamie Lynn Spears – had leaked and calling everyone I knew in the industry to try and silence web sites and gossip columnists. I loved the pace and the drama and the process of getting things done, but I really yearned for a simpler time when I was not the one with my head on a chopping block all the time.

'I won't do this forever,' I reassured my mum during one of my weekly phone calls home.

'Good, because your dad and I don't approve of how your boss talks to you and the intrusive demands he makes on your life. We've read about him, Sarah, and he sounds like a nightmare.'

'Yes, but I'm the lucky one. I don't have to work in the same office as him anymore. Well, not regularly, anyway.'

'Yes, well, don't get sucked in and start thinking all this celebrity business is real life. Or that America is the place to stay for good. We do worry you're going to meet some New York doctor or lawyer and stay over there, away from your family, forever,' she said.

'It won't happen. I really haven't met an American I fancy yet, so don't worry. American men are not for me. And I'm probably not for them either.'

This all changed one day in Hollywood on a celebrity shoot. The starlet was acting like a diva, being rude to the hair and makeup people and generally misbehaving. After a few hours of placating her and her team, while trying to motivate mine, I escaped to the garden with a bottle of water for a breather. There was the photographer's assistant, all 6ft 4inches of him, dressed in jeans that showed off his ass and a tight-fitting t shirt. He had longish, curly, blonde hair and piercing blue eyes. Nice, I thought, feeling a stirring that hadn't happened for months. A stirring that was so foreign to me I almost didn't recognize what it as: lust.

Luckily, my colleague emerged into the garden just as my inability to make small talk with a man I fancied was becoming apparent (all I'd uncovered was that we was called Noah and liked to surf). Her loyalty to me extended to inviting him out with us that evening, for drinks and dinner. He said yes. She told him where and when. We continued with the shoot and my first date in a long, long time was happening without me having to do a thing.

'You're very sexy, Sarah,' Noah's breathe was hard and heavy in my ear, a few hours later. The others in our group had decided to call it a night but we'd agreed to go on for another drink, spurred on by our raging hormones and mutual attraction, and ended up the corner of a dark bar in West Hollywood. He'd leaned in for a kiss as soon as we sat down, pulling me towards him in a manly grasp. My heart did flips and an unfamiliar, pleasant twinge worked its way down from there. 'Feel that.' He took my hand and placed it half way down his jeaned-thigh and pushed it up and down, over an impressive bulge. 'That's all yours if you want it.' This was more of a statement than a question. 'It's all there for you to enjoy, baby.' Oh bugger. American men – in my limited experience – all sounded like they were acting in a soft porn film the moment they got an erection. He stuck his tongue in my ear and groaned loudly.

'Thanks so much,' I replied, my overtly British politeness quite deflating his bulge I'm sure, if not his ego. 'That's really nice of you, but do you mind if we get going now. I have a 7am meeting I'm not prepared for it at all.' His eyes didn't shine with disappointment; the look was more of immense shock. He was a gorgeous man, after all. We carried on kissing for a few more minutes, then as we walked towards his car, he tried to dry hump me against a wall in a last ditch attempt to get an invite up to my hotel room, but the moment had gone. We swapped phone numbers – and he promised to look me up in New York when he visited the city for work the following month.

'Honey, you need to sort this whole situation out!' Mathew disciplined me harshly, as I recounted the tale of my missed sexual opportunity when we met up in Soho House the following week. 'You're either working or you're hanging out with poofs like me. It has to change, sweetie! Us gay men are fabulous but we're not going to shag you and we sure as hell aren't going to marry you. So stop expecting a straight man to be as pretty, charming and likeable as me and get your end away.' He was only half joking, I could tell. And he was right. Fuelled by our customary cocktails, Mathew watches over me as I send Noah a sexy text and wait for his reaction to come back. We only have to wait a few minutes. *Sounds good babe. In NYC next week. Lets hook up.*

Donning my sexiest matching underwear – a sheer pink set I'd bought in London the previous summer – I was nervous as I went to meet Noah in a hipster-heavy French bistro in Brooklyn. I showed up late to show I wasn't too eager, and he was already there with a group of friends (who eyed me up and down) to show he was not taking our date too seriously. We shared a few blonde beers and banter about England en masse; before his photographer buddies called it a night and we got a taxi to my place. He assumed what was going to happen next. 'I've been thinking about you Sarah,' he did the old nibbly ear business again. 'I've been masturbating about you.'

Would it have been wrong to muzzle him? He was so pretty when he didn't talk. I decided the best way to keep him quiet without illegally choking him is to just keep kissing, so we kissed for the whole $20 taxi ride (which it is assumed I'd pay for, like it was assumed I'd pay for his and his friends drinks) and we even continued kissing in my lobby, in front of my shocked night doorman, and in the lift up to my apartment. As soon as the doors closed, his clothes hit the floor of my lounge. Then he began taking my clothes off, and admiring my matching bra and knickers which I was pleased about to be honest because they were quite expensive, and pulled me into my bedroom and... As we walked to the Subway the following morning, and shared our awkward goodbyes before catching trains going in the opposite direction, we both knew we didn't have chemistry. I probably wouldn't have had chemistry with a laboratory technician at that point in my life.

Noah did unblock something though, so for the next few months I tried to get excited by the men I met... or could meet if I stopped working all the time and hanging out with gay guys. Katie, my deputy at the magazine and fellow single girl, and I went on an extended manhunt we christened 'Margarita Month.' Every evening would begin with a couple of frozen margaritas at the outdoor bar in Bryant Park and then we'd go somewhere we were sure hot, single men would be. So we tried the comedy clubs in the Meat Packing District, and the sushi bars around Wall Street. We even went to an Ultimate Fighting Championship match in New Jersey and a Yankees game in The Bronx. 'Nada! Nothing! Rien!' she quipped, night after disappointing night. 'We really are marooned on an island of gay men and single women.'

No one floated our boats. Disillusioned by the standard of men on offer, I accepted a date with an advertising executive we nicknamed Cat Man, whose clothes and apartment smelt of the three cats he had locked up in there all day long; cats who peed on his belongings in protest when he went away on business trips. I had another date with a graphic designer who tried to undo my bra under my blouse while we were out in a restaurant, then proceeded to fall asleep in a cigar lounge we'd gone to for after dinner drinks. I left him sleeping and pegged it. After a few months of trying to find a decent man in Manhattan, I gave up. I returned to my life of girlie dinners, early nights and business drinks and was much happier for it. I may have been over my ex-husband but I wasn't quite ready to move on to the next, and hopefully very real, love of my life just yet. And my women's intuition was telling me I wouldn't find him in NYC, packaged up in a Macy's bag, anyway.

Besides as this point, I only had eyes for one boy and he was back in England. Archie, my new, adorable little nephew had just been born. Yes, my younger brother James and his wife had had their first child and I was a besotted auntie. It felt a little weird and out of the natural order of things that my six years younger brother had the first child in the family, and got to decide what names would be given by the grandchildren to my mum and dad, but my overwhelming happiness for them and love for Archie dampened any shocking outbursts of jealousy or childish petulance. I wasn't ready for a baby of my own but it made the possibility of one, and the love I would one day feel for one for my own, all the clearer. If I loved Archie this much, I couldn't imagine the overwhelming joy my own baby would give me – and I felt excited for the future when I would be a mum for the first time. Forward thinking, I asked my friend Claire to post me a new egg testing kit that was available in England. It arrived a few days later, and I was happy to see a good result appear in the test screen. It couldn't tell me everything, or guarantee an easy conception but it told me one thing: I was still producing eggs. Now, I could put motherhood on the backburner again for a bit without worrying unduly.

***

The highlight of the year, and indeed my whole career up to this point, was the rather cheesy, glittery honor of being asked to be one of the judges of Miss America. I, along with my fellow judges (who included a breakfast news presenter, the casting director of High School Musical, an Olympic Gold-winning athlete, and a self-help guru) arrived in Las Vegas for a week of intense judging, discriminating and bickering. We were assigned security guards, for the state fans got a bit intrusive and aggressive when fighting for the title, and suites at The Venetian Hotel. For five days, we sat in a conference room – fuelled by terrible coffee and energy bars – meeting the 52 contestants (the British Virgin Islands and Puerto Rico were included) and listening to their awesome views on politics, religion and social justice. Awesomely bad, mostly. It wasn't their fault. They were young and desperate to win, brainwashed by right-wing, religious parents from some backward state, I figured. Progressive, this tournament was not. Anyhow, we somehow whittled the girls down to a smaller number, and then a smaller number – ready for the live televised final.

After a week of being wined and dined by every billionaire on the Strip, abandoning the gym in favor of the free mini bar, and sitting on my bottom all day watching 18 year olds strut their stuff, my Marchesa strapless, silver-beaded, grey floor-length gown was a bit of a struggle to get on. After a confidence boosting search for Spanx (which I thankfully found) and a trip a professional hair and make-up person, I emerged, blinking on to the judge's panel on stage, ready for the world. I was done up 'for television', which meant I looked horrendously clownish in person – all fake cheekbones, white panda eyes and penciled in lips and brows – but apparently fine on screen, which was more important. I had my own little support group yelping from the auditorium: my camp confidantes from London, Emma, David and Hasz, had flown in for the weekend, the magazine's publicist and a dear friend, Brian, had come to protect me and party from NYC and a few of my English chums from LA had driven up that day once I assured them I had tickets and there were lots of hot – if young and bible-bashing – women for them to ogle and ultimately, try to fornicate with.

'I'm all about the baton-twirler,' I decreed, impressed by the height with which she could throw her flaming sticks, do a few cartwheels, and catch them without injuring herself or the crowd. My new ubiquitous gay friend, the casting director, agreed. The others were torn in the talent round by the ballerina and the opera singer. I mean, it was all pretty pathetic, but they were young. And they needed college fund money. This was a good thing.

After the talent round came the bit of the show I'd been dreading: the swimsuit bit. Who was I to judge, velcroed by the pubes into my breath-restricting knickers? 'I feel most uncomfortable about this,' I confessed to the self-help guru, whose eyes were on stalks and mouth slightly slack. 'Think of it as it we're judging their health and their attitude to fitness,' he replied nonchalantly, and then voted for the clearly anorexic girl who'd mysteriously held on to her massive boobs. I voted for the girl with a runner's body. I'd always admired people that ran, having no desire to do so myself – unless it was to secure the last seat in a crowded cake shop.

My least favorite contestant of the final five won. She was blonde, and all-American, and gave cheesy answers. I was disappointed for my stocky, piano-playing, intelligent first choice. The television recording finished, we went back stage to congratulate the winner and get some press photos taken, and then I grabbed my fellow judges and my gang out front, and we limo-ed our way to the Bellagio and to a club opening. A PR acquaintance of mine had promised a fabulous night if I dragged everyone to Bond. For one week only, you see, we'd ruled Vegas: the judges' names, mine included had been blasted on constant rotation on 50ft digital billboards in the city. Everyone knew the Miss America pageant was in town and we were part of it. 'I feel like a rock star,' the self-help guru said, as we ploughed through the hotel en masse. I belled the PR on his mobile and as we approached the excited throngs he divided the crowd on the red carpet like he was Moses parting the Red Sea. 'This is pure class,' my friend David from London grinned. 'How can I ever go back to normal life now?' We got into the bar and were spoilt like the most VIPs of VIPs all night long: champagne, cigarettes, hookers (I'm sure), anything we were wanted were given to us for free by beautiful women wearing old fashioned cinema popcorn girl uniforms. Adrian Brody and some of The Killers joined our table. We danced on the banquettes and posed for photos. This was it. This was the most fun I could ever have being an editor in chief in America, I realized through my champagne glaze: dancing, laughing, and sharing it with my real old friends and a bundle of fabulous new ones. I'd reached my peak.

***

On my last day in Vegas, the self-help guru and I went to lunch. He was surrounded by fans – his books were best-sellers and he'd appeared in the hit film about positive thinking, *The Secret.* 'You saved my life!' one fan thanked him, as we nibbled on our edamame. 'My girlfriend is too shy to come over but she wants me to tell you thanks,' says a shy looking fellow, whose girlfriend blushes 30ft away. 'You helped her a lot.'

'Wow!' I tease, when the fan praise finally dies down and we're left to our tuna platter. 'I knew you were good but, well…'

My Armani-suited guru pal flashes his veneers at me. 'It's all about believing in yourself, and realizing what will make you truly wealthy. I'm not talking about money, or possessions, or job titles.' He swigs his sake and thinks for a minute. 'Let's think about you for a while, Sarah. You are young, healthy and have this great job. You have friends who love you – I met lots of them this week – and you say you are close to your family in England. So why don't I think you are happy? Why do I keep hitting a mental roadblock with you that stops me from thinking you are complete? That some things in your life lack harmony – and harmony is what we all need.'

'Ha!' I fake a laugh. 'Because you're right. There are massive things missing. Things that a great job and a good salary can't replace. Things like a sense of peace; an inner calmness; a deep, deep understanding of your purpose in life. I don't have those things..I thought leaving London and my unhappy marriage would sort me out. And it did on one level. But this new world I've created is manic, and stressful, and fake. That's it. I feel I'm building my life on a fake rock at the moment. And it's fun. It's wonderful most of the time, so I shouldn't complain. But I do know there has to be more to life than working like mad, drinking too much, shopping, partying, and making small talk with people who really don't matter!' Breathless, I stop my rant, half expecting him to look horrified at the barrage of words he'd unleashed.

'Well what are you going to do about it? We all have the power to change things for the better,' he reminds me. 'And your problems should be easily solved. You're young, healthy and have some money – boom – that's the big problems in life sorted right there. You work too hard; I can see that – boom – take a holiday, somewhere with no Blackberry reception. Read, swim, walk, think and plan what you really want to do. You say you're glad to be divorced – Amen, I hear ya – but do you want to stay that way forever? A single woman, burying her emotions and romantic needs behind her desk?' I shake my head. Of course I didn't. I wanted to be loved.

'I want to be in love again. And I still believe in marriage. I don't really regret getting married before, we were just too young and focusing on the wrong things,' I admitted. 'But I'd love to feel that deep, all-encompassing love again. I just don't meet the right men. I haven't met anyone suitable in the four years I've been in America.' I glumly twirl my stirrer around my club soda.

'Well make a list then,' he instructs.

'Of what?'

'Of what you want of course. On your plane ride back to New York tomorrow, take out a pen and paper and number one to twenty down the side of the page. And then – without over-thinking and analyzing, or getting embarrassed, because this list is for you and no one else, write down every single quality you want in a man. Create your dream man. This will help you focus. Writing things down always does. Some of the things will seem quite shallow or silly, but put them all down. And then, when the list is done – and do make sure you get to twenty, it'll make sure all your subconscious desires are out in the open too – pin it up somewhere you can see it every day, and reread it and think about what you've written. I'm not saying you'll manifest your version of the perfect Prince Charming immediately. But I do believe in positive thinking and making affirmations of hope. It can't hurt and it will keep you focused and aware of what you need.'

I'd always been a list maker. After a couple of years of marriage I put down in black and white the pros and cons of our relationship to see if it would help me get my head straight, and it did. It just took me a couple more years to act on it. So I promised my new positive chum that I would make the list the next day, and stick it to my fridge with the garish collection of magnets I'd collected from all over America.

It was hard to think of twenty things; you can only say 'kind' and 'thoughtful' so many ways, and at first everything seemed so generic

41

and obvious. But it wasn't long before I'd descended into a vacuous and random list of requisites I knew no man could fill. But this was a fantasy list, so I wrote honestly and with abandon:

1 kind

2 thoughtful

3 funny

4 intelligent

5 honest

6 sweet

7 handsome

8 nice body

9 strong – emotionally and physically

10 sociable

11 good family

12 good friends

13 confident – not arrogant

14 taller than me

15 blue eyes

15 English

16 likes to dance

17 Tottenham Hotspur supporter

18 sexy

19 likes to travel

20 likes to eat

The minute I got back to my apartment, the list went up on my fridge – and every evening from that moment on, whenever I'd open the door to grab some water or wine, my dream man would present himself to me. I figured ten out of the twenty things bound up in one man would mean I'd hit the jackpot. I was not self-deluded enough to imagine I could get all twenty.

***

With the list done, I took on the other idea my guru had for sorting out my head, and then ultimately my life. I booked a two week trip, something I hadn't done since my honeymoon over eight years previously; to places I knew would have sporadic phone reception at best: Tulum in Mexico and an Amazon cruise in Peru. I left emergency contact details and Katie, my brilliant deputy who I knew would keep the place running smoothly; pre-approved every page I could get my hands on; agreed the ideas and themes for the next four issues in advance and set up a time each day when I would be checking emails for problems and layouts. It was the most professionally liberated I felt since the day I moved to New York.

My fellow single Manhattanite Bethany accompanied me to Tulum, for a week-long stay at a bikini boot camp: a place to get your mind and body healthy by indulging in 6am silent beach walks, three hour daily yoga sessions and mediation under the stars at nightfall. I'd planned on going alone but she was going through a career crisis like me and needed to get away. So she tagged along last minute with a suitcase full of Eckhart Tolle books, bikinis and hope. I was glad for the company, and we contentedly shared a rusty old four poster bed under a mosquito net in a shack of a room, with no lock, that sat right on the beach. We quickly got into an old married couple routine. She'd blow out the candles each night after we'd read for a while (there was no electricity) and I'd run over to the senorita in the hostel's kitchen for fresh coffee and brown sugar every morning at 5.30am, to get us perky for our three mile, pre-breakfast silent walk along the sun-soaked shore.

'I've heard rumors there's an amazing old lady in the village who reads tarot cards,' Bethany whispered to me during one of our meditation sessions. 'She's been doing it for years and years, and lots of the women book to come here just to see her. You up for it?' I didn't know if I really believed in tarot cards. I mean, how could one pack of picture cards sum up the fortunes and futures of every person in the world? But Bethany was intrigued and I had nothing to lose, so we arranged to see her the following day.

Sitting cross-legged across from the old Mexican grandma, I blindly picked an assortment of kick-ass cards. I uncovered queens, warriors and goddesses. This could mean one thing only, I was convinced: that I was a fighter, that I would always choose the bravest, most daring path in life and that I weathered critics and criminals with class and grace. I was right to a degree. I was a fighter. 'You are always in battle,' the psychic octogenarian informed me. 'You have built a massive fortress to protect yourself. You have needed to because from a very young age you have had to strive for everything you have. But now you are locked in this fortress, and you have climbed to the top of the very highest turret and you are looking down at the rest of the world beneath you. And you are pleased to be alive, but you are scared at what will come next. You want to keep building and battling to protect yourself more. Does this make sense?'

It did, I suppose. When you're raised by a strong, single mother for most of your childhood you learn what it means to be a woman in battle and how being different, an outsider to the norm, means you have to guard against things happy, carefree children aren't even aware of. 'But I don't want to be locked up, scared, on my own forever,' I say quietly. 'Yes, I have fought to get high, but I don't know what to do next?'

'You know what the cards and my heart are telling me to say to you?' she grabs my hand with forceful meaning. 'Pull down the fortress! Pull it down! Demolish the turret! Place your bare feet on the ground again and feel life like it is new again. Stop protecting yourself. Stop feeling trapped. Stop being so proud of yourself and what you have done in the past that you can't go forward. Rip! Rip! Rip' For some totally unknown reason, I burst into hysterical tears. 'I'm sorry', I said, wiping the wetness dry with my sarong. 'I don't know why I'm crying.'

'I do,' she patted me on the knee, kindly. 'It's because you're thinking "but if I tear the walls down, will I be hurt and let down again?" And that's understandable. Also, you're thinking "but I've worked so hard to get this high, how will I ever be able to climb up again?" And that's a normal reaction too. But you know what you have to do?'

'Tear them down anyway?' I guess.

'Yes,' she smiles. 'Because you have no idea yet how much the goddess in you wants to be loved, and how the queen in you deserves it. And the warrior in the cards is laughing now, the warrior is telling me that if you think are a success right now, just see what you can achieve when you pull these walls down and start again. I don't know whether this means professionally, or financially, and I know you New York girls always worry about that. But I can see from the cards that what will happen next will bring you a true wealth, and true security.' I thank her – then make my way to the shoreline, where I walk and wail until it's time for mediation around the fire pit.

The following week I head, alone this time, to Peru. I made my way via plane, train and automobile to the summit of Machu Picchu swollen by the worst period pain of my life, altitude sickness and a stomach bug. I was horrendous. It was breathtaking. As I sat on an ancient rock, perusing the deep, sunken green valleys and red rivers below me, I felt tiny and insignificant. And that was perfect. It allowed me to step out of this tiny, carefully-crafted world I'd been living in and see, want, *feel* the bigger picture. We would all come and go, life cannot last, but we can try and make the most of every blessed, healthy, happy moment we are given. Why waste a moment when we have options? I didn't know what mine were yet but I knew I had them. I had my health and my brain and my absolute fear of rejection and failure to get me through anything. After sitting in silence until the sun started to fade and duck down behind the mountains' edges, I made my way down the hill to the local village, for hibiscus tea and an early night. The tree frogs chirped in the banyan trees outside my hut as I dozed, feeling excited and impatient for the future, positive my life was about to head in a direction – to a place – I had never, ever thought it could.

4

Getting Lucky in Kentucky

'The road of life twists and turns and no two directions are ever the same. Yet our lessons come from the journey, not the destination.'

Don Williams Jnr.

Refreshed – if not joyous to be back - my New York life returned to its normal groove of long-winded meetings, tabloid gossip, daily arguments with the London board and Beef Pho lunch breaks after my trip to South America. I was still an editor in chief who protected her staff like a lioness defending her cubs (we were all great friends so even the tedious meetings were hurried along by the sharp wit, sarcasm and great fondness I felt for my loyal colleagues) and the magazine was now selling one million copies per week, but over the last year I was starting to slowly admit to myself that I was over it all and after my trip I could not hide it. Yes, I had had the whirlwind life millions of people dream of. Invites to the Oscars, front row seats at New York Fashion shows, one on ones with George Clooney and run-ins with Britney (who decided to let her dog poop on designer dresses at one of my recent shoots) but when I slowed down for a second and pulled off the Prada shades, as I had been forced to on my much-needed holiday, it was glaringly obvious my life was a concoction of heart-stopping pressure and stress, thrown into a cocktail mixer with a splash of false and a twist of lame. The constant threat that I could be sued, fired, slandered or bullied at any time was harrowing. I managed a team of young creative types who, for the most part, were a delight but I also had to manage my bosses, a pack of flamboyant mavericks who too often turned anything good we did into something way off the

American track. For the four years I had been in charge of the magazine, I had to fight to take two steps forward for every one they made me take back and it was exhausting. My heart wasn't in it anymore.

After this epiphany, I couldn't go back to my old mode of behavior. Straightaway, I stopped arse licking the American Idol stars when they stopped by the office. I avoided album launches and the nonsensical talking rappers that came with them. I couldn't even be bothered to attend fashion shows anymore. A bag of freebies was a bit so-what and new photos of Jessica Simpson looking plump left me cold.

In my tiny apartment, my perfect man list was still stuck to my fridge.

It was in this mindset that I was thrown the most beautiful and unexpected lifebelt. At 11.40am on a standard Tuesday Russell Moffett's email popped into my inbox and my fractured, tired heart started beating wildly. Thanks to a mutual friend and after some investigative research to find out if I was attached or not, he sent me a message with a simple request: *'I hear you live in America now. So do I. I'm in Kentucky working as a software architect. It's a long story. Perhaps I should call you so we can discuss the merits and mayhem of working with Americans?'*

Russell was a boy I'd briefly dated at university in Canterbury. He'd attached a recent photo in case I couldn't remember him and I quickly gathered the girls and gays around my desk to check him out. We all agreed. Hot was the adjective of the day. His deep blue 'come to bed and/or Kentucky' eyes stared out of my screen. His gorgeous smile was just the same as I remembered. Lovely. I gushed until my co-workers got bored and returned to the jobs I was paying them to do, so I then forwarded his message to my university girlfriends, who would remember my long nights of Russ-musing, listening to The Cure while smoking Marlboro Lights out of my 3rd floor dorm bedroom window. 'At last! Bloody hell!' Hayley yelped across the miles, piercing my already excited brain with her own romantic delirium. 'I always loved Russell. Do you remember how we used to watch films and play drinking games in my house on Black Griffin Lane? And he's so handsome! You deserve this, bird, you really do. I knew you'd meet a great guy eventually, but Russell surpasses all my hopes for you.'

In America, I'd pretty much decided I'd rather be alone than lonely in a relationship, much to the worry of my happily-settled, kiddied-up friends like Hayley back home. But I knew I needed to be single for a bit, I needed to recover and regroup. I was a designer singleton. It was weird to be on my own again but it wasn't as horrific as it could have been, for someone who had been coupled up for most of their 20s. I was too raw with emotion to be good for anyone except myself. I'd secured an amazing bunch of man-less girlfriends to do cocktails with on Friday, chick flicks on Saturday and yoga on Sunday with Claire, a fellow Euro soloist; and my working weeks rushed by in the way of a typical New York singleton: late nights in the office, followed by a rushed takeaway in front of the TV or a trip to the gym, then bath and bed. I had been glad to be on my own, without the noose of a selfish man tightening around my self-esteem, and it was only since sticking the dream man list to my fridge that I'd actually began imagining I could meet not only Mr. Right, but Mr. Right Now. Please.

And now here was this email from an old university lover. And my positive reaction told me I was ready for something to happen. I could tell from the photo he'd attached that he was still as gorgeous as I remembered from our days as 19-year-olds, but with the added bonus that he'd stopped getting his Grandma to bleach his shoulder length hair and it was now a natural, shiny brown crop cut. After his first email, we communicated (re: flirted) electronically back and forth until, at about 6pm, he suggested that he calls me that evening. At 10pm my phone rang and, considering it had been 13 years since the pub-banter/snogging episodes of our youth, the conversation was easy. 'If you'd turned into a snotty media type, I was going to chat for ten minutes, wish you a nice life and that would be that,' he admitted, after we've been chatting for three hours. 'But you haven't changed at all. I've loved talking to you this evening.' I was hooked. When I got into work the next morning, an e-mail from him was waiting. He was hooked too. This glorious first week of e-mails and three-hour nightly chats (and an inability to sleep or eat) culminated in me booking a flight to Kentucky for that weekend.

***

Four days after that first email, with my heart hammering ferociously in my chest and my cheeks burning bright from an elixir of dread, desire and possible disappointment, I land at Louisville airport, the small city in Kentucky Russ called home, which until just a few days earlier I'd only vaguely heard of because celebrities flock to it for the Derby. I regret not packing my glasses now. Vanity had got the better of me but without them, I am blind and once through the arrivals gate, I am forced to squint unbecomingly to spot the man who would be meeting me here. It is no good, so I reach for my phone. 'I'm here but I can't see you,' I shakily explain, my nerves now taking its turn on my tongue, which seems to be sticking to the roof of my mouth and making me sound like a drunk, male Puerto Rican.

'Its fine Sarah, I can see you. I'm walking towards you now,' he replies. Before I can explain that I wasn't normally bright red and twitchy, he adds, 'and I'm nervous. Are you nervous too?' I force my desert dry mouth to form a sound I hope sounds like agreement. 'Nervous and excited, of course', he continues, as I pass under a giant 'Welcome to Possibility City' banner. 'I'm just going to grab you into a big hug until I calm down and can act normally. I don't want you to think I'm a total loser.'

And then there he is, a few feet in front of me. Russell. The boy from my student days at Kent University. The guy who used to drive me wild with desire when he played me Smiths songs on his guitar in the attic of his grotty student house; or tied his long, fake blonde curls back into a hippy ponytail and covered his head with a Tottenham Hotspur baseball cap. Russell. We didn't have a huge teen romance really. After a few months of dating (i.e. shagging and drinking in The Black Griffin), I got a bit disillusioned by his partying ways. He continued getting drunk with his mates and didn't seem too bothered. We were no longer love's young dream and going to the library (where I had previously hung out, on the off chance of bumping into him) became strictly off limits. At 19, once someone has seen you naked, you'd prefer never to see him or her again.

I hadn't seen Russell for 13 years.

Even under the harsh airport lighting, he is better in person than in his photo. And before I can say something stupid, or think about what I am doing, or even put my suitcase down, I am on my tiptoes kissing him. Before we even say hello, our lips are locked, our arms wrapping around each other, my eyes sneaking an up close glimpse of the one who had got away. 'Hello,' he offers as we eventually pull apart, that massive, gorgeous grin exploding over his face. My tongue is still stuck to the roof of my mouth so I just grab his hand and let him lead me towards the car park. I am now in such a frenzy the cool Kentucky night air feels like a welcome, wet slap in the face.

'*Calm down, calm down, everything is going to be good at last*', I try to tell my wobbly self. '*My mum thinks so.*' I'd called my excited mother while I was fighting my way through the Friday night traffic to get to La Guardia to catch my 8pm flight a few hours earlier. Far from being horrified that her daughter was flying 1,000 miles to stay with a virtual stranger, she yelped with girlish delight, 'Good for you. I've been praying for something like this to happen. Wahoo!'

Landing in Louisville, Kentucky that evening turned out to be the most important maneuver of my life. By the end of the night, we realized that although we now had these big jobs in America we were still just two kids from the London suburbs who loved our

51

families, our football club and an Indian takeaway on a Saturday night. By the end of the weekend, he'd booked his flights to New York for the following Friday to meet my friends. During that first weekend in New York together, strolling through Central Park, our tongues blue from Snow Cones, our shoulders gaining unattractive tan lines in the midday sun he said bravely, 'You know what could make me even happier than I am right now? It would be to know, with every part of my being, that you could be mine forever.'

By the end of the first month, we said I love you and meant it more that we'd ever meant it before. That simple, inquisitive email had led to a reunion people see in the movies but think can never really happen. Except it does. To two ex-lovers who'd travelled the world just to find each other again. I think we were both shocked at how love could be so instant. He too had suffered a few relationships based on games and insecurity, and the instant fondness we felt for each other was wonderful, and coupled with the physical attraction, it was mind-blowing. For the first time ever in a romantic relationship, I was my partner's number-one priority. In the past, I'd played second fiddle to jobs or friends or demanding mothers. It was wonderful to be a true significant other.

After two months, he proposed; back on the Kent University campus, kneeling on the sticky floor of Woody's, the Student Union bar where we'd first set eyes on each other as clueless teens. 'It's always been you, Sarah. I knew it from the first time we met all those years ago, and I know it even more now. I just knew you would be mine.'

He stumbled up from bended knee and into my arms, unleashing a beautiful diamond ring.

'I know its quick, that we haven't been together that long, but life is too short. When my father was diagnosed with cancer last year, it did many, many things to me, most of them bad. But his illness has also given me this huge appetite for life and I feel an immense need to stop wasting time with people and things that don't matter. My father has taught me not to be scared, to take chances, to love with all my heart. And I couldn't wait another day to ask you to be my wife.'

My family was waiting in a nearby Canterbury restaurant and this time, far from horror, my parents congratulated me on my engagement with genuine joy. 'This one is right,' my Grandma cuddled me gleefully. 'I can tell he loves you very much.'

She was right and my heart felt like it could relax for the first time in my life. This contentment I felt in Russ's arms, combined with the up-close look his father's illness gave me about what really matters, urged me to look at the other off-kilter areas of my life. I knew without doubt that my job wasn't fulfilling me anymore and there were thousands of people lining up, snapping at my stiletto heels, desperate to take my place, so shortly after our engagement – after a particularly savage and unjustified beating from my never happy boss over that week's front cover - I resigned. A weight was lifted immediately and my family celebrated my seeing the light. Russ, my sweet fiancé, said I should move to Kentucky to be with him.

'You've worked hard for a long time, let me take care of you now,' he insisted, during the first furtive phone call I made from my lunchtime Pho shop after I'd dropped my bombshell back on HQ in Blighty. 'I didn't really want to move up to your tiny place in Brooklyn anyway. We'll be happier down here. We can drink Mint Juleps on the rocking chairs on my porch every evening and watch the sun go down. I'll work as usual and you can be as busy or lazy as you want.'

Yes! This was all working out perfectly: my notice period would end just before our set wedding date. I could start my new life as a wife away from the aggressive, sky-high monster that New York had become for me, and without the pressure I felt to put my job before any relationship I had. For the months between my decision and the wedding, Russ commuted back and forth between New York and Louisville, taking a suitcase of my acquisitions with him every time he returned home to Kentucky. On weekends spent apart, I'd cram in bonding time with my girlfriends and electrolysis guru, while Russ converted an unused room into an office for me, complete with bookshelves, framed photos of us on holiday in The Hamptons and a beautiful glass desk with a sensible storage system. 'I want you to feel free to write, and read, or do whatever you want to do. I understand you're giving up a lot to be with me and I'm going to make it as easy for you as possible.'

My job had allowed me to enter American culture so uniquely and wonderfully I knew that one day I would sit back, take stock and think *wow*, but at this point it felt repetitive and shallow. Of course hanging out with a very tiny, glittery and pink Dolly Parton at a small gathering for the Golden Globes in Beverly Hills was something to call home about but it wasn't all fabulous; my boss was hard to please and bullied me into making incorrect decisions and even fashion week had become a chore. Sitting front row with the New York jet set made me feel like a garmently challenged elephant, despite the hard work of my Henri Bendel personal shopper.

I said goodbye to my swanky corner office overlooking the Chrysler Building the week before I flew home to England for our wedding. I wanted to be happy. I wanted to live a real life. Even my boss's last minute offer of a life-changing salary could not sway me. My heart was set on being a freelance writer, moving away from the city and making my marriage my priority. Was I petrified of handing over the reins? Hell yeah! During my notice period I broke out into cold sweats at night wondering how I'd cope without being arse-licked (let's face it, it happens) and without having a strict daily routine. Would I be able to stay motivated, working from home, with the constant lure of Oprah and the fridge? Would I start calling into QVC for Diamonique pendants and Princess Diana commemorative plates? Early on, I was made aware that people wouldn't treat me the same. I'd become a persona non grata without a magazine behind me and the sway that gave me. Without my grandiose job title, was I nothing? Was I dull? Would I suddenly be that girl who you tried to escape at cocktail parties? But I needed to be happy. So I stuck to my guns, quit and said goodbye to the most exciting city on earth, which had been my home for four years.

We were married a few weeks later in The Cotswolds, with the sentimental support of family, friends, a drunken man playing the piano and two wise-cracking blondes with trays of champagne. I wore an elegant Marchesa gown that suited me perfectly, and Mathew – my first friend in New York who was now back running a salon in the West End - curled my hair and placed an exquisite diamond band, picked out for me by Niria, the OK! fashion director, around my head.

'Honey, you look a-mazing!' Mathew caught me up in a bear hug once he'd admired my hair, his masterpiece. 'I told you life would get better once you got a straight man, didn't I?'

Unlike my first wedding, when I grimaced and twitched, I grinned all the way up the aisle this time; and when I reached Russ's side, he simply grabbed my hand and flashed his electrifying smile at me. His deep blue eyes were full of tears. Our humanist minister conducted a wedding filled with messages of family, friends, love and hope. After the ceremony, we walked out into the English country garden for a glass of champagne, waving to our gathered loved ones, as an old university anthem played: *Just Like Heaven* by The Cure.

'I love you,' I whispered as everyone else emerged into the bright sunshine to join us. 'So much.'

After a traditional British dinner of roast meats, local Gloucester cheeses and spotted dick, Russell's father, Peter, stood up in front of the crowd and gave a speech filled with such heartfelt power that the candle-lit room could hardly contain him or the emotions he unleashed.

'Lastly, on this wonderful day when we're celebrating the love of two very special people, I just want to thank Upstairs, whoever is listening,' my new father-in-law announced, looking upwards towards the heavens, 'for allowing me to be here today. I may not have any hair but I'm happy! And I'm so proud of you, son. Your mother and I couldn't have asked for a better boy.'

My two brothers and Russ's old school friends erupt into huge cheers. One of my bridesmaids Rose searches in her handbag for handkerchiefs to hand out. I watch as my lovely, sweet new husband clambers past well-wishers, through party popper debris and bow-tied chairs, to give his dad a hug. They hold each other tight until the music starts up and they are asked to perform a father-son rendition of the Zorba the Greek dance. They take each other's shoulders, and sway in unison, kicking their heels higher and higher as the music gets faster and faster. An identikit pair, living in the moment, the same wide grin blinding our clapping, laughing family and friends, who are trying to take photos with glassy eyes.

The next day, we fly as blissed-out newlyweds to my new home state of Kentucky. During our courtship I'd fallen in love with the place and its people. If you avoided the bible-bashing Rednecks, of which there were many, you'd find a generous and charming group of people who were heavily doused in that legendary Southern hospitality. Russ's friends welcomed me with open arms, and just through trips to the local coffee shop and yoga studio I met friendly, like-minded women who were keen to welcome me with a multitude of party invitations, home-baked goods and local know-how. My new friends were bakers, wine merchants, floral designers, theatre actors, lawyers, mothers, artists and truly the sweetest people I had ever met. If I had believed in past lives, I would have been convinced that when I wasn't writing the Magna Carta or getting my head lopped off by my husband, Henry VIII, I'd have been on the banks of the Mississippi, picking corn and trying to form a jug band. Kentucky instantly felt like home.

My accent acted as an ice-breaker wherever I went, leading to funny exchanges every now and again. 'Are you from England?' a young male server gasped at my new favorite place, The Homemade Pie Kitchen. I nodded proudly. I was thinking of getting something along those lines printed on a sweatshirt. I had to factor in an extra ten minutes talking time to even the simplest odd job. 'Wow, I've always wanted to go there,' he presented me with my usual: warm apple pie with cinnamon ice cream. 'Tell me; is it true the Eiffel Tower leans?' Torn between wanting a quick escape and the idea of breaking his dream, I muttered that yes, it did – a little bit – and left him smiling. I had to get to the launderette, a new weekly chore I actually enjoyed. I'd sit and shout at Jerry Springer on the overhead television with the other Hillbillies while my smalls got rinsed. It was different to the life I'd lived previously, a life which led to monthly dry cleaning bills of a $100, but in this life, I could appreciate the smaller things in life. I felt, perhaps for the first time in my life, that I wasn't in such a rush.

A few months into our new domestic bliss Peter dies. For better and worse, our marriage changes in many, many ways. I am forced into another journey of self-discovery and change just when I hoped my travelling days and sleepless nights were over for good.

***

As a person naturally disposed towards positivity, the ghastly head-fuck of depression comes as a nasty shock. Especially when everything should be so good. On the surface, my life looked so fabulous that an ex-colleague confessed she and the other fashion magazine gals I used to work with in London had set up their own Facebook group entitled 'Only Look at Sarah's Profile If You Want to Feel like Your Life is Shit.' Much of this rosy glow came from the aforementioned whirlwind romance, subsequent proposal and wonderful wedding. More droplets of sunshine came from my constant city-hopping, good friends and a general feeling that life should be grabbed with both hands.

So when my grip slipped and my carefully constructed path to contentment led me nowhere, I didn't quite know what to do with myself or how to move forward. The dark, creeping menaces Failure and Emptiness weren't companions I wanted to travel with yet they seemed to be hitching a ride in my coat pockets.

I began to look back at my former perky, glib self and not know if I envied her or wanted to smash her in the face. Despite going through my parents' divorce, my own divorce, a firing, a redundancy and a few painful fallouts with friends, I'd loved my life. 'Don't let the buggers grind you down', a feisty Great, Great Aunt Joyce had advised me from a young age – and it had worked for so long. Half of this was due to my natural jolly-hockey sticks nature... and the other half was due to the fact that until the last few months, I didn't know shit.

Grief is all encompassing. I soon realized that you don't *just* grieve for a person whom you've loved and lost; you grieve for the years you've wasted, for opportunities not taken, for unrequited loves and for changes that have been forced upon you. But of course grieving for someone you've loved and lost is the most terrifying and most real.

My father in law Pete was loveable, a joker and a tease - in the best sense of the word. Despite the fact I had only known him for 15 months, when he was cruelly snatched by cancer from his family at the age of 61, I missed him. Despite my personal sadness, following his death, I didn't feel I had the right to grieve for someone I had known for such a short space of time. I felt my emotions weren't valid. So I tried to focus on caring for my broken husband and the one positive I could lay claim to: the relief I felt that Russ had made his sudden move on me when he did and I'd got to know his wonderful, loving father at all. The whole time I'd known him he'd been bravely hiding what must have been – according to his doctors – excruciatingly painful symptoms and increasing stress and social embarrassment. Watching a grown man disintegrate in front of my eyes was something I'd never witnessed up close before. Grandparents had died, and old aunts and uncles, but at an age that felt appropriate and less disruptive to the order of things.

As I said, at the start of my husband's grieving process, I ushered myself into the role of caregiver and cheerful companion. How could I possibly understand what he was going through? I couldn't. My own father had abandoned me when I was a child and I assure you if I found out he had died yesterday, I wouldn't care. He means nothing to me. And I don't feel callous or mean for saying this. When your beloved daddy swaps you and your mum for a harsh woman in red lipstick called Rita, you learn to acquire a heart-protecting arsenal. My real father hadn't been there for me for 25 years and therefore I didn't understand my husband's loss. 'You don't get it, you can't,' was one accusation my angry, upset beloved would level at me. I handled this with all the grace of a child who was mentally stuck at the age she was when her father had walked out. I was *A,* annoyed he was calling me out on my emotional black holes and *B,* furious that he was so blind. He couldn't see what he had had and that I was jealous of it. Yes, I shamefully admit I was jealous of my destroyed, drowning husband because he could feel such strong sentiments for a father. Russ had had a man who loved him and his mother his whole life, cheered him on at football games and taken him up the pub for his first pint. He was feeling sorry for himself and taking it out on me... while I was feeling sorry for myself and taking it out on... well, no one.

And that's probably when the somber clouds started to appear above my head. Deep feelings of my childhood abandonment reemerged at a time when I knew I needed to be selfless and understanding. So I put a lid on it. I cradled my best friend in my arms each night, cooked him healthy meals and tried to be the perfect wife. He didn't fall for the act though. Russ is far too observant for that. So as much as he allowed me to cradle him and feed him nutritious dinners, *I* knew *he* knew that I wasn't able to see through the heavy fog of grief that hung in every room of our new home and in every conversation we had.

As a wife, I was a bit of a letdown. I felt I was anyway. And this made me even angrier. I was supposed to be getting it right second time round. The failure of my first marriage had left me with a clear to-do list: *don't bottle up your emotions, be honest about your needs, be firm when enough is enough and don't be so paranoid or insecure all the time.*

After his father's death, Russ wandered from anger to sadness and I decided to follow him down that road, disappointed that our first year of marriage wasn't turning out exactly how it should have. We were not in charge; we were not smug pleasure-seekers, thirsty for each other. *That* just wasn't happening, because grief deflates the libido quicker than you can say 'keep your pajamas on please'. Of course, being this ridiculously self-centered creature that had no firsthand experience of the death of a close family member, I tried to persuade and flirt and charm my way into his physical affections, trying to wipe from both our minds the pain that he was enduring in the daylight hours. After all, only months earlier we'd been unable to physically keep our hands off each other. We fitted, we bonded and I was missing the closeness that this intimacy brought.

And I missed the chance to make a baby. Yes, that was really the key at this point. Again stupidly and selfishly, I assumed a pregnancy would light up his life and help him forget his father. How dumb! As if his mind could focus on anything but his father – or more importantly, his lovely mother who was now living alone for the first time in her life, in the house where they'd raised their family together. A baby, I did get him to admit, would be something wonderful and help him move on, but the peeing-on-stick pressure I'd put him under since the beginning of the year was not going to fly. For the last few months, his lovemaking had been reluctant at best.

Patience is not a strong point of mine and I couldn't believe that after nearly 12 months of trying, we were still bump-less and not getting any nearer to getting one, despite the biological hindrances of our sporadic attempts. Friends seemed to be announcing their happy news every other week and I was finding it increasingly difficult to smile and congratulate them. I'm not a jealous person but the baby thing got me in a way nothing else in my life had. Wasn't it a woman's right to have a child? Well, hello, where were my rights, husband? 'I'm 34 years old!' was my constant battle cry, which Russ would ignore or occasionally sympathize with, while thinking, I'm sure, that he was now shackled to a totally insensitive lunatic.

The grief he felt from the loss of his father and the sadness I felt over the loss of my dreams of a perfect second marriage cozied up into a ménage a trois with the hatred I now felt for my old, failing body. I was angry that I couldn't get what other girls seemed to get so easily. And so I experienced another side of grief. The death of a dream *and* of a future. The death not so much of a baby but *the idea* of a baby. A baby that would make everything all right.

I had too much time on my hands at this point, which could have been part of the problem. Just before we got married, my resignation seemed like the right thing to do. I gladly swapped my appliance-laden condo in Williamsburg, Brooklyn for Russ' old Kentucky home. I went from living on a hamster wheel of hellish deadlines and crazy celebrities to a carousel of brightly colored horses and gumbo. Soon after I met Russell and started hanging around with the wonderful, *normal* friends he had down South, I was able to voice a scary yet enlightening truth: I couldn't give a fuck about celebrities. I hoped Jennifer Aniston would find true love but did I care enough to pay someone to follow her around on a first date? No! Poor cow, she needed all the help she could get - not a crew of crude paparazzi following her so people like me could sit in judgment and brainwash the nation.

A life of sudden domesticity was enjoyable at first. I felt like I was playing grown-ups, baking peanut butter cookies and buying Liberty print cushions, and I loved the immense security *and* freedom Russ wanted to give me every day. But after Pete's death, when the rosy glow on our marriage started to fade to grey, I twitched with the nagging fear that I had given away my true identity too quickly, or that it had somehow been stolen. I wasn't a Southern Belle. I was a NY-LON media maven.

Since graduating at 20, I'd worked like a dog to climb the slippery, steep ladder of media in London before being offered the massive job of editing a weekly magazine in New York. Now, jobless in the Bluegrass State, I was grieving for the loss of me as team leader, as a colleague, as an enthusiastic writer, as the nurturing editor. I had all this Leo energy bottled up with nowhere to go: pride and a need to lead (or to be bossy, really) was building into a volcanic rage that could only eventually burst and do damage. I'd chosen to be jobless at a time when many other poor sods were being shown the door. So again, I felt guilt at feeling saddened by my self-inflicted unemployment and bottled it up with my need for professional fulfillment. As Russ's grief got worse, I decided to throw that bottle out to sea and forgot about it – along with the 'letter to self' contained within it.

After a few months of slipping in an out of my most earnest role as loving wife, depending on if I could physically get up that day, I knew something had to change. I was lost. My husband was lost. Through no fault of its own, Kentucky hadn't filled our marriage with the 'unbridled spirit' it promises as you cross the state line.

But all was not lost. And Russ had a cunning plan to get ourselves going in the right direction again. With the help of his understanding boss, a get-better program from his therapist, our joint savings and my organizational skills, we decided to flee the real world and our ever-so-real depression and put it all in perspective by leaving America for a few months. We looked at a map, picked a few places we'd always wanted to visit, and did exactly what you are not supposed to do: we tried to run away from our problems.

5

Say Something Nice, or Say Nothing

'Time goes by quickly, and you cannot take it for granted. Appreciate how far you've come, and give yourself the gift of discovering how far you can yet go.'

Dr. Sonya Friedman

'I might end up murdering you on this trip. You are you so very, very annoying, my darling,' Russ glares at me across the table in a faux-Italian trattoria we'd stumbled upon in Chicago's theater district. You are the annoying one, I thought. And so I told him so. In pinched, hushed tones so as not to attract attention.

'You're the annoying one, Russell. I tell you something, you never listen, so no wonder I snap when after telling you the same thing multiple times, you ask me again. I could punch your face in.' He kisses me with gritted teeth and reminds me that he has poor hearing and an even poorer memory, as if this excuses everything and justifies his little outbursts at my expense.

Tell me: how is it possible to love someone so much you'd gladly die for them one minute, then they'd make you so angry you'd march out of a restaurant during lunch, if they dared mention an ex-girlfriend, for example? Is it passion? Is it heck! It's called lacking patience and peace. No matter how much yoga and mediating I do, I still have this fire cracker bubble inside me that throws my most Zen intentions off balance when that strumpet from his past is mentioned.

The freezing weather in Chicago isn't cooling our mood. In a bid to pack frugally, we'd gone without winter garb and hoped to fight off the cold of the Windy City by simply layering on the entire content of our summer-themed backpacks. I had coupled my chilly top half ensemble of three vest tops and a toweling hoody with skinny jeans that I hadn't realized no longer fitted and exposed my bum crack every time I sat down, got up or bent over. Months of comfort eating had made them stretch over my sausage like thighs to the detriment and exposure of my ample backside and it wasn't pretty - or warm - I soon discovered. When I felt unhealthy (and physically restricted), I felt miserable, so despite being the first day of our epic adventure, the air was a little doom and gloom. Even the mini Buddha we'd carefully selected as a travel companion, good luck charm and photo prop wasn't bringing much joy.

Today could have just been like any other stopover in any other American city. We'd both been to Chicago multiple times but never with each other, and we thought it would be fun to get out and explore rather than stay in the airport for twelve hours or hole up in one of those grim, grey airport hotels that promise in-room porn, a Starbucks franchise and little else. No, we had a spirit of adventure and so set off towards the Loop for Chicago's famous deep pan pizza. Four slices later, my muffin tops are even more exposed over the top of my trousers and Russ is ignoring my request to go to the Chicago Art Institute. He wants to climb the Sears Tower, despite the swirling, dense clouds and the security guard in the door who says there's zero visibility but an entrance fee of $18 per person.

'Any discount for no views?' my ever hopeful husband enquires. The humorless watchman shakes his head but we pay the price anyway and take the over-priced 103 flights up and stare out onto nothing for a good hour. Well, it is cold out and my ridiculous, Bermuda-clad soul mate can't bring himself to miss a photo opportunity at a famous landmark.

We spend the next few hours speed-walking around the Magnificent Mile, sucking down the scent of street Hog Dog vendors and wood-fire ovens, marveling at the iced over Ohio River and puzzling at the modern sculptures in the Millennium Park. We start to thaw out when we find a spot with a log fire and Stella on tap. A few beers and a few more pizzas later (well, we are in Chicago after all), we make our way back to the hotel for a few hours rest before our flight to Hong Kong the next day. Still hopeful and counting, I knew that today was day 15 of my ovulation cycle and this – on my self-evaluated, self-diagnosed measure of my fertility – was the best day for us to conceive. So despite the sore limbs, bloating and the stench of garlic coming from my husband's general vicinity, I go in with the normally successful cuddling, stroking and naked breast technique of seduction. I am greeted with snores and a fart; an uncouth declaration that his body was not to be played with.

So I go to sleep – or rather pretend to sleep – until the alarm goes off and I can act all hurt, try and start a fight, then be won over by the understanding yet firm tone my husband uses when handling my crazy drive to procreate and impatience at getting what I want.

'Perhaps now isn't the best time to get pregnant anyway,' Russ confesses. 'Do you really want to have morning sickness when you're stuck on a non air conditioned train for 12 hours with nothing to drink except putrefied mango juice?' I can tell from his tone he's expecting me to see sense.

'I can't believe you're saying this to me now,' I reply with theatrics and a few tears. Obviously. 'After all, I am a woman of 34 with only 12 chances of baby-making a year.' I retreat to the bathroom to whimper and steal toiletries.

'I had a dream about my father that seemed to last all night and has left me exhausted' he mutters after a few minutes of silence. 'He was still alive and well but then he seemed to deteriorate suddenly and I had to watch his death play out in front of my eyes again, as I had to in real life. I only woke up when I heard the death rattle. I heard it as clearly as I did when he died for real.' He mumbles that even the random yet exciting appearance of soccer legend Paul Gascoigne at his father's death bed didn't make it bearable. 'How did he face that moment alone? Did he know what that horrendous sound emerging from his chest meant? Why didn't he tighten his grip on my mother's hand and refuse to leave, or refuse to go if she didn't go with him? They always did everything together, so how could he have faced that nothingness alone?' Tears shine in his deep ocean eyes. The muted light of dawn creeps its way through the grubby, beige blinds and on to the bed where he sits, crumpled and smaller than his 6ft 4 frame should look.

The guilt I'd been carrying now for a good few months kicks in so I wipe away my tears and kiss away his. Then I kiss his left hand, return to the bathroom to fill the tub with steaming hot water so we can share a soak, and decide to look after him until the dreadful day one of us has to make the unknown leap his father did.

It was just as well I was filled with a renewed sense of caring for Russ because the crew on the 15 hour flight to Hong Kong wasn't very caring at all. Horrified by the lack of television screen in the back of our chairs and the dismal size of the bland airport food, he decides to stare lovingly at me for a few hours while we go over the details of our trip. I give it up to him in a way any doting wife who wants to earn easy points with her husband should learn to do: he'd backpacked around Thailand before so deserved kudos as the travelling expert *and* as a teenager, while I'd wasted my time studying the works of Judy Blume, snogging boys with long hair and smoking weed, he'd completed his Duke of Edinburgh Gold Award for outdoor adventure - which meant he could use a compass, light a fire with limited resources and fight off perverted Geography teachers in the dark.

My tempered behavior clearly works and while clutching my hands and soaring through the clouds, he whispers in my ear, 'You'll think it's impossible, but I think we're going to fall even more in love on this trip, I really do.' Well, a freshly-anointed pessimist is never disappointed, so I figured I had nothing to lose.

***

A 15 hour flight through a multitude of time zones brings disgusting, mind-altering jet lag. For me, this is usually accompanied by random sweating episodes and itchy skin. A sign that our little Buddha chap was doing some good – just having him nestled in my backpack made me want to be a nicer person, even if difficult circumstances, such as a smelly, drooling businessman falling asleep on me during the flight, made it difficult – was that Russ and I hadn't argued once. Normally with the physical effects of jet lag comes the psychosis… airports are the number one place for couples to fight apparently, despite the forced joie de vivre of being *en vacance*. But no, Russ, Buddha and I were a charming little travel trio and we got through customs, found the right bus and then disembarked at the right stop on Nathan Road without fisticuffs. Russ wasn't best pleased when we finally made it into our prison cell, sorry, hostel room, to discover not only would he have to twist his lofty, muscular frame over the toilet in order to take a shower in the 3ft x 3ft bathroom (he looked like a pornographic version of Superman in a phone booth) but that he was unable to rinse off the day's grease and airline stink because I'd failed to pack, or steal, shower gel or shampoo. 'Oops.' I wrench my mouth to the left in an exaggerated effort to show my regret.

But even then he just murmurs 'Well, this pathetic bit of soap will just have to do.' This trip was already doing us both the world of good.

***

'Every time we get lost, shall we call it an adventure?' I ask, playing origami with a Hong Kong train map.

'I think that's wise,' my peace-keeping husband replies, while surreptitiously taking photographs of a dinosaur-old Chinese man wearing a rhinestone Elvis T shirt.

So this is how we keep the peace. Russ has a genuine sense of adventure so this is a fine arrangement for him; I have a temper and hate getting things wrong so this is the best way to stop me swearing or bursting into tears. 'An adventure!' I cheer. 'This is fun! Yes, at this very moment I may be lost with sore feet and a desperate need for the toilet, but I'm achy and bursting for a wee while funny Chinese neon signs are dancing above my head, so this is fun.'

Will we get to where we need to go, that is the question? Our first mission is to head to Lantau Island to see the Giant Buddha and walk the Wisdom Path. Once we've battled our way through the terrifying Hong Kong metro system, where we are the only people A, not wearing face masks or B, carrying Hello Kitty handbags, we find the cable car to take us up to the summit where the Buddha has pride of place. Our ears pop and the cable car swings scarily as a Baskervillian fog swirls around us and all is lost from sight. When we should have seen the seated hero perched upon his over-sized lily pad, we saw nothing. Like our trip up the Sears Tower, we didn't seem to have much luck with weather at a great height. Why was everything so foggy and difficult to see?

I'd done my fair bit of Buddhist research over the last few years. I'd toyed with the idea of becoming one, the idea of enlightenment being appealing to someone who had lived with a sense of dread, pain and sadness since first visiting her real father in prison as a very small child. It wasn't the clanking, heavy doors I minded so much, or even the assortment of creepy, tobacco-dry characters I'd have to smile up to politely when my father introduced us; it was the useless ornaments my father would make me out of matchsticks that I was forced to collect as he spent year after year behind bars that really bothered me. They were embarrassingly shit and even then I knew it.

I'd spent my single days in hectic New York learning various Buddhist meditations and how to downward dog – the most unbecoming of yoga poses - while unlearning the desire to be in competition with my girlfriends or be envious of their successes. Yet being decent is hard for a tabloid editor. You feel propelled to comment on other women's bodies in a way that disgusts me –

whether they are too fat, thin or (gosh no!) have cellulite. You encourage your readers to want stuff, more stuff, bigger stuff, better stuff... just to keep your advertisers happy. You jump on a celebrity death or divorce like a stoned man at a Vegas buffet. It's gross and never sat well with me, and was certainly a crucial reason in me resigning. After four years running a tabloid in America, I felt guilty about feeding this petty, misogynist shite to people who should know better.

Russ, being a typical, Church-of-England raised lad knew little of Buddhism apart from it had something to do with karma, a word he frequently used and abused when discussing valiant wins by his football team or when nasty colleagues had been fired. Being a bossy cow, I therefore decide before he is allowed to walk the 300 steps to the mighty Buddha that we'd fall into the tourist trap and pay for two tickets to the 'multi-media, audio-visual showcase on the life of Siddhartha'. *Walking with Buddha* promised to be an 'enriching experience' and who can argue with that.

The film is quite daft really, the future Buddha shown as a handsome, pale-skinned Westernized cartoon character. But for some reason it really touches me. I cry a few tears and promise myself I'll try and become more patient and understanding. Thankfully Russ is at my side the whole time muttering 'this dude had it right. It all makes sense', and then finally, as we emerge, blinking into the bright lights of the ubiquitous souvenir shop, he concludes, 'I could be a Buddhist.' We are given paper leaves to offer at Buddha's feet, as he sat under the mythical Bodhi Tree. This particular tree was made out of plastic, but it did double duty as an incense burner, filling the altitude with lavender and sage, so we don't mind. Randomly, our leaves have the same message on it: *Pay little heed to other's wrongdoing, or what they have done or will do. Pay close attention to what you yourself have done or will do.*

Well, when you put it like that... My insecurities over being out of the media meat market – and even the amount of time it was taking me to fall pregnant when friends were getting a bun in the oven from looking at a baguette – seemed silly and out of place. I was in a race with myself, no one else. I had to chill out and calm down and know that if I want to change things, I have to do it myself. With our mutual sense of calm, we climb the steps up to the big guy, take way too many photos and descend for a vegetarian lunch at the Po Lin Monastery.

'You're so pretty even the Zen Monks are looking at you,' Russ declares, bombarding the paper tablecloth and his scruffy, hole-ridden jeans with bits of tofu, his deep blue eyes twinkling with what can only be described as devotion. This isn't true of course – the Zen monks are too busy queuing for their bok choi to notice a pasty Westerner like me – which makes me love him for saying it even more.

***

I couldn't really be a Buddhist because I do like a few hedonistic things, one of them being a crisp glass of champagne. One of my ex-dates thought this made me a complete snob. I'd argue it was my choice to have one good glass of bubbly over his 10 pints of Guinness, so he should stuff it (Which he eventually did. Permanently, thank goodness.) So this evening I was very excited about our planned trip to the Felix bar on the 28th floor of the famed Peninsula Hotel. Overlooking the harbor, with a delicious drink in hand and love by my side, what could be dreamier? Ah, the high life. This was the kind of thing I'd do all the time in London and New York and even though I didn't want the big city job anymore, I still wanted the bubbles.

'Have you seen the prices in here? They're taking the piss. This is disgusting.' Russ's eyes boggle cartoon-like at the slick menu. The thing is he was right of course, one glass of the house champagne was working out as $25, but this was my dream and I didn't think that had a price. I stay silent. An eyebrow lift would suffice. 'Well, I don't know why you want it so much. I mean why do you?' I just did. I'm a girl. A girl who loves champagne. 'Well, I'll just have a beer then. So we can afford your glass of champagne on our budget. I mean I'd like champagne too, but don't worry, I'll go without so you can have one.' We had a budget of $50 per day each, so this was pushing it. But I was taking a shower while sitting on the toilet and sleeping on sweaty sheets in a hospital bed so we could afford treats like this. I deserved it.

'Ridiculous!' Yes, he was still moaning? The waiter swings by, bearing gifts – well nuts, and mustard seeds – so we order... a beer and a glass of rose. Not the glass of champagne. This causes fireworks. Fireworks that quite outdo the spectacular light show we watch in silence 30 minutes later on The Avenue of Stars, after we'd necked our over-priced beverages in stony contemplation and made our way out on to the crowded street. As the lasers fade out and the throngs move on to the ferries and into the distance, my husband bravely – considering my mood – decides, 'If we can't get on and not argue in a beautiful city like Hong Kong, we've got real problems.'

We walk back to the hotel without uttering a word, holding hands but I'm sure mine felt limp and cold in his palm, my heart certainly did in my chest. We get back into our hell hole of a hostel, undress, and climb into our separate beds and pretend to be asleep. We didn't even eat dinner. So within our budget, I could have had the champagne after all. What bitter irony.

***

I'm not nice if I don't have regular sex. Russ is not good if he doesn't get regular sleep. Therefore it was wonderful to be woken up by a loving husband, apologizing for his behavior the night before with a solution to our woes: 'I think I am just tired, I can't sleep on these hard beds. I can't wait to move on to a nicer hotel where we can relax in a double bed tomorrow.'

Sometimes just stating the obvious, throwing it out there into the universe, is all that's needed to defuse a situation. I felt like Tom and

Nicole in *Eyes Wide Shut*. The sexual tension would destroy us if we weren't careful. Thankfully, we manage to get through our breakfast without arguing. I'd become quite addicted to yeun yeung, a Hong Kong local delicacy – a creamy, sweet hot tea – and I'd also taken to the other Hong Kong breakfast food of choice: fish fingers. Instantly transported to my childhood, when I would steal my brother's cod sticks while my mother's back was turned, I was delighted that it was acceptable to eat them before 9am. Russ insisted on going hardcore, sucking down noodles with dried fish and raw eggs while drinking a sour lemon tea. I did love his ability to eat and drink anything at any time. Except fruit. He had an aversion to fruit that I'm shocked didn't call for scurvy and bad skin. Any kind of animal: skinned and fried, for sure. An apple: no way. This was just one of the funny nuances of my new husband that I'd had to learn quickly. Getting engaged after two months of dating was a little rash – and allowed for many errors and uncomfortable realizations – but we both agreed to learn them on the job. I'd known instantly – from our first phone call – that I'd finally met a man that was worth it.

***

The next afternoon was spent doing what all tourists in Hong Kong are told to do, and quite right too. We climb into the Peak Tram and make our way up the hills of the island for the ultimate look down. Fog and mist beckon, once again inspiring thoughts of Sherlock Holmes mysteries, *not* oriental adventures. Suddenly, after an hour, the sun breaks through and burns the heavy grayness away. Blue sky emerges and the city comes into view. The Star Ferries dart across the harbor like Morris dancing boats, the futuristic skyscrapers plunge like gods down from the moon into the heart of the people, the beaches out beyond the buildings look frightfully still and calm compared to the cluster of life on Kowloon. As we take it in – at last, blue sky and a clear view - other things became clear too.

'Why have we come here?' Russ turns to me suddenly. 'I know why. To be with each other; to see the world, too, but to truly see each other and see who we are and what we need to be, as individuals and as a couple. We both need to chill the fuck out, be thankful for everything we have been able to do… and fight this black cloud that has been hanging over us for months now. We owe it to ourselves.'

We decide right there and then, up above the mayhem, that we aren't going to let the menacing fog weigh us down any longer.

***

'I've decided that my father's funeral was actually one of the best days of my life,' Russ says over the by-now ubiquitous fish noodle/finger breakfast this morning. 'I remember clearly walking in carrying my dad's casket and seeing Batesy, Fountain, Clowesy, Moring, Guil, Prov, Reasty, Sammy… all my mates from school, the same guys who spend their whole lives winding me up and taking the piss were all there for me. All there for my dad. I saw all your family as I was walking up the aisle too. They'd only known my dad for a year but clearly had grown really fond of him. All my university friends took the day off work to come too, fighting their way across London to make it there on time. I understood that day how much all these people love me and respected my dad, and well, that's what funerals should be. Realizing that life is too short not to make the most of the good people around you. Take the responsibility of friendship and family ties seriously. Treat people with respect and your family with dignity. My father's death may have made us lose our belief in heaven and hell and some divine justice from above, but I think we've both learnt even more valuable lessons about why you should be a decent person.'

I sit, sipping my yeun-yeung in dumbstruck awe. We were only four months into the grieving process, but my brave husband was seeing such time-defying truths in the moments surrounding his father's death that I was starting to fall in love with him even more (whether I chose to show it or not). 'I'm going to tell my mum that when I next speak to her. I'm going to tell her dad's funeral was one of the best days of my life.' I grab his hand and he flashes me his monumental smile, the smile I could always remember so clearly in our 13 years apart. 'I hope she gets what I mean.'

We take the Star Ferry across to Central Pier and walk, struggling under the weight of our backpacks, to the Cotai Jet terminal. We were heading to Macau, another Chinese territory a couple of hours away from Hong Kong. A friend of mine in Los Angeles was the PR guru for the Venetian Hotel in Vegas and she wanted me to go and check out their sister property over there.

Macau is widely viewed as the Vegas of Asia – and quite rightly so. The Venetian (the second largest building in the world, after a flower market in the Netherlands apparently) was surrounded by other Strip stalwarts: the MGM, the Wynn, and the Hard Rock Hotel. We felt a bit like we were cheating as we checked in. Thanks to my high-powered friend, we were deemed VIPS and greeted by the team as mini-deities, but they couldn't hide their disappointment as two grubby, Cockney backpacking types stumble off the shuttle bus. We are urged up to our rooms quickly to 'rejuvenate' before the official tour with the general manager, who would be expecting a noted journalist not a hippy with body odor. We didn't need telling twice. After four days in a hostel, taking showers while sitting on the toilet in a non-air-conditioned bathroom the size of a postage stamp, the thrill of a clean towel and marble under foot is intoxicating. Russ soaks in bubbles while I simultaneously drown under a power shower, our eyes locked the whole time, grinning at each other like children after Santa's been for a visit. How exiting to be clean! I'd never been aware of my own smell until this trip, and to remove the stench was delicious.

The tour is the usual hotel tour any journalist gets when they are invited to stay. It's a boring half hour of payback for getting a free room. You are forced to wander the conference rooms and the wedding chapel - even though you know you (or your readers) couldn't give a toss and it will never be mentioned in the piece you write. The hotel managers should have noticed by now, when they get the article in their eagerly waiting hands, that a 1,000 person meeting room is never mentioned. But perhaps they're just sadomasochists who want the freebie-hunters to pay for dumbing down journalism. The tour at the Venetian took extra long – it being so scarily large and all – and the things I remember are this: it's exactly the same as the one in America only there are fewer fat people in electronic carts getting in the way *but* there are more people hacking up god knows what and spitting it on the floor. Yes, it's a disgusting habit the Chinese seem to have that made me wretch constantly. The hotel is great of course - it had cost nearly $3 billion to build so it bloody should be – but it all felt too American and fake for a place in Asia, so determined to stay on whatever kind of track we were on, we leave the chain-smoking gamblers to it and do something 99% of visitors to Macau never do: leave their hotel, jump in a taxi, and head to the nearest temple.

We are blessed that the breathtaking A-Ma temple is just 10 minutes away in the main town centre. The temple is named after a poor girl who was refused passage to nearby Canton by wealthy ship owners but taken aboard by a lowly fisherman. The story goes that a storm blew up, wrecking every vessel but the one carrying the girl and the kind fisherman. On arrival in Macau she vanished, reappearing some time later as a goddess on the rocky hill where her temple now sits. We soon get lost in the maze of moss-covered paths that lead around the temple and reach clearings only by following the scent of joss sticks burning in mini shrines and chapels celebrating Buddha. Behind these lit-up meccas, statues of Taoist gods nestle in moon gardens, sumptuous green spaces guarded by ornamental lions, hidden by boulders in the face of the hill. Red and yellow flowers cover every surface and locals bustle around the courtyard gardens, clucking busily, bowing in prayer and smiling at us. I hover around the temple keeper's gatehouse, reading any information I can find in English.

I read about an idea that appeals to me greatly: the Chinese belief that there is no jealousy between the gods and so people can take advantage of all the good luck and good advice they can get their hands on. When it comes to religion, most Chinese believe in 'the more the merrier', a notion I shared whether it be planning a party and not wanting anyone to feel left out, to donating money to charity. I'd seen a bumper sticker in Kentucky only a week before on a truck, smugly stating 'Christianity is the best religion 'cause we're the only ones who have the resurrection of Christ!' That – in a simple car catchphrase – summed up everything I disliked about the idea of organized religion: the one-up-man-ship and competition wasn't very *Christian*, I thought. Anyway, as a result of this 'come join the party' attitude, the temples in Macau – like this one – were a combination of Buddhist and Taoist, as well as offering places to worship local gods and ancestors. All these religions celebrate the sanctity of life (which is why so many devotees are vegetarian), reverence for the Gods and your family and harmony with nature. This seemed to make sense. So I light 25 joss sticks (I never do anything by halves) and offer them in thanks to a fat, jolly Buddha who sat in his own little cave at the top of the hill, nearly setting my hair on fire in the process, causing a few locals to cluck even more hurriedly and run for water, and I buy two black and white Taoist bead bracelets for me and Russ from the temple keeper.

And then it all went a bit awry. Desperate to stick to our $50 a day budget, all we could afford to eat at the five star Venetian was McDonalds. Hmmm. McDonalds in Macau wasn't exactly what we had planned. We hadn't eaten for 9 hours though and were starting to fade. I ask hopefully for a vegetarian burger and the server just tuts. So a few hours after toying with a life of vegetarianism, I munch on a Big Mac while sipping diet Coke, feeling a little bit gross.

***

Our departure from Macau was always going to be a little tiring. We had to get our Cirque-du-Soleiled asses up and out of The Venetian by 11am to make it for the ferry back to Hong Kong, early enough to safely make our flight to Bangkok that evening. The water crossing was rough. I turned green while Russ clutched his sick bag nervously, urging me not to read. Thankfully, we'd avoided the many, many glamorous bars surrounding the casino due to lack of funds, and could therefore maintain a slight edge - and a modicum of dignity – over the hung-over Chinese who were travelling back across the choppy sea with us.

I spend the journey foolishly hoping that this could be a very early sign of pregnancy. Although, in my logical mind I knew morning sickness didn't kick in until about week 6, I was into the second week of my *Two Week Wait*, when all sanity and grip on scientific truths fell to one side and got carried away by a giant stork.

For those of you who have never felt the desperate need to fall pregnant the term *Two Week Wait* will mean nothing to you. I'd never heard of it, until after 9 months of desperately trying – mentally if not always physically, being geographically separated from my spouse while he was nursing his sick father over the pond – I joined the totally possessed and hallucinating group of women who feel every twinge in their uterus between ovulation and menstruation, and cling to every tweak as a sign that this month they could have hit the jackpot. Men know nothing of this. Even the guys who want a child as much as their partner, and who sweetly get excited watching their partner pee on sticks and are gung-ho when they are told to go for it. No, the *Two Week Wait* (let's call is TWW from now on) is a phenomenon for women, exaggerated by women, with heartbreaking results most of the time. Think about it statistically: the women who stress about their TWW are the ones who have had trouble conceiving. The more fertile of our species seem to have a few drinks one night, grab their bloke's penis, roughly mid-cycle, for a bit of 'how's your father' and that's it - preggers. The TWW nuttiness is purely for those of us who are looking for hope where there is little. I could spend hours on the many, many blog sites set up by women such as myself, yelling at the screen 'me too!', and 'yes, I'm bloated!'

As a rough looking Chinese man pukes into a bag a few rows up and wipes his mouth with an empty cigarette packet, my morning sickness daydream comes to an end. I am on a freaking ferry in a rainstorm, still jetlagged and sick to the stomach that I ate a greasy burger. My baby symptom checklist was turning me into a mentalist. It had to stop. Russ wanted a baby as much as I did, maybe more so at times, for the added bonus that it would give his mum something to look forward to again. Why would Russ want to have sex with someone like me though? I'd systematically removed the sexiness and romance from our love making, reducing it to a perfunctory task that left me lying in bed for an hour after the act, not from the afterglow but so I could keep my legs up in the air, my pelvis tilted and the sperm getting a helping hand from gravity. I'd become a stereotype. A sperm junkie. Madame Ovary. Someone who lived from period to period like a woman on the verge of a nervous breakdown. This trip could change that. I should be too busy to live by an ovulation calendar. I'd deliberately left my cycle monitor at home. Perhaps I should try and leave my baby obsession there too.

6

Where Attention Goes, Energy Flows

'Thought is action in rehearsal.'

Sigmund Freud

More boats. Our hotel stood majestically on Bangkok's bustling river so the quickest way to get to the historic area was by longboat. The throat-clogging smell of rotting vegetables excited the local fish, who jumped and flipped above the surface of the water as we swayed down the gang plank and on to the long, thin vessel. Bangkok was different to Hong Kong and Macau. Not as clean, not as modern and the locals didn't seem as interested in what we were doing. This surprised me as I thought the once British Hong Kong and Portuguese Macau would have been more used to Westerners than the ancient and decidedly oriental Thailand. One way we could get their attention was by opening our wallets. 'No money, no honey' seemed to be the catchphrase of the day, plastered on signs and t shirts all over the city. The minute we disembarked at the stop for the Royal Garden Palace, we were surrounded by smiling faces, persuasively leading us to their tuk-tuks, informing us that the Royal Palace wouldn't be open till 2pm but that for a reasonable 60 bahts, they would take us around the city on a special tour – with shopping! This scam – which of course we fell for being naïve fadangs (a derogatory Thai word for foreigners) – was apparently the petty crime du jour, the Royal Palace in fact being open from the minute we arrived in the district at 8am. We could have been upset, but decided to look on the bright side: we had yet to become one of those irritating, pompous know-it-alls you have 'done' places and felt they knew more than the nationals. Yes, we spent a few hours getting carted through the smog with the promise of bargains at various cousins' jade stalls but that was part of being here. We were clueless Brits being taken for a ride – literally and metaphorically.

When we were released from our goose chase, we quickly made up for lost spiritual time: dousing each other with holy water at the shrine of the Emerald Buddha, buying friendship bracelets from an orange-clad monk in the shrine of the Lucky Buddha, and then trying to take in the unimagined, blinding beauty of the Reclining Buddha – a 15 meter high, 46 meter long capturing of the moment just before Buddha left the earthly world and reached Nirvana. If Michelangelo's David is worth gawping at for 1 hour, this is worth at least two. The mother of pearl eyes and feet are so intricately decorated that it's quite unbelievable. Around the walls, the many tales of Buddha's teaching are told through paintings. Our guide chose to share the meaning of a mural on the front door. A rich old man, surrounded by his wife and many concubines, was worried that his hair was getting thin and grey and that his stomach was getting bigger and his bones older. So he went to the Buddha and offered him as much money as he wanted to stop it getting any worse. The wise one informed him that none of this mattered: we can't control the body, as we can't control life or death, we all get older so worrying and obsessing over physical attributes is a waste of time. We come into this life alone and we leave alone. Once we are aware of this, getting older and the thought – and sometimes physical signs of approaching death, as the rich old man had seen – of death, become less scary and more just another step in the path of enlightenment and non-suffering. It all made sense and my eyes welled up with shameful tears. Yes, I was a girl who sometimes let a bad hair day ruin her life. How pathetic.

As our guide escorted us through the many temples, he stopped under a tree, where a stone penis-shaped object was surrounded by bottles of soda, cookies and flowers. 'This is where women who want to make a baby come and ask for help and leave little presents,' he said pointedly to me. 'You come back and ask for help after I've finished.' The tears started to well up again. He probably said that to every thirty something girl on vacation in Thailand with her husband and a desperate look in her eye but it felt very personal and poignant. Not knowing how to pray to Buddha, Russ and I returned and sent our own little message of positivity out into the universe. We kissed and told each other, 'I love you very much and would love to have a child who was half you and half me, who would become his or her own person with our help.' We kissed again. Bowed to the over-sized, decorated penis, finger tips together in a prayer-like stance under our noses, and walked off hand in hand to catch the boat back to our hotel.

The evening took a totally different turn – giant penises still played a part, but this time they were in the trousers of red-faced, puffy sex tourists, roaming the streets of Patpong, eagerly chatting away to pretty, young Thai girls who wouldn't look twice at them if their money couldn't buy their honey. It was a sad state of affairs in my mind. We sat people watching – well prostitute watching - in a bar, sipping on Singha beer and being alternatively tickled with the humor of it all and dismayed by the tragedy. Geeky young men were rabbiting away excitedly to Asian Lolitas, thrilled that finally a woman seemed to be interested in their computer game record. I didn't need to hear what the girls were saying. The universal female language of facial expressions showed me what these charmed nerds couldn't see… 'Yeah, yeah… we'll listen to this rubbish, buy us a few more drinks to get over your nerves and then let's talk cash. Other men were more confident, just walking straight up to girls or lady-boys on the street and disappearing up dodgy looking staircases or into darkened alleys. Fat men, disabled men, men with lazy eyes, covered in scars, long greasy hair in pony tails… they were all getting lucky tonight. And lucky with women who were beautiful and probably seemed so sweet compared to the pushy, demanding women back home.

'I think its fine' Russ announced. 'If the women are safe, the men get what they need and it stops them from assaulting women in the real world. And these women get the money they want. What's the harm if they all use condoms and know the score?' I saw his point. I was the only person who looked depressed in the whole bar. But still? We could dress it up with fairy lights and vodka red bulls but everyone here was being taken advantage of!

After a few beers and desperate to get to bed – we'd been up since 6am and seen about 2,300 Buddhas since then – we decided the last, must-do, infamous sight-seeing tick off our list had to be done. It was now or never. And a feather in the cap for every Bangkok holiday maker. Yes, the pussy ping pong show. This is the *family friendly* entertainment offered for those not keen on the whole whoring scene but fancying something a bit naughty or rebellious. The pussy ping pong show was the honeymooners special really – straight, happy couples would go to see it and be put off any kind of vaginal freakiness for the rest of their lives. Friends of ours had seen a woman launch a dart from her va-ja-ja and burst a balloon in Bangkok last year and Russ persuaded me we needed a better story than that for him to go up the pub with next time he was back in London. These are not as hard to find as you may think. Touts hassle you with ping pong invitations the minute you step on the street. Attracted by the big fluorescent 'Super Pussy' signage, we headed into the venue, up some dark stairs and paid our 100 baht for a beer and a promised thrill/shock of a lifetime. Immediately, a Madame pushed us into a booth with a seriously overweight German couple who seemed to love the attention of a handful of nubile young women with no tops on. And then the next two minutes went into slow motion.

Five or six prostitutes clambered around us, shaking our hands and shouting 'pussy dance for you, pussy dance $3.' I was hyper aware of the day-glow lighting and remember thinking how funny it was that Russ's teeth and eyes were glowing green, and how my handsome husband looked a bit ridiculous and scared at the same time. 'Pussy show, pussy for you.' They kept shouting, ignoring me, and climbing over Russ, who turned into a Hugh Grant caricature.

'No thank you, I'm here with my wife for a drink and the show, no thank you, no dancing.'

'You don't want this,' one of the prostitutes unleashed her breasts, pushing me out of the way to wiggle them in his face, 'or this?'

Now it was the pants down, and a shaved fanny was dangerously near my shoulder. I looked up to see a woman on stage sticking a beer bottle up her own business and pretending to enjoy it. Next to me, the German tourist was getting a fanny show of his own while his drunken wife gurned with a medieval pleasure, touching the girl's breasts. And then the atmosphere turned.

'Give us 600 now'. We explained, we'd paid the entrance fee, the 100 bahts for the beer and show, and didn't need anything else, or want to pay for anything else, thanks you.

'Pay now, pay, pay, pay,' shouting and vicious faces were scaring me now, as more prostitutes gathered, smelling the blood in the water and climbing into their degraded shark tank. The Madame sneered at me.

'No way, we're leaving,' I hurled back. We both got up. The Madame grabbed my bottle of beer, smashed it on the Formica table and held it aloft, swiping it past my face.

'Touch her and you'll know about it,' Russ pointed in her face, grabbed my arm, pulling me down the stairs and into the neon street.

'Ping pong show sir, you like! Come, come!' Touts swarmed again.

'Get out of our way,' Russ shouted as we power-walked to the nearest tuk-tuk and escaped.

Back at the hotel, we showered, and rubbed our hands and feet with antibacterial gel with a new fervor. I was disgusted with myself for having paid into an industry which exploited women, exploited lonely men and exploited the trust Thai people have in their own country. Russ felt disgusted that he'd put his wife in that situation. All this regret and upset, and we'd only been to see a woman fire a ping pong from her nether regions. Imagine how some other wasted tourists would be feeling the next day? I just hope they'd made a trip to the Patpong chemist beforehand (I'd spotted a pharmacy sensibly positioned between two sex bars that's stock was about 90% condoms). What fools we'd been? Just because Bangkok is famous for its red light district and depraved easiness, it didn't mean we had to play a part in it. I'd never have dreamt of seeing such a thing elsewhere yet I'd just added to this nasty game. Bangkok to me could have been the city of golden temples, delicious lemongrass and mushroom soup, dried squid stalls and brightly decorated longboats. Now it was a city of depressing sleaze and aggression. My inner compass had failed me.

***

Thailand is known as the land of smiles, a notion pushed by the tourist bureau I'm sure, and it's as if most of the people have been trained to be flattering and sweet, except for the con-artists and prostitutes we'd encountered the day before of course. Everyone else has been beyond delightful, something Russ put down to their firm Buddhist beliefs.

'Share with me the principles, how do you Buddhists stay so calm and happy? What are the rules?' he asked a random man in the car park of yet another temple.

'To be a Buddhist monk is very hard, you have over 200 rules, but to be a good Buddhist person is very simple. You have only five rules, and it you do these you will have a happy heart and a calm brain.' The rules all made sense: Buddhists should not kill, lie, steal, be sexually deviant or get dangerously intoxicated by substances. Apart from my aforementioned weakness for champagne, I could pretty much do that I was sure. The others were a no-brainer. 'And when you become Buddha,' our new enlightening friend beats his chest like Tarzan, 'you feel happy inside. Not from outside but from inside.'

I wasn't entirely sure that the Thai Buddhists never lied though. Even the sweetest ones I met seemed to stretch the truth a little, including an adorable waitress serving me my green curry, who insisted, 'You beautiful like beautiful girl in Avatar. You have same face.' Her flattery fell a little flat when I thought back to the film and its three female cast members: the blue creature, the Hispanic girl and the pushing 60 Sigourney Weaver. Each one of them would have been high praise indeed, but not at all realistic seeing as I was a chunky, 34 year old, English blonde.

The Thai people are driven by beauty and appearance, not in a bad way but in a very open way, a way that enjoys aesthetically pleasing people and things. Within 48 hours of being in Bangkok I was praised for my height, my dress, my hair (numerous times, and I assure you it was a bleached out frizz ball). We were asked how old we were all the time, and how tall. This isn't considered rude in Thailand, just important public information. We were also asked if we were married, had children, and when we answered in the negative, why not.

Our taxi driver on the way to the airport had a very firm grip on what he found attractive. 'My wife was beautiful and gave me two beautiful sons. But now she's so fat. She steals my sons' food when they are not looking. She's always eating. And she's 180 lbs. Can you believe? It's not good no more. I love her but she can't stop eating.' He kept taking his hands off the steering wheel to visually illustrate her massive girth, then shaking his head in despair.

To make him feel better about his wife's largesse, Russ volunteered information about me. 'She's 160 lbs, so there's not that much difference between them,' he consoled our chauffeur, giving my left thigh a hearty whack.

'Bloody hell, Russell! Cheers,' I groaned as our driver checks me out in the wing mirror.

'Don't worry, you hide it, you don't look big fat like my pig wife,' he offered.

Russ agreed with him and gave me a peck on the cheek and a wink to prove it.

I'd beg to differ – since landing in Asia, rather than slimming down with stomach bugs I'd put on weight – and even squatting over toilets to pee while wearing a heavy backpack had done little for my increasingly wobbly thighs. I should diet I suppose, lay off the coconut milk and street food. But one of the monks did say that we Westerners paid too much attention to our appearance and that as long as we were healthy, we should turn our minds back to what's inside, rather than out. I toyed with the idea of losing weight through starving myself as a teenager, but the idea only lasted a few hours, thanks to my good friend Andrea – who'd wrestled me to the floor and fed me a Malteser. So I figured the monk didn't need to worry about me, but I should squeeze in some exercise on our backpacking tour. My muffin tops would probably thank me for it.

7

Appreciation Nation

'A healthy body is a guest-chamber for the soul; a sick body is a prison.'

Francis Bacon

In 1975, the year I was born, Pol Pot and his Khmer Rouge party came into power. For three hours after his election, the people of Cambodia celebrated, believing his political campaign message: he was going to unify the war torn country and bring a new kind of change and development to the nation. But after three hours, when people started to go missing or be murdered, something was clearly wrong. It took Pol Pot only 180 minutes to change from being the people's Obama to their Hitler.

By 1979, when I was four years old and a tomboy in a tutu, excitedly going to my first Tottenham Hotspur football games with blue and yellow ribbons in my hair, Pol Pot had killed around 2.5 million of his own people. Including children and babies. He had to kill them too you see, in case they grew up and learnt of what he did and sought revenge. Complete families had to be 'destroyed'.

Walking the blood-stained corridors of the notorious S-21 is an experience I will never forget, and should not try to. My heart was numb and my head racing as I tried to make sense of the macabre beastliness of this unfathomable period of the world's modern history. That this had happened in my lifetime, 30 years after the world saw off Hitler and his monstrous regime, was beyond cognition. The only way I could begin to grasp the true horror was to try and relate the numbers, the figures, the faces, the statistics, somehow to my own life. It started the year I was born. When I was an adored toddler, Cambodian three year olds were being thrown in the air and used as shooting practice by groups of prison guards. When my wonderful mother was struggling to save money with no support from my hopeless father, the Khmer Rouge decided to save money too – by not shooting their victims with expensive bullets, but holding them by their feet and bashing their heads against a tree. When the Vietnamese took over and started to dismantle the vicious regime in 1979, the first visitors to the killing fields, 10km outside of Phnom Penh, found a tree covered in brains and hair next to a deep pit filled with over 100 bodies of naked women and children.

Not one Cambodian could explain Pol Pot's beliefs or aims to me. 'His own people, his own people,' was all they could say while shaking their heads incredulously. 'He wasn't like Hitler, who killed the other, who killed those who he thought would harm Germany,' my tour guide tried to explain to me. 'He was a Cambodian who chose to kill Cambodians.' He also killed his friends and his colleagues. Again, I tried to make sense of this madness: this would be like me deciding to murder 35% of English people, including my Kent University friends and my former team at *The Mirror*. That put a perspective on it that made everything even more unbelievable.

I have two brothers who I adore. They can be annoying, of course, yet they are truly two of the great loves of my life – my link between the past and the future, allies against my parents' craziness. By the time she was 13 years old, my tour guide had lost all of her brothers to the brutal regime and her mother and grandparents. Unfathomable loss. Unfathomable pain. How could she take foreigners around the prison, pointing out key photos (mug shots of women, with a baby's hand grasping at their chest, their faces out of shot; Buddhist monks, stripped of their robes and humiliated with their identification label pinned through the skin on their neck; young boys with broken noses, eyes like pools of dark water) and describing her own recent history in such detail. 'We want the outside world to see what happened to Cambodia, to understand my country. This can never happen anywhere ever again.'

Russ and I had been snap happy for the entire trip, joking that we would trap our friends back home and bore them for hours on our return to Kentucky. Today, there were no photos to take. A photo couldn't capture it, only our hearts could. How can a hastily taken shot of a building, a former school turned torture chamber, symbolize the story of a teenage girl who, excited by the prospect of a hot date, burst into a British love song from the 1960s and was killed for it? A guard heard her voice, took her away from the village to question her. Deciding the hippy ditty was a sign of her disloyalty, she was killed, her blood-soaked clothes returned to her village to remind the other teens that singing, or dating, or love, would not be tolerated.

The S-21 Prison is in the heart of Phnom Penh, a city deserted by the fearful during the regime and still suffering today from the mass destruction, arson attacks and vandalism of that time by the Khmer Rouge. Buddhist temples were used as pig stys and schools used as concentration camps. After all, the monks, teachers and students didn't need them anymore – they were amongst the first to be imprisoned. After the end of the regime, no one knew there was a prison in the heart of Phnom Penh. The Vietnamese stumbled across it by smell. The stench of death was so strong it could be detected two miles away. Following their noses led to this hell on earth, instruments of torture flung around the floor and a gallows erected in the once pleasant gardens. Cells no bigger than a single bed, windowless and covered in blood and urine. Again, that this was uncovered while the Western world was dancing to Abba and enjoying package holidays to the Costa Brava, coating their eyelids in glittery eye shadow, was beyond me.

We weren't happy that we went. But we're glad we went. To witness the instruments of such cruelty and to hear the tales of genocide from the people that lived it is humbling and shocking but a necessary part of any visit to Cambodia. How can you understand the people, their begging, their smiles, their reaction to foreigners, without seeing this? I saw nothing special, I did nothing special. Russ and I followed the well-trodden path of around one million other Western tourists coming to the country since the late 1980s. But the experiences, however packaged up in a neat 5 hour excursion – complete with a stop at a gift shop and toilets – will change my outlook on life forever and make me even more grateful for the blessings that life has kindly given me. When I look in the mirror and begrudge the onslaught of wrinkles on my forehead, I will remember my tour guide, who slept on mud beds in rice fields for a few months when she was 10 years olds because the Khmer Rouge had destroyed her home. She was forced to work for 18 hours a day, 'until the moon shined bright', for two bowls of soup a day. The reason I'll think of this and not Botox when I catch a glimpse of my ageing reflection in a mirror? 'The mud and rain made me look like an old lady. I was an old lady child. And the heavy equipment I had to carry gave me sore shoulders and bent back. I was 10 but I look 90 years old.' My tour guide actually manages to smile at the bad luck of it all. She can persuade the corners of her mouth to turn upwards and her eyes to crinkle at the ridiculousness of it all, which is more than many of the plastic men and women I know can do.

***

Bright tangerine monks, waltzing in crocodile lines, barefoot and shaded by Clementine parasols, are energizing to the eye, unlike our darkened men and women of faith back home, suffocating in black. I'd always been shocked by the ridiculousness of Christian spiritual costumes. Apparently, aged three, I'd embarrassed my poor mother in the John Lewis department store on Oxford Street by standing on a restaurant chair and yelling 'Look Mummy, a penguin! A penguin!' as a pious nun walked past. The excitement must have been too much because I then proceeded to wet myself.

Chasing the barefoot monks down the unmade roads linking rice fields and concrete schools, were motos, driving in both directions carrying whole families to work, children balanced on seats, parents' laps – whatever they could get a grip on. Skinny cows searched for grass next to statues of elephants. Banana trees twinkling with the gaudy gold delights of the imminent Chinese New Year lined villages on stilts, balanced above murky looking water covered in the most beautiful water lilies I'd ever seen. The road to Siem Reap – described by our guide book as 'blissfully smooth' - was filled with holes, bumps and terrifying. But we were glad we chose this 6 hour journey, rather than the boat. It's between bustling cities, in the small villages, that you can witness the real lives, however fleeting, of the people we'd flown 6,000 miles to get to know. Every village had a Cambodian People's Party headquarters, and a bottle shop, where old Pepsi bottles were filled with petrol and sold off to people who could only afford a tiny bit of watered-down fuel. Dogs wandered around aimlessly, thin and dreamy, ignored by the children playing soccer. Old women balanced baskets of fried cockroaches and ears of corn over their shoulders, toothless grins greeting them in every house, for they were the Cambodian equivalent of the ice cream van. The litter was what really hit me. It was everywhere and included everything, whether strewn singularly or gathered in piles. Mounds of rubbish upon rubbish, next to toddlers playing and monks praying.

'It's disgusting they've let the countryside get like this,' Russ shook his head, dismayed at this urban ruination of the pastoral scene. I argued they had more to contend with than being tidy. It wasn't the litter being thrown around the fields and roads that bothered me, but the landmines.

Between the kaleidoscope of characters through the window and catching up on the news in the Phnom Penh Post (pig's head thrown in Muslim mosque in Malaysia, Obama disappointing in America, restriction of freedoms in Indonesia…) the long, hot, bumpy ride flew by.

We arrived in Siem Reap hungry and thirsty – for lunch and a new adventure. We dumped our backpacks in our $7 per night hostel and headed straight back out to sample some Khmer cuisine. I was thrilled with anything including Bok choi, lemongrass and mushrooms and Russ lusted after the Cambodian equivalent of a Thai red curry. Sat in a small pedestrian walkthrough nicknamed The Alley by locals, you could sense what this town was about. The French influence was still there, the restaurants were fine and much more sophisticated than the ones in Phnom Penh, and lots of the old architecture remained, with plenty of space for people watching on iron-balconies on the third floors of grand 19th century buildings.

As we ate, the by now expected parade of beggars and book sellers approached our table. We'd agreed in Phnom Penh not to give money to children anymore. Not only did the children make more money than their fathers (the cute factor pulled heart strings), throwing the whole system and hierarchy of family out of order, but it encouraged their parents to keep them out of school – short term gain rather than long term planning. Siem Reap's inhabitants had been badly affected by landmines and it was easy to tell. Amputees were everywhere, begging for anything we could spare. We'd decided that we could spare everything we had. A week's rent for a Cambodian was the same as a Sunday brunch for us back home in Louisville, so who were we to say no? An experienced Dutch traveler we'd met had told us if we were going to give to people on the street that the landmine victims were the ones to give to. Without a national health service to rely on for care, they were also seen as outcasts by society, freaks within their own people. With this in mind, Russ and I – who were still on a budget, however loaded we must have seemed to Cambodians – decided to give money to every amputee who asked us that day, instead of having dinner.

The child rule got broken near the end of the day when we met Kim. We were sitting, drinking water and getting some shade when he approached with a huge smile and one leg. His other leg had been blown off at his hip bone a few years earlier. He swaggered over, a bundle of postcards and books tied round his front with a krama, a traditional Cambodian scarf.

92

'Where you from?' he asked with a grin. Our answer – London – unleashed a barrage of facts that won us over (we weren't naïve to the fact the kids were probably trained in scam school to charm tourists in such a shameless way, but Kim had a twinkle in his eye while doing it that was totally charming): 'London is the capital of England, your Prime Minister is Gordon Brown. You like to play football. And your population is 65 million but you have minus two. You know why?' We shook our heads. 'Because you two are here with me now in Siem Reap! Buy some postcards please! Look, they're very, very pretty and you can send to all your friends. I have monks, I have temples, I have monkeys,' he flicked through the cards like a Vegas dealer.

'I don't have any friends, I've only got one and she's here with me,' Russ joked, clearly smitten with this child.

'Ahh, really? I'll be your friend then.' And they shook hands on it.

This little artful dodger wasn't going anywhere so we bought 10 postcards and asked about his life on the outskirts of this beautiful ancient city. 'I have six sisters and three brothers, my mother is very busy,' he laughs. His father? 'My father dead. Last year, he got hit by a moto at 7am. And we thought he was ok. But then the next day at 7am his head exploded, his brain went whoosh and he was dead. It was funny. From 7am to 7am. It took one day for my father to be dead.'

'My father died last year too,' my grieving husband confesses to his 12 year old confidante.

'I'm so sorry,' replies Kim. 'I'm so sorry that you no longer have a father.'

This shakes us both to the core. That a 12 year old with one leg, a beggar who watched his father's brain explode, was giving his heartfelt condolences to Russ. He'd already told us he liked reading and we thought we could send him some English newspapers and magazines from home to read. 'Write down your address', Russ hands him a pen and paper, 'and we'll post you some books from England. Would you like that?' Not understanding, Russ continues, 'tell us where you live, we'd like to send you some things.'

Ahhh. He gets it. He grabs the pen and starts to scribble. 'Here is the Old Market, you know where that is? Well, from there, follow the river around the bend and keep walking, keep walking, keep walking. Then cross the road where you'll see an old man and ask him where Kim lives and then you'll find me. Come and see me!' With his fresh dollar in his pocket and spotting fresh donors on the horizon, he's off, quick as lightening on his crutches to charm the next holidaymakers, leaving us – two bedraggled backpackers – bedazzled, humbled and a little bit guilty.

***

Cambodia represents heaven *and* hell on earth and today we got to see the heavenly side at last. Angkor Wat: the largest religious building in the world, a series of Buddhist-Hindu temples built around 700 years ago. We had decided enthusiastically the night before to be up and out by 5am in order to catch sunrise over the lily pond facing the largest temple. It was a battle to stir ourselves in the darkness, chase down a tuk-tuk, avoid the many potholes (I did end up down one actually, no harm done) and get to the pond's edge for the first glimpse of pink. But it was worth it. Everything you've ever dreamed of, Angkor Wat cannot disappoint. Even the most temple-fatigued traveler will find something to willingly gawp at.

As the moon disappears and the sun rises, we head away from the gathering crowds to a little-talked of building down an unmade road. Suddenly, from nowhere, a monkey darts at me and launches himself at my leg. Looking up at me from my knee, the monkey seems bemused – does he want a play fight or is he warning me to stay away? Unable to communicate and scared shitless, all I can do is fling my leg around, jumping up and down on the un-monkeyed foot, while Russ laughs so much he forgets to take a photo. My attacker jumps off and rejoins the little furry gang that have gathered in the trees, while I try and rub off the dusty monkey paw prints that have covered my leggings.

The temples don't have a deeply moving, spiritual effect on either of us – it's too touristy and busy for that. We both felt more in the tiny temple we'd discovered in Macau. They moved us aesthetically – to see the huge faces glaring down at us from the Bayon temple, wry smiles tempting us to go in and try to climb them was exhilarating – but it's hard to feel like you're entering another realm or witnessing God's work when you have Japanese tourists pushing you out the way to get the shot they have seen in their guide book. Mother Nature had more of an influence in the wonderful Angkor Thom, famous for being Lara Croft's base in Tomb Raider and therefore even more clambered over by tourists, and was wonderfully decayed by gigantic trees and their crawling roots. Branches dripped down into the walls of buildings, proving that nature could outsmart even the most carefully planned building. Piles of rubble decorated the walkways as giant trunks had decided to make their home where the temple previously had.

After seven hours of temple jostling, an elephant ride, and a tuk-tuk accident on the ride back to the hotel (again, no harm done, it was just a bit hair-raising!) we decided our weary feet could do with a massage. I'd been told about a place nearby called Seeing Hands, a massage centre where the services were performed by blind people, giving them a job in an otherwise jobless world, and where the profits went to a local care centre for the hard of seeing. I'd been warned that communication was difficult – as you'd expect without the usual hand signal stuff that you could usually do with foreign masseurs – and they certainly wouldn't win any awards for their rubdowns, but it was a good massage for a good cause.

We arrived down a back alley, followed by a pack of dogs and children and a man pointed upstairs to a balcony. In for a penny in for a pound, we climbed the stairs, shouting 'hello, hello', and 'massage'. A 40-something lady and a youngish boy, he would have been 20 at most, emerged from a dark, dirty room and beckoned us in. We were here now, so the cobwebs and their filthy robes couldn't change our minds.

'Two 30 minute foot massages please,' we held out our hands to the lady, the boss we assumed, so she knew there were two of us and both spoke so she knew she had a man and a woman.

'Ok, change and sit please.'

Seeing as they were blind, Russ decided modesty was unnecessary, saying 'Let's just get changed here', so we stripped there and then with them in the room and got onto the dirty, holey beds.

Let me start by saying neither of our feet were touched, which is odd for a foot massage. Russ had his scalp massaged for about an hour while I just lay there watching. After an hour, the woman found my thighs on the neighboring bed and shook them forcefully for about 10 minutes. She then returned to Russ, who was then pulled about for a further 20 minutes. My dear husband had an expression of *I'm going to kill you when we leave here*, as they flipped him over and both started massaging his bum, climbing up onto the bed to get a firmer pummel. But we held hands throughout, sometimes having to face opposite directions so as not to catch each other's eyes and rudely laugh, and truly admired these brave, hard-working people. Seriously, I don't know how they even crossed the street in Siem Reap. The driving was bad enough when you were fully sighted; let alone finding a way to survive without the key sense of the human body. As we stifled out giggles at the absurdity of lying in this pitch black room, upstairs in a strange house down a back alley in Cambodia, my husband being fondled by a pair of blind masseurs, we were thrilled to have done it.

***

I awoke at 3am with the most agonizing stomach pains. I knew my dreaded period was due any day, but this felt different. I couldn't lie on my left or right or on my tummy. Just on my back, flat out. My head was pounding as my teeth felt too big for my gums and my ears felt like they had balls rolling around in them. I wasn't sweaty, which was weird considering our budget hadn't run to air conditioning and the room had felt sticky the previous night. In fact I felt cold. After a few hours of silently writhing and inwardly groaning, I moved to the bathroom in the dark, hoping that sitting up on the loo would relieve whatever was taking over my body. After a few long minutes leaning my weary head on the sink, a fanfare of gurgles announced the arrival of Gangee's revenge. The relief was short-lived as a lurch upward made me know I was about to vomit as well. Lovely. Top and tail, I was a walking (well, crawling) tourist stereotype. My jolly hockey-ness had got me nowhere. As I'd gamely thought I would eat and drink like the locals, sit around dirty homes and shake hands with all and sundry, my sanitary Westernized body had other ideas. *You silly cow*, it was saying. *This is why Americans carry around hand sanitizer with them – in America!*'

As soon as Russ stirred, bringing me water and a hair band, my legs gave way, and he took me to bed, laying me out flat once again to continue my pathetic moaning and groaning. At dawn, I ushered him out. It was that undignified, messy illness that makes you want to wallow alone, so that hours could pass and night come again without too many distractions to puncture the clock. He busied himself with Khmer meals, buying jewelry at the old market and getting another massage. He'd return every few hours to check on me and show me his purchases but was forbidden to tell me what he'd eaten – the thought of food made a flood of metallic saliva flow to my mouth and I couldn't imagine ever enjoying a dinner again. I tried to tempt myself with my favorite things (beans on toast, nooooooo…. Mushroom pizza, yuk…….. Mum's roast dinner, I'll vomit) because the idea of not being interested in food for someone like me was too weird. I realized I hadn't been this ill, or physically vomited, for years – perhaps six or seven.

Through my lack luster, limp body something twinkled in my brain. Aha! Morning sickness. Again, I *did* know that officially morning sickness didn't start till about week six of pregnancy, but I was always so impatient for everything else in the world, it made sense that my morning sickness wouldn't be able to wait to start making me crazy, my baby hormones taking over. And I'd normally have got the first signs of cramping by now, and there weren't any. Perhaps this was it. Perhaps morning sickness really was as brutal as they say. My trip would be bloody miserable but it would all be worth it for a baby. My mind leapt forward to the very long train and boat trips we had yet to take. They wouldn't be pleasant of course, but it would be do-able. I'd try not to moan too much so that Russ could still make the most of this much-needed trip – and I was excited to see these new places too – and in a way it would be exciting to tell our child that he or she had been on this adventure with us.

When Russ returned after his final expedition of the night, bringing gifts of a beautiful handmade straw ring and a bottle of water, I casually dropped my theory. 'Honey, you've got the shits. You don't get diarrhea with morning sickness, I'm pretty sure,' he sat down on my bed (another budget saver in hostels was sleeping in small single beds rather than double ones). 'We're in Cambodia and you're running around non-stop in the heat, eating food washed and prepared on the street, ignoring my advice about having drinks with ice in and playing with the village kids. You were always going to pick up a sickness bug somewhere and you have. Now go to sleep and you'll feel better in the morning, I promise.'

I didn't. I hadn't slept a wink and my stomach still felt like it had a small animal using my intestines as a warren. Somehow I rallied; well I didn't have a choice. We had a tuk-tuk, two flights and a bus to catch. We were leaving Cambodia, a place that had opened my eyes so much when I first arrived and had sadly left me trapped in a dark, airless room, fearful of leaving the toilet. We were heading back to

Thailand, this time down to the Adaman coast in the South – a glorious hotspot of holiday glee to many, many people.

8

Wear Sunscreen

'Quality is not an act, it is a habit.'

Aristotle

Now, I may be seeing Phuket, our first port of call, through the weary, cynical eyes of someone who hadn't eaten for 36 hours but the place was worse than a disappointment – it was a dump. And I don't mean in the way that some may have described the dirty, dusty, rundown streets of Phnom Penh. Patong, our chosen destination on the island of Phuket, seemed to be a place filled with scammers, players and partiers. The result was a plethora of my vegetarian nemesis, McDonalds (indeed the local tourist maps had their logo printed obtrusively on every other street corner), prostitutes catcalling chubby holidaymakers ('let me kiss your body all over' they'd offer, laughing when worried girlfriends looked upset) and effeminate looking men in immaculate makeup, jutting their snake hips towards passersby and blowing smoke in their faces. The beach was pretty and there were smiling faces too, but the general air was menacing and mean. At the hostel, a fellow traveler was recounting the tale of her camera being stolen when she asked a passerby for directions and another retorted with a tale about a cab driver scarpering with the substantial change she was owed. Everyone was on the make. Not just the locals, the visitors too seemed more of an in-the-know bunch that we'd met around Bangkok, Honk Kong or Cambodia. They were there for the cheap girls, cheap gems and even cheaper suits, not the rich culture we'd seen in the northern Thai capital. These are all massive generalizations, snatched from glimpses, and by a tired, nauseous person at that, but the energy didn't work with mine – or Russ's – and we decided to get the first boat out the next morning.

***

As we cruise towards the gigantic cliff faces of the Phi Phi islands, I feel a familiar dagger like pain in my groin and then my heart. A thickening of agony circling my hips and lower back confirms that my monthly friend has arrived and, as well as the Andaman Sea, I am now cruising the crimson wave. Too exhausted to get myself emotionally wound-up, I just search for painkillers and a tampon in my cavernous backpack and get on with business.

Docking in Phi Phi is a relief. The standard Thai hustle bustle is there in all its topsy-turvy glory but there's more a sense of welcoming than 'show us your cash'. We quickly and easily find a cheap hostel within walking distance of not only the ferry port but the beach and bars. It has a pool and breakfast is included (result) but A/C would push the price from a doable $35 per night to $50. Therefore once again we agreed to roast as we slept. The result of these nightly toastings seemed to be bad skin. The sweat and dirt of the hostel world did not agree with my complexion and I don't think I'd ever looked so rough. Add to that the green tinge of constant boat rides and a bout of sickness and I wondered if Russ would ever be able to muster the arousal to actually get me pregnant. At this point, I certainly wouldn't want to shag me.

The beautiful Thai islands that form Phi Phi were the worst hit by the Tsunami in 2004 but you wouldn't know it. Despite death washing down every alleyway and through every palm tree, the spirit of the place is bright and exciting. Every single freestanding building was completely destroyed by the treacherous waves, businesses were ruined and lives were lost. Yet six years on and the village was rebuilt, the travelers were back and the place was bustling once more. I'd been friends back in New York with a model who had survived the disaster by clinging to a tree on the island, breaking her hip bone in the process, yet more painfully, losing her fiancé to the sea. Despite the sunshine and calm sea we encountered, I imagined her in every tree I saw and hung to Russ's arm tightly.

***

We're thrilled to have a breakfast included in our feeble room rate, so set our alarm to make the most of the buffet. The plan was to gorge ourselves first thing so we can make it through till evening without spending any of our much-needed and quickly-diminishing cash. Before I've even poured a juice, a Chinese man has coughed up something nasty and spat it in a flower pot. Then a German dude is having a sneezing fit over the pineapple and mango platter – without covering his nose, mouth or turning away. I tut loudly, pull faces at both of them which is meant to say *I'm English! We don't do things like that in England and I think you're disgusting!* I resist the urge to run back to my room and take my place at the toaster. As I wait for my slices to pop up, I'm aware of a whirling dervish at my side and before long she's trying to nudge me out the way to get at my toast. 'Excuse me, it won't be a minute and then I'll be out of your way,' I offer her with a smile – a not very sincere one, but a smile. She grunts something in a thick Israeli accent and carries on pushing me, so I push her back, my toast pops up, I yank it our as quick as I can, say 'see it wasn't difficult to wait, was it?' in an overly-loud voice and march back to my table.

I don't like to think I'm one of those awful travelers who wander the globe with a passport and a sense of superiority but to be honest, the places we were going and the people we were encountering were starting to get to me a little. I was starting to feel like one of those doddery old birds in an E.M. Forster novel, referring to 'good, old Blighty' and moaning about the heat, dust and mosquitoes. And I didn't even live in England! That was the joke. I'd lived in America for five years. I'd been warned once you left your home country – wherever it was – the first thing you unpacked were your rose tinted glasses and that you never saw your birthplace the same way again. You didn't necessarily want to go back (we knew we did, but still couldn't totally commit to a date) but you saw it as the perfect place, a blend of nostalgia mixed with shock at how the rest of the world lived and thought would have you place your, well, place on a pedestal.

Before I turned into a character from Downton Abbey and started polishing the hostel's cutlery, Russ shoved me on the path to the beach for a day of chilling out. Fate struck a blow as we were sandwiched on deckchairs between two groups of Aussies. In their early twenties, they were doing their annual pilgrimage to get tanned. Phi Phi was their equivalent of Ibiza and they felt they owned the island. Apparently this meant they could A, talk very, very loudly, constantly, about absolute gibberish and B, squeal even louder than they talked while C, using the word babe in every sentence. I'd always loved the Australians in Australia, but I swear the minute they leave their country they become a bit annoying. Why do they insist on talking as if everything they say is a question, their tone goes up at the end in a way that after a few hours had my teeth on edge? The bimbos on either side of me (for that's what they were I'd decided, eradicating memories of me and my girlfriends at the same age on the same sort of holiday doing much worse) were shouting over our heads, sharing their sex bruises while slagging off each individual friend as she disappeared on a smoothie run. I didn't like the last part especially. Hey, we've all had a few sex bruises but I didn't like the bitching about friends behind backs. Bloody Aussies.

It struck me that Russ and I must have looked much older than we realized that afternoon on the beach, sat under our umbrella – him reading up on a computer project he'd be taking on when he got home, me reading a book about the life and teachings of Buddha. The girls either side of us made us feel mature but we still assumed we could fit in physically. Yet as the day wore on it became clear all the beach dudes selling things up and down the shore line had other ideas. While we'd be offered the all-you-can-eat-buffet nights and sunset cruises, everyone else seemed to be offered all-you-can-drink cliff jumping tours and booze cruises.

'How old do I look?' I threw poor Russ and unwinnable question. Too old, he must have been ogling the tarts either side of us. Too young, he's after something.

'I think we look about the same,' he wisely replies, 'about 29.'

'So why aren't we being offered the booze cruises?' I protest.

'If you want to go on a booze cruise, we can go on one – but I warn you, it'll be horrendous being hung-over in that room with no air-con.'

'Of course I don't want to go on one, the lads selling them look like monkeys who couldn't steer a bicycle let alone a boat, but I want to be asked.'

Convinced that I must have aged in the 17 days since we'd left America, I put on another coat of Factor 50, wrap myself in a damp towel and try to remember what Buddha said about ageing: worrying about it is futile. We all get old, we all suffer, and we all die. Ah good, that's cheered me up.

As the sun goes down, the Australian ladies are reaching excruciating levels of shrieking as they plan the night ahead. 'It's like soooooooooooo important that we go to Stones bar, not Rolling Stones bar.'

'Oh. I. Know. It's like soooooooooooo important.'

'So, so, so important babe.'

'Oh, so, I know babe.'

As this mindless banter continued, two English chaps arrive, kneeling at the babes' loungers, clearly recognizing some easy targets and coming in for some action. Colin and Kevin were a walking embodiment of the typical Brit in Phi Phi: they were decorated with wooden beads, wore flip flops and long board shorts, and had very red faces and white hairless chests – all rubberstamped with the ubiquitous Celtic band tattoo around their bicep. I wasn't expecting a brilliant meeting of minds (I knew they'd be let down by the opposing side already) but the English lads brought nothing to the party. In fact, they made it even worse.

'Yeah, it's a real pisser that all the clubs on Phi Phi have to shut a 1am now, not 6am. Two Thai dudes shot each other a few weeks ago so they're showing the dead some 100 days of respect thing. But they're not exactly respecting our need to par-tay are they ladies,' this delivered with a certain twinkle seemed to induce giggles of agreement from the fillies. 'I mean we come here, want to flash our cash, and where can you go to get wasted after 1am? Nowhere. It's pathetic. They need to get their priorities sorted. That's why we go on these boats, get hammered all day long, tell the captains they have to plug in our iPods so we can play our good music, then we don't mind going to bed at 1am if we have to.' What charming lads. The Queen would be quaking in her Hunter boots if she heard this but they did me a favor. I was starting to think to be born English is to be born better than anyone else. I realize within a few minutes of listening to Chimp 1 and Chimp 2 that it's not where you're from, it's where you want to go, that really says the most about you.

***

Today I felt how fragile my happiness was and that any allusion of self-control or calm I had was a self-perpetuating myth that I really needed to expose once and for all. It all started as dreamily as you'd expect while holidaying with the man you love on a tropical island, with no plans to make except where to have dinner, no decisions except whether to scuba dive or snorkel. My meltdown today really scared me, because if I can't be truly content and at peace with myself under these circumstances, what hope did I really have? My battle to get to know myself and to become a better person – which was the sub-reason for this world tour – was clearly failing. And I didn't like to fail.

Back to the not-so-difficult decisions to set the scene: I decided to snorkel and Russ decided to scuba dive, him being a far sportier, brave type than me (and I had the added excuse of a twisted tube in my inner ear which caused immense pain when I had dived in the past). We board the dive boat with a mixed, up for it crew of Irishmen, Swedes and Thais, and listen carefully to the safety briefing while waking up on sugary donuts and tea. We sail off towards Maya Corner, our first stop and the infamous bay where Alex Garland (or Leonardo Di Caprio if you're a celluloid type) got into trouble. Yes, it was the beach from *The Beach* and therefore the hottest spot in town. By the time we throw in our anchor at 9am, dozens of other small sailing boats have done the same and the sea is dotted with the splash of a blue flipper and a ripple of bubbles from 10 meters down. Russ gets tanked up and poses for me, the adoring wife, snapping images of my brave boy venturing down to the depths of the ocean, and then I quickly squeeze on my fins and mask and jump in the warm, turquoise waters and float around the top. Immediately I spot a Hawksbill turtle so decide to meander along the reef with him, slowly seeing what my new leader sees and enjoying the sounds of the sea, the gentle drilling and nibbling of a zillion hungry marine creatures, filtering the seabed for tasty morsels.

Time flies and my back bakes, I grab onto the boat's ladder and pull myself out of the saltiness and into the arms of the weathered Irishman and his bags of tuna sandwiches. Russ emerges minutes later, as excitable as a performing seal in his black wetsuit, proclaiming the joys of diving again (it had been seven years since he'd last done it) and eager to refill his oxygen tank and jump back in.

He had his wish an hour later as we sailed around the coast to a coral garden of local legend. He and the fellow divers sunk straight through the azure waves and once again I followed, a little timidly thanks to the promised proximity of black tipped and leopard sharks. All I had to do was look out through the surface of the sea towards the horizon and I'd see their fins.

My octopus's garden was what I imagined heaven to look like, if there is such a place. Blue mushrooms swayed against orange flowers and reeds of deep red. Trumpet fish swam two by two through the ripples a few inches from the real world while the parrot fish darted between the black and white stripes of the angel fish, near the bottom, using starfish as goalposts for their ocean Olympics. A few kicks away from the coral, I pushed my way into a snow globe. I'd entered an underwater disco where two billion tiny blue fish had decided to simultaneously do the electric slide while wearing silver cat suits. Around me they swept to the left, then the right, catching sunrays and glitter on the scales as they performed a dance routine just for me.

This blissful moment gave me the one thing we all live for: to feel alert and true and in the moment, to acknowledge that whatever went before and whatever will happen in the future, whatever memories haunt your mind and whatever fears lurk unknown, that you are present and in a simple state of utter being. Those minutes in my marine nightclub were intense and complete. I was alone and my mind was blank. I was feeling the water swirl against my skin, my heavy ponytail float and drag with the waves, my eyes whirling around my head in a daze of color and movement. And then my school of techno fish moved on to the next bar, I heard the muffled horn of my dive boat and I came back to the real world and all the complications it brings. I hadn't seen a shark, and all the divers felt so sorry and rushed over to share the evidence from their underwater cameras, but who needed sharks when you'd experienced a private dance recital. We sail back to harbor, sun-crisp and red-cheeked, bleached out and salty, happy with our lot.

When gurus tell you to 'live in the moment' my underwater experience was what they meant. But it's easy to do in the Andaman Sea, not so easy in a queue for petrol when your partner is being factitious and you're running out of cash. I got that. I tried to remember the fishy feeling but within hours I could sense that feeling of completeness dissipating quickly. A trip back to the very real world of home via an internet café showed how pathetically far I was from this point and hence my despair. Two bits of good news received via email left me in a mood. I got a message that a friend of mine was eight months pregnant. A friend of mine who'd never wanted kids, who hated kids, whose husband felt too old for kids, was eight months pregnant. I hadn't heard from her for a few years now – she was one of those girls I loved at university but haven't had much in common with since, especially when geography got in the way and I moved stateside. Russ got an email from his mum sharing the good news that his much younger cousin and his new girlfriend were also expecting a baby. It was unplanned so quite a shock at first but now they have got their head round the idea; they are looking forward to it.

In a flash, I become the bitter, weak person that I am ashamed to be. A bitch. A jealous cow that is envious of other people happiness. 'Oh good, everyone can have a baby apart from us,' I sarcastically celebrate to Russ as tears well up in my eyes.

'What is wrong with you?' he barks back without missing a beat. 'This isn't you? You're one of the good girls, the one who is happy for others and encourages them to be great.'

'Well it's just really hard to always say "I'm so happy for you, how lovely, have you thought of names yet" when each new bit of bloody baby news just highlights how my shitty body isn't working.' I knew it was my body not his – thanks to the paranoid health checks I'd made us do the month before. His sperm was chipper, my ovaries had a cyst. My cervix had an above average amount of fluid in it, whatever that means (but I'd crossed my legs in the bath like some demented nun since I found out).

'I try to be happy, I try, I am, I am happy for all these other people. But I'm tired, tired of always saying congratulations and my heart hurts from it. I only ever say this to you. You know to everyone else

I'm the perfect little actress, all smiles and merriment. But if I can't tell my husband the truth, who can I tell? I can't be alone in this Russ, I can't.'

At this point, he should have just held me tight and said something comforting like 'we'll get there, darling, we'll get there' while rubbing my sun burnt shoulders. But he doesn't. He stays a few meters away. 'This baby thing is making you nuts,' he says, glaring at his monstrous wife and shaking his head. 'As I've said, this bitch isn't you. You really need to sort yourself out.' He turned his back. 'I'm heading to the pool. I need to cool off.' He shuts the door and I'm on my own.

***

Another battle of birth, death and rebirth that I was dealing with on this amazing tour was that of my career. Travelling for a good length of time delivers the double whammy of opening your mind, so that everything you have valued or beloved in the past is up for questioning... while giving you much more time to analyze it, criticize it, berate yourself and eventually, hopefully, set up a new set of rules and regulations to live by. The sad death of Russ's fabulous father was out of our hands, and so for the time being – until I wished to be poked and prodded some more – was the possible birth of a child perhaps. So my lazy days on the beaches of Phi Phi were spent mulling over the birth of my career (the inexplicable urge to be a writer from the age of 10, work experience at local newspapers from the age of 14, a lucky break at the age of 20 and then the scary, dizzy climb to the top), the death of my career (resigning from one of the most talked-about, juicy jobs in media at the age of 33) to the rebirth of my career (what the fuck do I do next?).

A year earlier, when the time came to announce my resignation as editor in chief of the magazine, no one could believe it was my choice. After all, what kind of fool actually chooses to walk away from possibly the most fun, interesting and gossipy job in the world?

So when the press quickly redefined my quitting as me being 'ousted', 'dismissed', 'fired' – and of course terribly bitter about the whole thing – I wasn't surprised. I mean, *was* I mad to walk away at such an amazing time in the life of the magazine? Ever since it's conception three years previously, it had been my baby, so how could I leave it now it was starting to grow into something huge? I had to believe that giving up this dream job was the right thing to do though.

When I took my first job as a beauty assistant at *Tatler*, a posh glossy in London, at 20 years old, I became instantly addicted to the heady world of media. In my eyes, there was love, life and magazines – and the third on that list was my priority. I relentlessly pulled myself up the career ladder before me, reaching upwards for promotions and recognition at fashion monthlies and daily newspapers. I worked like a dog. No task was too embarrassing (I once posed in a leotard on a see-saw to accompany an article I'd written about my IBS) or dangerous (I worked undercover as a nanny in controversial day cares around London). The thrill of the deadline was intoxicating, as were the adrenalin-fuelled chases for a story or an exclusive. Of course the vain satisfaction of seeing my name in print was a shameless pleasure too. Proprietors and editorial directors could scream and swear at me, publicists make ludicrous demands and lawyers send threatening letters… but I'd give as good as I got. I'd take it all in, enjoying the circus surrounding the drama and news I could help control and manipulate. Angry bosses would explode at me in front of smug colleagues – sometimes for the benefit of smug colleagues – 'You're a back of cunting piss, Ivens. A fucking disgrace. A stupid little school girl.' One boss once actually spat in my face. I'd go bright red (and wipe off the aforementioned saliva if needed) and carry on with my work. I couldn't miss a deadline. My imposter syndrome drove me on to believe I was going to be found out any minute: I was just a comprehensive kid from East London, the product of a broken family and a working mum. I was a young woman whose arse was too big to comfortably fit into skinny jeans and whose boobs were too big to hint that I had a brain, and was not in fact, a total bimbo. For all of the reasons listed above, I worked my butt off. I gave 100%. And then 100% more. Just to prove my critics (and there were many) wrong. Through hard work and determination, I started to leapfrog get noticed, climb ranks and make some cash. And I adored it. I loved – and still do love – journalists. They are mighty fine drinking companions and exceptionally gifted storytellers. You simply won't find better company on a miserable, rainy night in a city full of workaholics – as my colleagues and I all were.

So when I was offered the job in New York, I had to say yes immediately, even though I didn't know a soul over the pond, in case they snatched the offer away. Retrospectively, if I'd actually known how hard it would have been for a 29 year old like me to do it, I wouldn't have taken on the challenge. Launching a weekly in a crowded market with a boss desperate for quick results should have been career suicide. But, as I repeated to myself at the time, what doesn't kill you makes you stronger and for three years I balanced the long hours, nasty rumors, frequent scoldings, frustrating meetings and having my Blackberry as a bed companion with the many, many pluses.

My old bosses in London were still lurking around, scared to stop all communication in case they got stuck for an editor who possessed both a brain and the ability to work hard while dealing with their bullshit. Within a few months of leaving, the magazine had been through four different editors in chief, each bringing their own dramas until they got fired, each time leaving the magazine in a drearier state than when I'd said goodbye to it. Fearing for the future of my 'baby', they persuaded me to become the editor at large for a chunk of time – and change - and after each disastrous editorial sojourn, I'd be somehow encouraged back in for a few weeks, pick up where I left off, running the show from Kentucky in a way that highlighted quite how easy the job could be if you had the trust and respect of the team, a good head on your shoulders, and the ability to look at a photo of Brad Pitt and make a story up about his relationship with Angelina by the length of his beard. Sadly for me though, or perhaps more for the lovely team I'd left behind in New York, I didn't care too much for Brad's beard these days.

It had been the year of Michael Jackson's death and my bosses had decided to run a photo of the tragic star, clearly moments from death – if not actually dead – on the cover. A decision I thought was horrific, and told them so. There were also tacky shoots with Tiger Woods' mistress, she getting paid a lot of money to say nothing but sell her dubious dreams for the future. There was a premature celebration of the demise of Jade Goody, who had had a tragically public death to cervical cancer, leaving behind two photogenic little boys. Then there was the constant celebration of 'stars' who weren't stars, unless getting their tits out or, oops, accidentally leaking a sex tape to all and sundry made you a star these days. I couldn't even spell their ridiculous names and I didn't want to have to learn how to. Celebrity wasn't what it was. Even from when I started back in the last 90s. At least the ladettes were comedians with their own television or radio shows, and at least the footballers played football. Today's crème de la crème were obvious wannabes, creeping around the shadows of a more famous friend (normally in the guise of stylist or drug dealer) until their moment to get a reality show, porn shoot or clothing line came. Cynically, I could see it all happening and predict the brainless bimbos we'd be putting on the cover 12 months down the line. Oh for those golden days when girls wanted to read about Julia Roberts, or Madonna, or Kate Moss. These celebrities couldn't sell magazines for toffee. To get the sales, you had to get the reality stars. And that made me even more depressed.

I politely declined all offers to stay involved with the magazine around the time Russ's dad finally passed away. I needed to focus on him now, and I knew I was trained like a Pavlovian dog to answer my Blackberry even at the most private moment with my husband. I had to let go once and for all. There were a few suggested ways we could make it work, that I could still be involved but much less, but knowing how my boss and his crew worked this would have meant me still being available for them whenever they needed me but for less money. No, a clean break was what I needed. When it was my baby and I had control over the content, I made sure it was a pro-woman, positive book – despite its tabloid tone and subject matter. I'd brainwashed the staff to repeat the mantra *naughty but nice* – we could cheekily point out the flaws of celebrities, but we could never be cruel – but with me gone from the top spot, the cheap shots were coming out quick, desperately trying to keep sales up to make advertisers happy. In the long-term, I couldn't see it working.

So, why, when I made my daily pilgrimage to the beach internet café to check my messages, did it hit me so hard in the solar plexus that I was no longer needed by anyone? I realized that somewhere my ego or sense of self was linked weirdly to my former role at the magazine. I tried to get my head around this as I made my way back to my lounger, rhythmically licking at a chocolate Cornetto, hoping that the ice cream would somehow lessen this weird nagging in my heart, making me forget about it and remember how lucky and free I was: on a beach, on a backpacking trip with my husband, in Thailand. It wasn't that easy. You see, for years now, whenever I'd been out and about, people asked me what I did for a living, and I was almost embarrassed to tell them, because I knew – not big headedly, just matter of factly – that it was very cool. Or at least, they'd think so. Everyone loves a bit of Hollywood gossip and they're lying if they tell you they don't. So for years now I'd felt judged and accepted because of my career rather than who I was. I was confident that I was a nice girl from a good family with a great group of friends, but I still felt deep down that my job was the most interesting thing about me. When getting bad service in a restaurant over the previous few months, my husband would occasionally joke to me, 'Don't they know who you used to be?' It was supposed to be funny, and it would have been had I not been a bundle of insecurities. I'd snap and say 'I still am somebody you know' and huff and puff at him. He'd laugh and bear hug me, squeezing my ridiculousness out of me. Or at least hoping to. He was actually pushing it into my heart and making me wrestle with it internally.

The few weeks travelling so far had taken me from Buddhist Temple to Buddhist investigator and on the beach that week I'd been reading Deepak Chopra's book on the compassionate one. The hardest part for me to grasp about the whole philosophy was ego-death. I'd sort of got my head around living in the moment, the fish had helped with that, but to lose all sense of your ego and to not worry about job titles, or career plans, or bank balances, what would I be without those things? If you're no longer pushing and fighting and clawing your way to the top to get a bigger house, better car, more creative fulfillment, more respect, what was the point?

I had assumed by resigning happily and with free will, waving goodbye to Manhattan and my corner office and expense account, I had seen this light, that my ego-death was well underway and I was truly becoming an enlightened being, happy to take life day by day, returning to university to study for a Masters in English Literature where no one knew about my past career, and accepting low-paying but interesting pieces of freelance work here and there 'to keep my hand in', as my dad would say. Even deciding to come travelling was part of this: we could have used the money to get a fancy sports car or put it towards a mortgage on a swish house in a better area, but we decided a trip with each other and learning about the world would be better for the soul.

'Let's have a cocktail tonight to celebrate me being out of the B-list business,' I announce to Russ as we're walking back to our hot-house hostel. I didn't feel as calm as my jolly tone was trying to convey and he knew it. But a strawberry daiquiri in a beach bar can help a lot of things. And perhaps we could bury my ego in the sand afterwards?

**

It was with a sigh of relief that we waved goodbye to Phi Phi. It was indeed a beautiful place with an interesting array of people – Aussie harlots and Mafia families included – but we'd been there for four nights and it was starting to feel claustrophobic. The traveler's life, even though we were only a month in, had really struck a chord with me and I was ready to pack up my back pack and get moving again. The hostel which we'd loved on first inspection had lost its glow. The owners hadn't changed the towels and tutted when we asked for more toilet paper. We were both covered in mosquito bites each morning and a putrefied smell of sewers was starting to waft through the sink plughole. It was time to go.

Luckily, although I'd resigned from a top job, my skills as a writer were still employable. As we were planning our trip a few months earlier a few editor friends had asked me to pen travel pieces for them and a few PRs had invited me to stay and review their Asian properties. It was hard to get US journos out that far, so everyone was a winner. Especially me, I figured, as I was unsure at that point how my luxury loving past was going to cope with a hostile, hostel future. Apart from my skin, which had been spotty since the first night in Hong Kong when my pores discovered they were going to have to shower while sitting on the toilet, I was actually enjoying living the low life; although I'd be lying if I didn't admit to being as pleased as punch at the thought of getting to our next stop: the new Ritz Carlton resort in Krabi.

***

Now, I'm a floozy for a five star hotel and this place has turned me into a total tart. We were shown to our room, if you can call it that, by our own personal butler, Tanya – a sweetheart who informed us she would do anything we needed, even unpack our grubby backpacks, and run us around in our own little golf buggy rather than letting us risk walking and getting a bit hot and tired. As soon as she left us to unpack (we turned down her kind offer, more through embarrassment than kindness), we ran around like demented drunks. We had our own pool! We had a bathtub in the garden! We had a huge bed made for jumping on! The bed, we actually found out later, was the biggest in Asia, two king size beds pushed together with custom made linens. The mini-bar was stocked and free, a true delight and respite from our strict $50 a day diet, and all around the rooms – for we really had 'rooms' – were little gifts: a straw hat, a new toothbrush, some beer. Paying guests would need around $2,000 per night for such decadence but we were getting it all free. My ego, or my past ego, was certainly still beneficial in a few ways. Perhaps this was the key: just writing a few things that I believed in, things that I wouldn't have to exaggerate and that wouldn't upset anyone. I could still get occasional arse-lickings and get to see how the other half lived without selling my soul up the Hudson to do it. We would never, ever be able to afford to stay here without my reputation as a writer and after a few weeks in dreary hostels, we felt like the luckiest people in the world.

It's easy to achieve a Zen like state of mind in such a place. Sitting in a cabana, sipping the water fresh from a young coconut, watching the coastline's 200 islands bob up and down in the waves in front of me, thoughts and emotions floated to and fro in my mind. No memories anchored themselves to me; no worries were buoyant. This was the feeling my yoga teacher back in the Bluegrass had tried to get me to learn for 12 months... but I couldn't. There was always something to stress about, a tick needed on my to do list. Today was different though, I didn't even need a book or an iPod. The day literally drifted away before me like a sailboat making a peaceful journey on a very clear, calm day. The sun came down and I hardly noticed. Tanya, our butler, had to come and tell me it was nearly dinner time and that she'd filled my bath tub with oils and petals if I fancied a soak before eating.

There were a few other journalists staying at the same time as us, which I was thrilled about. As a group, they are great storytellers with the confidence to deliver the funniest, most outrageous lines to a group of strangers and the social skills to do so without taking over or appearing pompous. As much as I didn't miss my Manhattan media life, which towards the end had been filled with moneymen and advertisers, I did miss the writers so it was great to be in the company of a few again.

One was an older British chap who, after his third rum punch, openly discussed his strange set up at home – a collection of ex-wives, a few children all over Asia and a current wife, 'who has changed, I don't know her anymore.' This was all delivered against the clock, because his latest mistress was flying in from Hong Kong to join us for dinner. He wore the classic old English fop in Asia outfit: purple, suede loafers, baby pink trousers, a powder blue shirt and a fedora. Long, grey hair completed the look. He was the kind of chap who would love to have been born Argentinean but was in fact born along the Thames Estuary, so escaped as quickly as he could to the Orient to build a new life and sense of mystery for himself.

The other journo was a wonderful girl from Sydney called Mary, who I immediately adored due to her doppelganger-ness to my ex-colleague and great friend in New York, Katie. Russ noticed it straightway too, remarking that she even did wonderful things a'la Katie, such as ordering mojitos at 11am and taking the piss out of the British journo we'd been too polite, or perhaps patriotic, to laugh at. She was married to a South African called Drew, who was a decent chap too, so it wasn't long before the four of us had ganged up and were boozily eating dinner en masse. Mary was there to cover the resort for an airline magazine in Singapore, which she'd just become the editor at the impressive age of 32. She loved it. The magazine and the ex-pat life in Asia, thrilling us with tales of Singapore Slings, cheap taxis, funny local customs and the nuances of doing business in a United Nations style set-up. Of the five million people in Singapore, over two million were foreigners. It sounded like an intriguing way to work and live and Russ and I found ourselves quite openly envying them and their life. I do think once you've left your home country once – not to go backpacking or for a brief secondment in a foreign office for a few months but to actually *set up* a new life – you realize how easy it is to do and the negatives give way to the very, many positives. Russ and I had now lived in the US for nearly five years and although we worried from time to time about our roots and planting them firmly in the familiar, we also had cut the apron strings to our mother land and were tempted to keep moving, exploring and learning.

By the end of the night Mary had told me about a job going at her company, editorial director, overseeing nine in-flight airline magazines, being a corporate spokesperson and essentially her boss. 'I think you should do it!' she enthuses. 'You'd be perfect! Here's my card. Think about it. We can talk some more but I think you'd be perfect and they'd love you. I'd tell them about you.'

The thought of it made my head buzz. I could tell from his expression it made Russ's head buzz too. How exciting and how perfect. It had only been a few months but I had missed nurturing a team. 'You're a great editor, you were born to be an editor really,' admits Russ, as we sway our way through the palm trees towards our villa. 'I could easily find work in Singapore too, and it's virtually tax free over there so we could save some good cash to try and pay off the house. And it would be an adventure.'

I nodded in agreement because I agreed with everything he said. But what would this mean for my ego – and more importantly perhaps, considering we were both about to turn 35 and I had a cyst on my left ovary, our baby plans?

***

By our third and last day living the high life, we were kind of scared to enter the real world again. My only deadline each day had been an 8am yoga class and a glass of wine at sunset, at 6.30pm. Although at first, Russ had been horrified by the idea of a butler, he came from good working class stock, readers of *The Mirror* who had never had a cleaning lady, by day three he was calling Tanya to wipe his arse. Not literally of course, but he'd turned into a real Little Lord Fauntleroy, throwing a tiny fit if he had to walk somewhere or his pad Thai took a few too many minutes to arrive.

'I haven't been treated so well,' he announced, after a waiter had brought some cold towels and a mini prawn cocktail to our cabana, 'since I lived at home with my mum.'

I warned him not to get used to it again. His mother had already done too much damage and her little prince – despite being a modern man – would quite like his hair to be stroked on demand, or breakfast in bed, if he thought he could get away it. His mother could have ruined him but she actually just made him into a guy that realizes how wonderful women could be and how you should look after them to keep them sweet. His father had been the same. Shortly after he died, his mum crumpled in my arms, and professed through tears how Pete had been the best husband in the world, 'never making me jealous, never flirting with other women, always being faithful and spending time with his kids. He was there for all of us.' His death had left such a huge hole in the family that even a stranger would not have been in doubt by the size of Pete's huge heart and love for his family. Russ was already shaping up to be the same kind of man.

I'd had a nightmare the previous evening which made me cling even tighter to Russ that day. It wasn't one of the usual death dreams we'd both been having since grief and loss had become part of our daily lives; it was a strange dream that I was still married to my ex-husband. I felt trapped and angry and it all felt wrong. I woke up a few feet away from Russ in our massive bed and quickly rushed over to groove my body into his when I realized my error.

'I put out my arms to hold you in the night and I couldn't find you,' he murmured sleepily, 'this bed is too big.' Relief washed over me. My ex was an extremely bright, creative man but we got married too young, as my parents had warned, and I had felt trapped for much of our time together. My relationship with Russ couldn't help but be easier because we were older and both been through our years of trying to prove ourselves. We still wanted to travel and do new things but remarkably, we seemed to want to do them together. Or so I thought.

As I spend the day thinking more and more seriously about the job opportunity in Singapore, and getting back into the business somewhere new and exciting – I'd realized I was done for the time being with London and New York, but in Singapore or Sydney or Hong Kong it could be fresh again – Russ has been doing some thinking of his own.

'I always wanted a baby with you but now I'm finally at the point where I am 100% ready and I feel that it's the only thing missing from our lives. I feel like this trip is a big adventure for the two of us, the swansong of it just being me and you, and now we need to introduce a third little person into our world. To form a new gang, a new family. When we get back from our tour, a baby should be the absolute priority for us both. I understand now, I understand how couples in love get to the point where a baby isn't a hassle or the end of lie-ins and nights out. A baby becomes a great new adventure.'

This is a good and bad announcement. Good because over the year we'd been trying I'd never truly felt that Russ was as gutted as me when I came on each month. He'd give me a hug, and then say 'there's always next month – where shall we have lunch?' He didn't understand my paranoia and our racing biological clocks. Now it seemed he did which was great - but what timing! After my night of tossing and turning and feeling trapped, Id woken up relieved, to a feeling of freedom, and I wondered if a baby could get in the way of that. All day I'd been trying to convince myself that we had more time and perhaps we could squeeze in a few years of Singapore Slings and corporate conversations before I embarked on a full time life of motherhood. Madonna had got preggers over 40. My mum was 38 when she had my little brother, William. Perhaps my clock wasn't tick-tocking as fast as I feared?

***

Obviously not being able to pay our own way at the luxury resort, after our two free nights, we were ceremoniously dumped in Krabi

120

Town, on the steps of a cheap hostel near the bus station. Our charming driver tried to carry on the Ritz Carlton style by calling Russ sir and carrying our backpacks to the check-in counter for us, but we refused, muttering something about getting 'back to the real world' and grabbing our bags off him with a warm thank you and goodbye.

We'd become more and more chilled as our tour had gone on, which was the great traveler's calm I'd heard about, and we'd arrived at the hostel without booking and with little thought about how we were going to make it to Malaysia the next day, relying on the business-minded Thais to make it easy for us. Sure enough, there was a room for 500bahts, about $20, which promised warm water, free Wi-Fi and A/C (the triple whammy for backpackers) and a sign up sheet that offered a bus to Penang the following morning at 7am for 600 bahts. Done and done. We didn't even bother to unpack. We just retrieved our toothbrushes and clean pants from a side pocket and thirstily downed two frozen strawberry daiquiris. Our time in Thailand was coming to an end.

***

Even when you're not in a tuk-tuk, driving in Thailand isn't fun. There's a lot of swerving, sudden breaking and shouting. And the road through Southern Siam down to the Malaysian border is pretty dull. Apart from the change from Buddhist country to Muslim province, represented by the lack of temples, the change in the women's dress and the type of food offered at our occasional roadside toilet breaks, it's a bland trip of well-made road, blue sky and galvanized iron tin hut homes. Our fellow pilgrims weren't any more interesting. The young Thais, squashed up the front with the cheap tickets, occasionally conversed with each other and looked back and laughed at their sun burnt travelling companions. The driver clearly just wanted to drop us off and get back home, or to a bar, as quickly as possible, judging by the constant near-misses and head-banging bumpiness of his driving. The fellow Westerners slept off weeks of wandering and partying and we were no more exciting.

Russ listed to Eminem on his iPod. This choice in music was his way of ensuring I wouldn't ask him to share his headphones (rap was the one type of music I couldn't suffer) while I must have looked ridiculous, covered in bites and spots (one night back in a hostel and my chin had become a breeding ground for Thai flora and fauna).

The ten hour road trip certainly gave me time to think. Bored of looking out of the window or picking at my split ends, after the third hour I decided to mentally make a list. Why did I want a baby? It had been such a driving ambition for the last 12 months, I was shocked by my ability to throw it out and welcome in a new goal, and one I didn't think I'd wanted, like getting back into media full-time.

My reasons for wanting me and Russ to have a baby (maybe two or three babies, time permitting) were:

1 because that's what married 34 year olds do;

2 because I'd like to see how a mixture of me and Russ turns out;

3 because I love Russ and it's a further commitment to him and him to me;

4 because I feel the experience of being pregnant and being a mother would be a great one for me as a woman, spiritually and creatively;

5 because I don't want us to grow old and be alone;

6 because sometimes I look at my nephews and niece and my heart could burst, so I can't even imagine the love I would feel for my own child;

7 because my mum and my mother-in-law, and my dad, and our siblings and my mother-girlfriends would all love it and I could be part of their gang and understand them more;

8 because it's the normal thing for someone of my age to do (as opposed to backpacking around Asia or going back to college to get a Masters with lots of 23 three old poets).

Oops. My reasons weren't very inspiring or kind or generous. They were really about me. Did other women – my good friends, even, who were mums – have better reasons for procreating? I didn't think I believed in God so I couldn't pretend procreation was my duty to Jesus. I actually thought most of us were busy destroying the planet with our taste for excess and self-centeredness, so I couldn't pretend I thought a new baby would make the world a better place. My baby would just use more petrol and paper and create more demand for nappies and Toys'R'Us. I couldn't even claim to have a yearning, burning desire to be a mother that came from my very core. I had never desperately wanted to be a mother before I met Russ, hit 33 years and mentally decided it's what I should do next.

Is the love of your husband, a selfish desire to create a mini version of you-and-him and a fear of growing old without the traditional closeness of a family good enough reasons to have a child? Were they easy enough things to let go of if you couldn't have a child? Some of my reasons could be fulfilled by adopting a child, and I felt selfish for wanting my own flesh and blood when there were so many other beautiful children that we could give a good home to. Do other wannabe mums think about the planet and God when they're thinking of making a baby… or did I, again, simply have too much time on my hands?

9

Life's Not Measured by the Breathes We Take, but the Moments That Take Our Breathe Away

'A man is but the product of his thoughts. What he thinks, he becomes.'

Gandhi

The first thing that hits any first time visitor to Malaysia is the intoxicating combination of Indian and Chinese cultures that have blended over the centuries to make a marvelous culinary heritage. It became quite clear, very early on, that Russ and I would be gorging ourselves on the curries, rojak, laksa and spicy, fragrant noodles 24/7. Well, if not 24/7, at least for three meals of the day. And yes, to the horror of our Western bowels, that did include breakfast. Once you've gone to the spicy and hot, it's hard to turn back to a bit of toast with apricot jam.

The second thing you will notice is the wonderful sense of humor possessed by the majority of the Malay people. I don't know where it comes from, we hadn't witnessed anything like it in the rest of Asia on our trip so far, and it was quite a delight. Especially after five years of living in America, where irony is not dead as some snooty Brits claim, but a wicked wit is not admired and encouraged as much as it is back home. Here in Penang, it certainly was and Raja, a Malay-Indian version of Robbie Williams, insisted it was all to do with the British invasion of Malaysia, way back when in the early 19th century. It seems we not only imported our system of law and education while we were stealing their sugar and spices, but a sort of *oops-where's-my-trousers* form of comedy that was still going strong today. Within the first day the locals were happily having a laugh at our expense – and we loved it.

When trying to cool off in the 90% humidity by a swimming pool, Russ asked where the toilet was to be told, 'We can't afford toilets. All tourists must piss in the pool!' His horrified face scored lots of back slapping for the jovial pool boy and a wash of relief from Russ, once he was pushed in the direction of the little boys' room. When looking for the dining room in our hotel, the duty manager informed us 'You've eaten too much already. We've been watching. No more food for you two tonight.' This wasn't quite so funny, as we *had* been eating too much and our expanding tummies and thighs couldn't hide it. A look of panic crossed the manager's face as we angrily pinched our back fat and we were ushered to the buffet without further ado. After dinner, sat outside with a delicious papaya and raspberry concoction, Russ spotted a monkey on the roof. A monkey, how wonderful… until a lovely chap called Suleiman informed us 'You must be blind! It is just a giant squirrel. You have squirrels in England, no? Well, we just have bigger ones.' It was quite clearly a monkey but his persistence and local knowledge made us doubt our own eyes, until Suleiman gave us a wicked laugh and suggested we move on to something stronger – like a margarita.

Very quickly during our tour, my saddlebags had taken off at a rip roaring pace and my bottom was struggling to pull itself off from the floor. I'd fooled myself into thinking carrying a backpack a few hours a day – not that, even – constituted a workout routine than would allow me to indulge in each Asian delight, coconut-milk enriched or sesame seed-oil based, that I came across. Since marrying Russ, I'd started to eat like a 6'4", naturally muscular, sports-obsessed dude. This is because this is how he ate. But he fitted the description. I was a 5'11", naturally soft, book-obsessed girl. My diet and my profile didn't match and no amount of bag-lugging in hot climates was going to make it. Being a naturally lazy beast with a spiritualist bent, I didn't do what Russ did for our four days in Penang and join a gym (that would have been far too much like hard work, and quite frankly, the extra sweat wouldn't do my already troubled complexion any favors), I found the local yoga guru and signed up for 3 hours of tuition with him.

8am felt like a dreadfully early start to me but of course Vega had been up since sunrise, drinking eight glasses of water – lukewarm, with fresh lemon squeezed into it – and stretching the early morning into life. I emerged from bed ten minutes before my class and belted it to his studio, complete with last night's make up and a full stomach of vegetable korma. Something about my ramshackle, Western appearance threw him off instantly and I secretly wished I'd wiped off my smudged eye liner and sprayed some deodorant. 'Your balance is wrong. You have not been to the toilet this morning and you have a full stomach. It's all wrong.' He was right of course. I'd barely had time to clean my teeth let alone go to the loo, the process of doing a number two could not be demanded but had to come naturally, once a day, in its own time. I'd always admired Russ's ability to go for a dump almost as a recreational activity, a sort of *Hmmm, I've got 10 minutes till the footie starts and I plan on eating a lot of BBQ tonight. Where's my iphone?*

My unbalanced bowels meant Vega couldn't do everything he wanted with me that day, so our meeting was split into two 90 minute sessions – and I was expected the following morning, same time and same place, but with an empty stomach and a less active brain. For this class then, we would focus on my breathing and aforementioned full stomach. Different to the Western yoga I'd practiced before, this lesson seemed to be about making as many embarrassing sounds, faces and bum maneuvers as possible. He had me walking round the room on all fours like an elephant.

'Go, go, go, I will watch you. Come on, slow elephant, old ladies in my village in India do this for 15 minutes!' Shaking with laughter like hyena on speed, 'shake your whole body with your laughing, louder, ho ho ho!' And the most humiliating, sticking my tongue and bottom out at the same time, 'like a rabbit.' Hmm, now I'd had rabbits in the past and I didn't recall them stretching their tongues out and pushing their bum to the sky simultaneously. 'You have good tongue at least; it's very, very long.' I don't think he meant this to sound creepy, but when you're on all fours with you bum in a young guy's face, it can't help but sound a bit off.

Clearing my mind, however, seemed to be the most difficult of the tasks. I was worried about farting. This was a fear that haunted me in yoga classes wherever I was. I was scarred by my first ever lesson, taken with colleagues from *Marie Claire* some 13 years earlier, under a railway bridge south of the Thames. An energetic downward dog had led to a loud escape of air from a designer chum's behind. I was torn between laughing and pitying her, while trying not to blush in case someone thought it was me. It was never mentioned – we were in England after all – but I'd never been able to totally relax in a meditative state in yoga because of that one noisy interruption. Now, today, with a tummy full of curry, a humid pavilion, and my bottom in the air, my ass-clenching had taken on a new kind of all-consuming, physical strength. Sensing my discomfort, or a waft of garlic naan, Vega backed off to sit on his own mat and instructed me to sit up with my feet tucked under my bottom.

'This is the best position for digestion,' he taught, 'especially if you make two tight fists with your hands and press them into your stomach for a few minutes while bending forward.' So I dutifully followed his cue for a few minutes and desperately needed the loo within minutes of finishing my class.

Issues with my nether regions could not have come at a worst time. The curries were fabulous and Russ and I were both secretly thrilled with our guile, swooping into local joints with a laissez faire attitude to the menus, asking with a smile if we could instead be brought what the locals around us were eating. 'No, no, no need for plates or forks, we'll eat it off the green paper sheets with bread and our right hand how you are, that's fine.' Gosh, we felt down with the Malay. But we were fast approaching my baby-making time and I desperately wanted everything to be as smooth and fragrant as possible. I was worried about getting sick again – and yoga had reminded me of the horrors of flatulence. So I did what any good British girl who loves curry would do in such circumstances: I vowed not to touch the garlic naan, just the peshwari one from now on... and to avoid sparkling wine and fizzy water. I could not, however, give up a decent tikka masala.

I prepared for our monthly seduction routine (for my new rule was that it had to still *feel* like a romance, a game, rather than a quick delivery for purely baby reasons) by retrieving my one decent yet crinkled dress (Russ' favorite) from the bottom of my backpack, actually brushing my hair for the first time in weeks (it was resembling a bleached blond bombsite) and complimenting him on everything from his ever-wildly growing locks to his hazelnut tan (this wasn't hard, to me, my husband was totally delicious even when teeth-grindingly irritating). He could sense from these maneuvers what time of the month it was without me having to spell it out and did his own little getting ready for baby routine: giving me appreciative looks that make me feel wanted, sleeping without his boxer shorts on and kissing me tenderly.

All of this behavior came more naturally to him now than it had over the last few months, a sign that our holiday was working. We hadn't had any big discussions about my baby obsession since we were in Thailand, and although the excitement and possibility of a job and new life abroad had reared his head and was waving to us across the bed sheets, we still knew that a baby was truly the one thing left for both of us to achieve. They'd be other jobs, other cities, other adventures, but having a baby was the only one with a to-do-by date firmly tattooed on it. And it was the only unfulfilled ambition that 'turned me from a sane person into a nut job', Russ reminded me over dinner that evening.

So, we started getting on with it. A great, fun chore for both of us, especially with the sunshine and warm waters rushing into our hearts and long, lazy days spread out before us. This was the perfect time, we decided, to throw the net open wide. I'd left my ovulation monitor at home but it generally said to go for it between days 13-15 of my cycle, so we'd decided to do that… and throw in a few extra either side of those times for good measure. After my difficult trip to the doctors a couple of months back, we'd been told not to go at it like rabbits for a short time but to do it every other day to allow the sperm to gain strength and speed. So this was our new game plan. And if you could put aside our year's worth of disappointment and tension, it was actually a really fun game.

***

As if reading my sex-focused mind, Vega greets me with visible dismay and a shake of his head when I show up at his yoga pavilion for our second session. A propos of nothing he decides to share his philosophy for a long life, his advice moving from my back-bottom to my front as it were, as if he could smell my husband on me and didn't approve or something. 'When a man meditates, he breathes 20 to 25 times a minute. When he runs he breathes 30 to 35 times a minute. When he is with his woman and doing physical things with her, he breathes 70 to 75 times a minute. Now, you only have so much breathe in your life so the man who meditates will live the longest and the man who…' he raises an eyebrow to check I get his drift. Yes, I get it. Do I buy it? No. There were a thousand other things that determined how long you lived, and this felt a bit personal – a bit like a death wish on Russ – after the wonderful evening we'd had, tumbling around and enjoying each other a mere 10 hours earlier. I was a bit cynical of his Eastern mysticism and wise words after that. And the rest of the class was filled with less enthusiastic elephants, rabbits and giggling than the day before.

I wasn't a total cynic however, and was determined to at least investigate, if not wholesale buy, the new teachings that were available to me. The Indian spiritual element of Malaysia, the yoga, had stretched my body but not my mind, so I was hoping the Chinese element, my Chi energy flow, would be more enlightening, or at least get me in good physical and mental shape for making love, making whoopee and making it to Kuala Lumpur without putting on 30lbs.

Chiang was a jolly little soul, standing at least a foot shorter than me, but with pudgy, strong hands that promised a thorough rub-down once my Yin and Yang was balanced and my Chi element uncovered. I sat in something he proudly described as a Tibetan hut (I'm not sure why, except that Tibet seems to immediately be a symbol of peace if you are anything but Chinese, paradoxically, I assumed) and started answering questions. My favorite color was green, closely followed by white. I liked the afternoon but was not so keen on mornings and late nights. I loved sour, spicy food but could like without sugar. I enjoyed a nice breeze and a bit of sunshine, despairing of harsher climates, be they too hot or too cold. I undressed and put on the ubiquitous paper knickers and a robe, was given the quick physical once over... and then the results were in. I was metal. I had metal Chi. Metal energy. It didn't sound promising, cold and formulaic in fact, but a gaggle of Chi-mastered gathered and seemed very pleased, almost in awe. 'Metal is the element of beauty and protection. A person with a metal core balances inner and outer beauty and has a strong need to protect herself and the people she loves.' Spot on so far, I liked to think. 'Metal personalities hold themselves and others in the highest regard, living with principle and reason.' Well, yes, that was true of me too, I felt. I was very proud and stubborn yet I could respect and openly admire the best in other people. And what was this tour about if it wasn't an open search for a life of principle and reason – a pleasurable but somewhat desperate hide and seek for answers to life, death, ego, love and the big one: what to do and be between now and the end?

Chiang decided I wasn't as balanced and wondrous as my description however, and a few oils were needed to bring my various sides to peace, 20 minutes of reflexology was required to join my mental with my physical and a few chiming bells and a back rub would release any remaining unrest. Well, it was certainly more enjoyable than sorting out your inner issues, the Western way, with a handful of prescription drugs or a trip to a therapist (the former I'd never tried, the latter I had and rather enjoyed. Well, it's just a chance to talk about yourself for hours and gain sympathy rather than a firm kick up the butt from people who know you too well). I left floating on air, oiled up and superior, and totally ready for a dip in the outside bath Russ had running on our balcony. 'I thought we could relax in the water together until sunset,' he announces as he opens the bedroom door. He's looking breathtakingly gorgeous, tousled and tanned and pumped up from his workout at the gym. Sticking to our every other day rule could be tricky if he keeps tempting me with his handsome self and an outdoor salt soak…

***

We'd heard rumors that Malaysian train travel was quick, clean and wonderful. Hmmm. We arrive at Butterworth station, the closest bit of mainland to Penang at 6am to find a toilet sink full of sick, a few dodgy types looking at my cleavage and woman who kept farting, loudly and with abandon (she clearly hadn't suffered the cruel out casting of a Western yoga class). No matter, we had a few good books and bottles of water and we'd be in Kuala Lumpur by 2pm, just in time for a late lunch of curry, rice and roti. We would have indulged right there and then of course, we now woke up craving something hot and spicy (fanar fanar) but all that was being offered on the platform was a selection of identical dry, white rolls and some luminous sweets that looked like they'd win in a battle with your molars.

It wasn't long into the seven hour journey that my unpredictable bowels felt the need to be relieved. As much as he could chose to go the lavatory to fill a few spare, dull minutes, Russ could also store it up for hours, like a camel full of shit, if the facilities weren't up to his hygienic standards, so he urged me not to go. It wasn't that easy, I tried to whisper as I got up and swayed backwards, following a smell that can only be described as living hell. At the end of the carriage I was presented with two options: a sit down or squat, described both literally and graphically on the signs, left and right. I unenthusiastically peaked into the squat, having developed quite a technique in Thailand, but couldn't imagine being able to stand firm as the train grinded to sudden, jerking halts or spun in one direction on the rails at a breakneck speed. So I did the American thing, taking the sit down but spending a few minutes preparing my throne with masses of toilet roll and a few deep breathes. The sensation was quite pleasant, I have to be honest. Ok, so I didn't love the idea that my ablutions would immediately whoosh down the toilet hole and on to the track (images of playing children and railway maintenance men making such a discovery flooded my mind) but the cool breeze up from the open air straight to my cheeks relieved the slight burning from the reappearance of last night's Indian delight. It wasn't the coziest toilet experience of my life (I normally like a few Molton Brown products dotted around to make me feel at home) but it wasn't as bad as an experience on a seven hour trip through South East Asia could have been.

We arrive at the hotel in not much of a fit state to do anything but sit by the pool. The air was thick with an exotic grime that coated our skins with salt and spice, an unusual situation for two pale-skinned Brits to find themselves in. After a quick trip to the gym – Russ to build muscle, me to gawp at him lovingly – we crash by the pool, while the sparkling, startling Petronas Twin Towers spy on us with a glint in their eyes.

That evening, in the bath, I picked up our bedside copy of The Qur'an. I didn't read that much of it. It got to the point that I always get to when reading religious books: I couldn't suspend all sense of logic, good sense and science long enough for it to seep into my brain and to take up residence. I couldn't even buy in to the coolest of the bunch, Prince-Siddhartha-cum-Buddha, and his followers tales of monkeys and elephants wholeheartedly. Even in my teens when my parents were worried about my ever-increasing interest in the American Evangelist Billy Graham, they needn't have worried for it wasn't his talking in tongue, crazy hand waving, promises of hell and high water for the non-believer that got me going. No, it was that the woman round the corner who was Chigwell's administrative arm of Graham's UK tour would give the local kids free chocolate Hobnobs if they went along and listened. My equally choc-tastic mate Andrea and I would nod our heads approvingly, even join in for a sing song around the piano, and then put our hands out impatiently for our sweet reward. Not everlasting life but a biscuit. God had nothing to do with it.

I loved the idea of religion, the pomp and circumstance, the traditions and the singing. I loved churches and cathedrals, temples and mosques. But I loved the colors, the smell of the ancient and the quiet calm more than the believing. When a boyfriend I had at the age of 16 kissed me, told me I was going to go to hell because I didn't go to church every Sunday, then went in for a grope under my bra, my mind was set: if heaven was where dull church-goers, hypocrites and he was going, I'd rather be in hell with the gay boys and the animals. As my wise Auntie Jilly said to me once, 'Father Christmas, the Easter Bunny and the Tooth Fairy don't exist either, but we don't go to war or limit people's human rights over them, do we!'

So, I closed the Qur'an a few chapters in with some new insights and an old opinion: all religious books can offer comfort, help and moral guidance if read by people with good hearts and good sense but it's important to remember they were written a very long time ago by people who couldn't even imagine the issues we have today.

***

The day began in the marvelous way any woman madly in love'n'lust with her husband who wants to conceive a child dream of: with a firm nudge in the buttock, a nibble on the neck and a whisper in the hair, 'Are you awake?' A furtive glance at the clock alarms me that its only 6am and I am yearning for more sleep, but it's also day 15 of my cycle, we obeyed the one-day-off, one-day-on rule and I had felt a twinge in my ovaries during the night. With all this evidence, you can imagine what happened next. After the deed was done, Russ had a bath while I did a headstand for 5 minutes in a way that baby doctors and my yoga chap Vega said was beneficial. I stayed, in all my naked glory, upside down, boobs rushing my ears on either side of my head, until my neck felt like it was going to break off and Russ called out for breakfast.

Eloise, a friend in New York, had told me I had to visit the Batu Caves, a series of old Hindu temples half an hour outside of Kuala Lumpur. Guarded by a giant, 43 meter high Lord Murgan statue, the site is impressive immediately. Gathering our energy and removing our shoes as the locals were doing, we begin the 272-step climb to Temple Cave. With the 90 degree plus heat, I struggle on, thighs taut, bottom clenched, telling myself this mount will let me off the gym for a few more days, while Russ springs around, trying to take photos of the monkeys who leap about the steps, seemingly posing for photographs and being rewarded for it with coconut by the temple guardians. Some monkeys were tiny, some skinny, and one had the most enormous pair of testicles. They hung off him, mimicking the coconuts he was munching on, while he wore the most uncomfortable expression on his face, trying to balance on the wall without crushing his oversized manhood. I'm not normally this interested in balls, I must assure you, but they really were that eye-catching that it was impossible not to mention them.

'He looks like you this morning,' I joked to Russ unsuccessfully, never being good with Benny Hill humor and grimacing rather than gurning for I actually found the whole sight rather repulsive. The monkey seemed to turn to me, look me up and down and smile. I freaked out and looked away, while Russ took a step closer to get a snapshot. Suddenly, the monkey leapt at him, teeth flashing, and balls swinging. He growled, Russ fled and I ran up the next flight of steps as fast as my hot, chaffing thighs would carry me.

'He had it in for me', he panted (Russ – not the monkey) when I finally reach the peak. In full Mother Nature mode I explain my theory: it is spring and he has giant balls (the monkey - not Russ). 'You were threatening his manly position on the steps and you had a wife who was ovulating, currently walking around filled with your essence. If dolphins humped sexually charged scuba divers,' I reasoned, 'this little man-to-monkey showdown could make total biological sense.'

'Uh-oh,' he pulled me with him into the dank, dark cave. 'I think we've entered the next stage of your cycle when you get a bit ridiculous.' I would get upset, but I'm definitely not at the stage in my cycle when I get sensitive and weepy (that's day 24), so I let him win me over again with a Ganesh the elephant friendship bracelet and a swig of his warm water, and we follow the cool breeze and rainbow-colored lights to a series of shrines and sherbet-dipped worshipers.

***

We'd climbed all there was to climb in Kula Lumpur (the Petronas Twin Towers, the Menora KL and the Batu Cave steps), so our last day in Malaysia was spent doing what we had learnt to do best in Malaysia: eat lots of curry while the locals good naturedly took the piss out of us. 'I love these dudes,' Russ laughed, meaning Malaysians, 'they have a really cheeky sense of humor.' The day before, not realizing that tickets up the Petronas Towers were free, Russ asked the security guard how much it was to get up to the suspension bridge.

The extremely official looking guy, pulled him to one side and said in hushed tones, 'well, sir, how much have you got?', before slapping his back and yelling, 'It's free! Its' free! I had you then didn't I?'

'They really seem to know how to have fun,' Russ reminisced as we packed up from the poolside and made our way to KL Sentral to catch the late afternoon train on to Singapore.

With full tummies from breakfast and only two ringgits to our name, we unwisely decide we can go the eight hour journey without any food. So instead of doing what we would normally do, which is rush around the station concessions stands searching for on-board

135

worthy snacks, we window shop and read The Straits Times, the local paper. As the tannoy announces our imminent departure, Russ, still scarred from the open air experiences of the train from Penang, pays a last minute trip to the station loo, while I attract a gaggle of giggling Malay girls who are gathered around me while their friend takes photos. They must have had *pose with giant blonde English girl* on their wish list for the year. I grab the girls and they pose around me, laughing and saying 'thank you, thank you' while reaching up to try and touch the top of my head, then collapsing in more giggles when they realize they can't. We then have to do individual shots – and there is about ten of them – and a crowd has gathered by now and I'm laughing too but simultaneously getting redder and redder. When Russ emerges from the loo, even taller and more tanned, they literally let out a scream of delight and foregoing any of the shy, polite hints for photos they'd played on me, just rush over and start snapping, obviously identifying him as mine, and therefore open to posing, by our matching backpacks. The girls look thrilled as they rush one way for the train, while we rush the other. We can hear them laughing all the way to their platform. What fun the Malays are! I might add a return visit to the next list I stick to my fridge.

10

Express Yourself

'Language is the blood of the soul into which thoughts run and out of which they grow.'

Oliver Wendell Holmes

After what seemed like a never-ending ride into Singapore, we arrive, just after midnight, sweaty and starving. The station is nothing like we'd imagined, a shockingly low grade place with locals hanging out, sitting on each other's laps and drinking warm beer. We'd expected something all together sharper, sleeker. 'It's a bit grubby,' Russ, using his usual non-diplomacy grumbles to our taxi driver. 'It's dirty! I'm shocked.'

After a few repetitions of his visual discovery, which our polite driver does his best to agree with without being disloyal to his country in Singlish (the very strange English the Singaporeans speak), I bark 'Alright, enough!' as in 'shut it, big mouth!' He shuts it and we get to our hotel, via China Town, in less than 15 minutes. So tired, we can't sleep, my limbs jump around the bed like I'm on a bicycle and Russ's stomach grumbles further complaints. So far, so not good... and this was a place I was asking for a possible job in?

Sleep is so impossible that at 7am we decide to cut our losses and just get out and see what the place was really about. Everyone had declared it to the cleanest city ever, not in a sterile way but in a delightful way that meant backpackers shoulders could relax after weeks of travelling through Thailand and Malaysia. We weren't disappointed. Everything was so neat, from the roadside shrubs to the men's hairdos. Our new friend and chauffeur explained that if you were caught littering, you'd get a $200 fine. If you were caught a second time, you'd get a $400 fine. A third time? Well you fool; you'd have to pay more money and do community service. The local newspapers and television channels would be invited to film your work, gathering rubbish from the beach for example, and you could very much expect to be named and shamed in public, on page two of the newspaper, the next day. I thought this was a marvelous idea. In fact, the *Keep Britain Tidy* campaign could benefit from similar punishment methods.

'People from outside think we are barbaric because we are hard on crime', our man in Singapore continues, 'but I think it's a good thing. For example if you murder or rape, you get lashed as well as being put in prison. And believe me, once you are lashed, you never want again. Men can only take four lashes before they fall over and cream has to be applied.' What a ghastly job I thought, but if it worked good.

'So you must have really low rates of rape in Singapore then?' I asked.

'No', he replied matter-of-factly, 'but we don't have any litter.'

I didn't really know what to make of it all really and was pleased to get to our first, highly recommended, destination.

The Singapore Flyer is an unashamed replica of The London Eye… only a little bit bigger, as everything in Asia is, in a bid for eyes and ears to turn East instead of West. From there, the city spread before us; a building site of a place, desperate to be higher, richer and more fabulous than anywhere else. It was the old school that interested us more though, so we left the Flyer and strolled past plastic pandas and angry looking tiger statues to the harbor to pose by the famous symbol of Singapore, the Mer Lion. Half fish, half lion, this water feature was more than a tourist attraction by a sign to the world of Singapore's past and future: as a strong, defiant sea port. From there we fought the humidity along Beech Road to lie in the grass at

Singapore Cricket Club, a charming square of grass sandwiched between the skyscrapers. A delicious slice of colonial times, you could practically hear the ladies chinking their teacups through the sweltering heat while their men cheered each other on to bat with a *jolly good show* here and a *this one's for Blighty* there. The sweltering midday sun demanded an earlier stop than we imagined at Raffles Hotel, the home of the Singapore Sling. We head straight up to the Long Bar for a cocktail and some monkey nuts, along with every other expat in Singapore. It was a bit of a shock after being pretty much just with each other or just locals for four weeks. It was worth it though, not only did we get a sugary spike but I'm sure you could hear the ghost of Somerset Maugham typing away as we walked past the Billiard Room.

That evening, we'd been invited to our new friends Mary and Drew's apartment for a sunset barbecue on their roof deck. After meeting us in Krabi and her telling me about the job at her company, we'd stayed in touch – she putting in a good word for me with her boss – and thought it would be fun to meet when we got to their adopted home city. Their apartment made us want to move there even more. Somewhere between getting out of bed and languishing at the bar at Raffles, we'd fallen in love with the place. And in general, travelling around Asia had made us love the continent and not want the adventure to end. Disappointingly, I hadn't heard from Mary's boss, despite a very impressive email from me and thumbs up from her, one of his trusted editors.

'The first thing you have to understand about him is it is not personal. He's just got a million things to do, a few editors who are going mad and trying to do photo shoots at German concentration camps, and I have to chase him all the time. But he's a great guy, so creative, and I think you'll really get on. He's English with a wicked sense of humor,' she reveals over a Sapporo and sunset combo. The great thing was though, I wasn't too bothered. Travelling had really opened up my mind to, well, keeping my mind open. As long as Russ and I were together and earning enough money to eat and sleep without any anxiety, then all would be well. You can't spend four weeks seeing people living hand to mouth yet happy and get back on the hamster wheel with any real kind of dramatic urgency. As Russ said in the taxi home to our hotel after a lovely, long evening with like-minded people, 'if he wants you, he wants you. His loss if he doesn't. We'll just go on to the next adventure.'

***

'His ears must have been burning because he's just emailed me saying he's got in touch with you,' was the message I got first thing the next morning from Mary. His was the next email I opened and true to what I imagined, it was the email of a busy man who wanted to get stuff done. After a few niceties it came down to two things: what are you doing now and where are based. I replied that since I had resigned in December, I'd been travelling around Asia and writing travel features and that I was based in Kentucky, which is always a shocker for people who haven't been there and seen for themselves how beautiful it is. He quickly responded that 'the only problem would be when and where we could meet – perhaps Asia in April (a no-go for me) or London at some point?'

My heart sank a little, but not much, and I replied in a jolly manner that I'd be in touch with him when I was back home in England in the early summer. I had to remember: I shouldn't be disappointed because I wasn't desperate for the job. In fact, I was supposed to be chilling, enjoying being a newlywed, getting pregnant and doing my Masters. Singapore was probably a mental idea anyway. I had to stop trying to run away from decisions.

***

Our liking for curry had turned into a bit of an obsession, the first question out of Russ's lips when arriving at a new destination being 'Do you have a little India?' In Singapore, the response was yes.

'And you can buy everything you need there,' our hotel doorman enthused, 'except guns, bridal gowns, coffins, cars and alcohol.' We assured him that these five items were not on our list and questioned him further about the food. 'Well, s'ok but the Hawker Centre at Newton Centre is better! More choice! More flavors! Just don't touch the seafood.'

Done, we agreed. Get us there.

Hawker Centers are an old Singaporean tradition. Hundreds of stalls and shops selling every kind of food you can imagine set up next to each other, enticing taste buds with delicious aromas and low prices. I settled on some Chinese noodles while Russ went for a Thai chili soup – it was a culinary United Nations. After twenty minutes of watching Russ sweat like a pig, for it really was too hot to be consuming something that spicy, and being told off by the waitress for using too many paper towels, we had to go back to the hotel to take care of business. A baby-making shag. 'I'm really not in the mood for this', my paramour complained and I wasn't surprised. He was still running a fever from the chili, his stomach was bloated and he was stressed about the pressure to perform. I showed no mercy though, I was a woman with a mission, and even though I couldn't be arsed either (which was totally out of character), we had to give it a shot before the window of opportunity slipped by for another month. So we did it, by numbers. Then we packed up and headed to Changi Airport for a fish therapy pedicure (when 500 fish nibble away the dead skin on your toes, a Japanese craze we'd been desperate to try) and more importantly perhaps, to catch our flight to Denpasar, the capital of Bali in Indonesia.

11

Follow Your Own Star

'Let nothing dim the light that shines from within.'

Maya Angelou

We were a bit worried about this leg of our tour. Decency Laws were being talked about on the news every night, meaning that Indonesia, a Muslim country, was getting very serious about women's rights and privileges and not in a good way. We'd been warned not to touch each other in public and certainly not kiss. The mood felt different the minute we stepped on the national airline. In the in-flight magazine there was a list of prayers to be said to stop the plane from crashing. It made sense I suppose that if you were going to pray, in a plane in difficult skies would be a good place to do it. Or start, in my case. There were prayers typed out for Muslims, Christians, Catholics, Buddhists and Hindus. Jewish people weren't allowed into Indonesia, so they didn't bother typing up anything for them. Far from being helpful, we flew through a thunderstorm and came within a mile of two other planes. We were so close; Russ swore he could see people looking out at him from their windows. He got sweaty again, this time through fear *not* chili and was visibly shaken by the time we landed in Denpasar to a huge warning sign that said smuggling drugs would lead to the death penalty, no questions asked.

'It's going to be ok,' I reassured him. 'Seriously Bali is almost hippyish in its attitudes to people and places. Once we get to the hotel, you'll be fine.' He gritted his teeth, gave me a look that screamed *you'd better be right*, and said, 'Now, where did that guy go who just took our passports and money saying he was sorting our visa out?'

Bali had better prove me right or my husband might drown me in the Indian Ocean.

Russ's nervousness about Indonesia wasn't helped by the fact I was now most certainly at the psycho stage of my cycle. He'd worked out over our time together that for the first week I was clingy, second week horny, third week psycho and fourth week, just a bit of a mess. This was the third week and even I felt sorry for him. The poor sod couldn't open his mouth without me yelling at him or making some sarcastic comment. When I was like this he refused to give me kisses and would even turn down my offers to stroke his hair (his favorite thing of all time) when I realized what a beast I was and try to sidle up to him and his affections once more. So, despite waking up to the deafeningly glorious sound of birdsong, in a beautiful villa overlooking a volcano and the ocean, we were having a miserable time. This made us both feel worse, the nastiness in the face of such perfection, and if I could have flogged myself for my selfish, hormonal spoiltness, I would have. I couldn't stand the way I was so ruled by my body, and I also feared that due to the clockwork appearance of Nasty Wife, nothing had transformed hormonally within me at all, and therefore, I was a failure once again. There was no baby. Russ had gone all out whenever and wherever I asked him to and yet still I was an infertile, dried up, childless being. My ample Wyth of Bathe breasts and hips, synonymous around the globe with motherhood and fertility, were simply objects which needed to be disguised or despised when trying to fit into a bikini.

***

The next morning Russ and I awake before sunrise for an early morning trek through the rice paddies and coconut tree valleys of Ubud. We followed the sound of the crickets, pulled coffee beans from their pods, said hello to passing, laughing children, and stayed alert while crossing bridges made of nothing but two canes of Bamboo. Our bodies became super sensitive, to the flies biting us and the dew dampening our hair into a cobwebbed frizz, to smells of gardenia wafting up river and the certainty of each foot we were placing in front of the other as we marched through the uneven hillsides. Nature was overwhelming us to the point of silence. Our senses were shaken while our feet ached. Our voices could make little impact amongst the chorus of rainy season in Bali. We were just two other breathing, moving, beating creatures amongst millions. The landscape humbled us and quieted the fears and fires within our chests. Rather than talking for once, my husband silently and protectively helped me keep balance and avoid any angry bulls. He didn't want me to fall in the water and drown and I didn't want him to get trampled on by an angry animal. That was a start at least.

After lunch, we ventured to the other side of Ubud to visit a traditional Balinese medicine man. We didn't really have any medical problems that we fancied discussing with him – we didn't discuss this, we each knew the other just didn't want to share certain things – but it was something to do and the locals had great faith in it. This particular chap was a fortune teller too.

'I went to see him twenty years ago to ask him if I would have any sons,' explained our driver Hardi en route to the healer's family compound. 'He said straight out, "You'll have two boys", and I did! I do! Two boys to make me proud and look after my ancestors, my animals and my temple when I get old.'

Every family in Bali has a lot, an area divided into three sections: one area for the gods, one for the animals (cows, pigs, chickens and ducks) and one for the humans. Generations live together in this space, they're born there and they die there. As we cruised to the east of the town, we saw a colorful funeral procession leaving one compound for the community temple, a carnival float of pick'n'mix rainbow fabrics, held aloft by strapping young men.

'We wear black when we are very sad at the temple,' Hardi reveals as we drive slowly past out of respect. 'But most of the time when we are mourning we wear bright colors and lots of white. Black is not a good color for us.' Having sons is key in Balinese culture for it is only men who can look after the temple and the other worldly possessions.

Women work hard here ('Harder than the men,' smirks Liv, a Westerner who works at our hotel, when I remarked on the back-breaking work I'd witnessed in the paddy field by the girls while the men drove around smoking on mopeds) but are still not considered as important as the guys. The ideal number of children for a Balinese couple is two. School is free but the uniform and certain books are compulsory and expensive and if their choice is between having a third child or clean water, sensible parents opt for the water. But if the woman doesn't conceive a son in the first two tries, it has to be third time lucky. And then fourth. And then fifth. The rules were too concrete and sacred for me to even mention a simple change of property policy without seeming rude or naïve but it did remind me of a problem Jane Austen brought up as ridiculous 200 years ago.

The medicine man takes a while to arrive on his front porch. We are told by his grandson to take our shoes off and sit on the bamboo mat on the floor, underneath a canopy of trees decorated with bird cages and plastic flowers. There is a framed photo of the guru nailed to the wall above our heads so we get an idea of what to expect. We can hear coughing and slurping from inside a dark room and then suddenly a very modern, beneficial electric fan appears in the porch doorway with some mumbled Balinese. 'He's worried in case you are hot,' his grandson informs us. 'He thinks it is not hot where you come from.'

A slurp and a stutter and our man is sat down beside us. For a man of 90 years, he is remarkably agile, bending his legs into the kind of twist my Kentucky yoga teacher could only dream of. He doesn't so much as look at Russ and immediately starts flirting – yes, flirting is

145

the only word for it – with me. He clearly knows who the more interested, gullible party here is.

'You very pretty, very pretty.' He starts inspecting me, which is all part of his service. 'You have good, big ears.' I did, I hated them. I was nicknamed Dumbo at school and it wasn't because I had a good memory. I felt better about this since learning than Buddha had big ears too and it was considered a physical sign that someone was a good listener. 'Yes, big ears are good. Very strong and pretty. And Chinese people like big ears. You have good forehead. You have three lines in it between your eyes which means...' he paused.

'I'm old?' I suggest.

'No, no,' he giggles like an overgrown raisin, 'it means you are very, very, very smart. You understand. You could be a success again if you want. You were a success. You can be a success again in you want. Perhaps publish. Or open a pretty salon for ladies.' Interesting, would it be back to life as a journalist or a new life as a manicurist? They sounded equally appealing at the moment.

'You have good nose, good cheeks, left and right, with dimple in the left, I like, I am very happy to meet you. You have lips like cherries. I like them. You are very, very pretty. I am lucky you came here today.'

At this point, Russ, who never liked to be overlooked, coming from a family of women who fussed and fawned over his every move and referred to him as God, burst in with a 'Steady on, are you trying to chat her up?'

The healer kept looking at me and just said, 'Your husband is a lucky man.'

He only found two problems in my future that had got in the way in the past, therefore making me think he did have genuine skills and persuading Russ to get a body reading too, for in the car on the way there he'd been saying it was a load of clap-trap and he wouldn't be splashing out on the equivalent of $25 for such an exercise in silliness. My problems?

'You are too impatient. This was good for job but now it's bad. You need to learn to be patient. You understand?'

Russ nodded emphatically while I humbly admitted his diagnosis was correct. He then grabbed my left wrist and felt my pulse.

'You have too strong sexual energy. It's crazy. You like the sex too much. You want to have it three times a night but he can't do it like that and you need to be careful of your husband. So if you must have sex three times a night, let him rest between times. Give him some food and water and then let it start again. It will be better for you that way,' he adds with a wink and a chuckle.

This is really all too much for Russ. He was thrilled to have an outsider agree that I was indeed a sex maniac who wouldn't leave him alone.

'See honey, see! Now it's my turn.'

He wiggles he's way in to the hot spot for his Balinese breakdown.

'You are very handsome, very handsome.'

Oh right? He said this to all the Western punters, did he?

'You are the King and your wife is the Queen. You will both live to 100 years old but you must be together. Without each other is bad. With each other is very good.'

He throws in a few Russ truisms ('you love travelling', 'you can be a bit lazy and you need to work harder if you want to be successful', 'you have very good knees') and then cuts to the chase. 'Why don't you have children yet?'

'We're trying', Russ admits. 'But you're the fortune teller! You tell us!' Russ was only pretending to be joking and I was practically sat

147

on the healer's lap with my over-sized ear clamped to his mouth to hear his answer, but the healer was chilling and laughing and seemed to be having a lovely time in the afternoon heat.

'You've only been married once and you will only be married once. This is very good. Very good for you.' He didn't say this to me so I guessed somewhere my palm told the story of my starter marriage and subsequent divorce. 'And you will have two children. Very good. Make me happy. Very lucky. You will have two children.'

This makes our afternoon, for a few hours anyway, until somewhere during our walk through the Monkey Forest, my paranoia comes clawing into my imagination and the realization that he said Russ would only be married once and would have two children led me to the conclusion that I had long feared and suspected: that I was infertile and we'd have to use Russ's pristine and powerful sperm to impregnate some other woman if we wanted to have a child that was even half our own. As the other tourists laughed as two monkeys put on a live sex show for us (a lifting of the tail, a sniff of the bum, a leap, a balancing act where he uses her knees as a foothold and she clings on to his furry ankles, a push, and a scarper to a safe haven for the lady monkey five seconds later), I turned a perfectly lovely – and probably totally made-up – prediction into another clue in my game of Maternity Mystery.

I managed to forget that I was in Ubud, walking streets filled with carvings and offerings and ancient temples. I stopped smelling the gardenias and hibiscus. It became all about me again, me and my lack of bump. All the talk of ancestors and protection had done something to me: it had absolutely confirmed that I wanted to have my own child. The list of reasons I'd excavated on that exhausting journey to Malaysia had popped into my head and I'd burst all my doubts one by one. I didn't just want a child that was a symbol of my love for Russ, or for our joint devotion to each other. I wanted a child so that when one of us died, the other wouldn't be alone. That we'd always have someone to talk to, to care for and to care for us. Yes, I adored my brother's children and Russ's sister's little girl, and they'd always make us feel included, but I didn't want to be that tiresome aunt who was always on the *we'd better invite or she'll be alone* list. I wanted my own unit, my own family, my own fulfilled future.

'Remember, we can always adopt,' Russ reminds me over dinner that evening, when I reveal my fears.

'Yes, you're right. I've thought that too but I'm not sure that's what we should do, or could do, yet. I'm not crying out for any child, I'm not yearning to be a mother in general. I don't coo over babies in the street. It's something more tribal and more basic than that. I want to carry on our ancestors, like the Balinese do, carry on the circles of history that is above questioning or change. With rules and honors and agreements, a passing down of stories, of property, of the past.'

'I agree with everything you just said. I'm just putting it out there as a future option. I'd never have thought I would say it but after spending time in Cambodia, I can imagine us adopting from somewhere like that. Giving a better life to a child that didn't have any other options.' Environmentally, I knew it was far more appropriate to adopt a child than bring another one into this crowded, abused world. So what were all these deep-rooted feelings of self I was experiencing? And would this baby torment ever end? I was bored of spoiling every romantic meal I had with my lovely husband with my fear of the unknown.

***

Our old friend Buddha was starting to pop up again everywhere, in the bustling towns we walked through and in the little artist enclaves set on hilltops that we saw from our car window. It was a perplexing sight – a plethora of Siddhartha's on an island famously 90 percent Hindi in a country famously 90 percent Muslim.

'Tourists love his head,' explains our new holiday chum and tour guide extraordinaire Raka, during lunch in the pouring rain overlooking Mount Batur. 'Foreigners come to Asia and they love his head and want to see his head. And Balinese love foreigners who come to Bali and want to give them anything they want. Even Buddha heads!' So Ganesh and the Compassionate One share shelf space around the green isle and the famously laidback locals don't mind. 'We both believe in Karma and reincarnation,' Raka justifies, 'and we both believe in harmony and kindness, Hindus and Buddhists. So why not share heads?' Well, it seems fine by me.

Mount Batur is now covered in complete grey, mist is swirling around our table top like a smoke machine at a school disco and for the first time in weeks, I'm shivering with cold. 'Time to get down the mountain to the rice paddies before you leave Bali with the flu or some bad luck!' Raka motions for us to get to the car.

Every village in Bali seems to specialize in something, even if that something seems to be totally useless and seemingly not very profitable. Buddha heads I can understand, but Pinocchio puppets? Yes, one tiny hamlet sold nothing but wooden replicas of the Italian midget who wanted to be real. I counted more than 100 in all sizes and colors, hanging from multiple shop windows. We left that one village and I never saw him again. Most peculiar. Many of the little places we drove through offered "Antiques – made to order!", a wonderful phrase with its irony lost on the Balinese who despite trying their best (and speaking English much better than I spoke Balinese of course) weren't on the whole natural linguists. I would repeat the simplest question, such as 'Is it going to rain today?' about five times, in exactly the same way, only slightly more desperate each time, until I got an answer. And even then, it was 50/50 if the reply would be 'Yes, Ibu!' or something totally leftfield such as 'We don't like fish because we believe the devil lives in the sea, Ibu!' (That is a real response to that question, I assure you).

Whatever words they used though, only the most blinded, hard-hearted fool could not fall in love with the Balinese and their island. A few days in and although Russ and I aren't totally smitten with each other (our affections at this point seem to fluctuate like the cloud cover over Mount Batur), we were both smitten with the island. What's not to love about a place decorated with nature's candy? Coffee beans and cacao grows freely and abundantly, coconuts are the most worrisome weapon I've encountered and the water-drenched rice paddies have given me an even deeper love for the Biryani dish at my favorite Indian restaurant back home in London. The only things outnumbering the smiley, oaky faces are the mutts that roam the streets, smart as whips and well cared for of course, in a land that places animals and trees on pedestals as well as gods and humans? When I asked Raka why there were so many, he shook his head at my silliness. 'Dogs are doorbells,' he chuckled. 'We need to know when we have visitors!'

Early in the morning and mid-afternoon the furry alarm systems are briefly outnumbered by children, cuddling and swinging their linked arms, making their way from school yard to family yard in matching orange uniforms, waving as we pass with such big smiles I feel guilty for ever not wearing one. As we crawl along the island from twisted mountain roads to the coastal paths of East Bali, the Indian Ocean comes into focus, Lombok glistening in the distance, the sea as smooth as a turquoise mirror, daring you to disrupt its calm with a boat or a swim. The cooling breeze of the mountaintop surrenders to the barmy whip of a tropical paradise. We make it to our next hotel just before sunset. And for a reason too pointless and ridiculous, Russ and I decided to have digs at each other. While we were in the middle of our silent treatment I had to cut the frosty air by asking him to remind me what our glacial glares were for again. Apparently I'd made a sarcastic comment. That prompted me to remember he'd been thoughtless. We were tired and too hot so we silently motivated ourselves to get into our swimming gear and descend the steps to the pool to watch the sunset from the water. We walked in sync, step by step, dropped our towels on neighboring loungers and sploshed through the chlorine in unison. Then he swam to one end of the pool, I swam to the other and we watched the most dreamy, mesmerizing sunset we have ever seen in our lives alone.

***

'Do you two play games with each other?'

'Mental games, you mean?' Russ and I answered at exactly the same time, to the shock of the American woman sitting on the deckchair next to us, the next day.

'Well, no,' she replied after a beat, 'I was thinking more like golf, or cards. My husband and I take playing cards with us to dinner every night so if we ever run out of something to say, we have something to do. I'd kill him if we didn't play games. I would have killed him by now.' She sneaks a peak at her other half, a sun burnt creature busily doing laps of the pool. 'We've been together solidly now, just the two of us, for seven whole days,' she adds in a conspiratory whisper.

When Russ reveals that we've been together solidly for five weeks, alone, expect for a few chance encounters with travelers like herself or the odd friendly local, she squeals in horror. 'How do you do it?' she begs me. 'And really, you don't play golf?'

The news of our vacation length is enough for her to drag her man from the pool. 'My wife tells me you've been travelling together for five weeks,' he strides over, politely holding out his hand and shaking ours in the confident and friendly way only Americans can, 'you deserve a cocktail. Four vodka and tonics please,' he calls to a nearby waiter. 'And you really haven't played any golf since you've been away?'

A few vodka tonics later, we move on to the local rum and lemonade and we've totally fallen for this couple. They are everything we've grown to expect, love and laugh at in Americans of a certain age. In the five years we'd lived stateside, both together and apart, we had begrudgingly become more and more comfortable with the American way of doing things. Swimmer Husband asks me what the difference is between living in England and living in

America and I answer him as honestly as I can. And honesty is easy due to my growing devotion to his country.

'Well, when I lived in England, I thought of the UK and America as family, as the same. I simply imagined that America was the cool kid on the block, going for it, causing trouble and having fun, while England was the slightly older cousin that lived across the road, half the time cheering him on, admiring his pizzazz and chutzpah, but the other half of the time covering his eyes and shaking his head, trying to warn him, "No, no, young cousin, we did that 200 years ago and it's really not quite right". But when I moved to America I realized this great bond, this imagined family unity was only true politically and historically, and that morally and culturally I am a European. I don't mind boobs but I hate guns. I'm pro gay-marriage and pro-choice. Yes, before I moved to America I was English. Now I live in America, I am English and I am a European.'

'Honey, if that's your criteria, forget being from Connecticut, I must be from Belgium. And that calls for another cocktail'.

Baby-making is always at the back of my mind. I know that I'm midway through my Two Week Wait, the dangerous zone that mixes expectation and dread with imaginary symptoms and hormonal fluctuations. Normally, at this point of my calendar I turn into Sandra Dee, banishing the slightest swig of coffee (my Kryptonite) from my daily life, avoiding smoky bars, turning down boozy nights out with my girlfriends. I felt guilty as my head got fuzzy and my voice got louder. I mean, I'd been avoiding hot tubs and massages for the last week or so in case it damaged the sperm and egg tango I hoped was going on inside me. Here I was now, drunk on Vodka and munching through bowls of peanuts, the only thing we'd eaten all day, being nibbled by mosquitoes as the sun goes down. Sensible Sarah knew it was time to put the drink down. Satan Sarah, or it could have been Sane Sarah, was tapping me on the shoulder, telling me to live a little and that as soon as I actually got pregnant, I could start living the life of a paranoid nun, but not before. Please.

So we drink into the night, learning too much about them really (not only do they travel with playing cards, but porn playing cards which Russ and I are alarmed to have whipped out for a viewing, being in an Islamic country where porn is illegal). They also travel with dildos, uppers and downers and running outfits. Ahhh. This makes us feel like home. Their joint openness, addiction to prescription medication and inability to function if they don't do a three mile run every day is two a penny back in our adopted homeland. The honesty was refreshing – I still don't know if any of my best friends from school have dildos and yet I know the shape and size of my new Golf Wife's one. He looked like he'd just got showered at his fancy Country Club while she looked like she'd been bonking her personal trainer. They had the fancy, successful look about them. He'd been to Harvard, she'd bought him a Masserati for his 40th birthday, she couldn't join Facebook 'because I'd look up ex-boyfriends and have affairs, I just know it' and they'd both always wanted to go to the Kentucky Derby, so we invited them to come visit us and we meant it.

Russ and I had been living in this fantasy world of love and all-conquering, problem-solving, temper-muting love at that. We'd waited so long to find each other and put up with so much shit before from ex partners that we tended to put each other on a pedestal. This was good, I'd read, shortly after we started dating. As long as you take it in turns to be in the top spot, and it's not the same person delegated to worshipper on a constant basis. But spending the day with the Americans, who were so honest about needing extra things in their relationships (dildos, golf, alcohol and drugs) to make it work, and banning others (Facebook, holidays longer than seven days) to keep it on track, highlighted how naïve we'd been. So we could wind each other up. So we couldn't bear the sight of each other sometimes. Sometimes we didn't even want to share the same sunset in the same pool. But that was normal.

We head up to our villa after the customary swapping of emails and fond farewells (they are leaving in the early hours of the morning so they will be gone by the time we wake up) to find a four-poster bed, complete with mosquito net, torch and a guide book to the stars of the Indonesian sky, lit up by candles in our front garden.

'I thought this would be romantic,' Russ pulls me into his chest for a hug. 'I've only ever slept outside before with the lads on a hiking expedition. I thought it was about time I got to watch the stars with my favorite person.' I tiptoe to kiss his gorgeous mouth.

'You are the best, rabbit,' I tell him, unleashing the term of affection reserved solely for him, much to his chagrin for there is nothing spectacular about a rabbit, expect it is my favorite animal and both our Chinese year signs.

And we undress, naked in the frangipani breeze, and make love under the mosquito net without once – thanks to the Vodka tonics and the stars above our heads – thinking about my ovaries.

***

Russ was starting to get itchy feet. Despite us travelling from village to town, up and down and around mountains and out into the ocean, he wanted to get off Bali for a bit. We'd been staying in beautiful hotels, another time of excess luxury thanks to my writing skills and good relationships with helpful PRs, and although I adored every second of it, my husband was convinced the nicer the resort the more removed you were from real local life and real local people. I would have agreed with him perhaps until we travelled to Thailand and Cambodia and realized that unless you actually moved to a country and worked there, or raised children there, or bought a house there, as we had both done in America, you weren't seeing the real country at all.

'In five star hotels we mix with business gurus and we chat to the hotel managers and get information. In hostels we mix with Australian teenagers with dreadlocks and we get ignored by whichever mafia family we are asking to fix our blocked toilet.

Neither is real Russ. Just because you have a private swimming pool in one and no air conditioning in the other, it doesn't show one is more down with the community than the other.'

He kind of got it, I think, but he liked to think of himself as the hearty traveler type, after all, he'd backpacked before with his mates, while he liked to think of me as Ms Fancy Pants. 'You're allergic to pikey places,' he concluded when I came down with an eye infection at one ghastly hostel we'd stayed at on the trip so far.

'If you mean allergic to smelly toilets, dirty towels, blood stains and squashed mosquitoes on the wall, then I quite agree,' I'd replied with indignation.

To placate his minor strop, and to see more of Indonesia, we decided to jump on board a fast boat to the Gili Islands, a set of three miniscule Robinson Crusoe-esque sand patches off the coast of Lombok, the next big island along from Bali. I was actually getting beach fatigue at this point – Oh look, another strip of golden sand! Ah, turquoise waters! Wow, coconuts washed up on the shore! – and would have preferred to return to Ubud and sit drinking papaya juice in the local markets or visit the local temples to make offerings but Russ was a beach bum by nature. He'd been a life guard at his local lido when he was in his late teens and I think the dream of an outdoor life of sea and surf had always appealed. Sadly for him, growing up in the suburban sprawl of Hertfordshire, the pool was only open for a few weeks every summer and he only got to make one dashing life save ('and he may have just been kidding around, to be honest'), but it didn't stop him wearing wooden beads round his neck or getting blonde highlights done (by his Nan, with a plastic cap).

***

At the end of Gili Trawangan dock, newcomers are greeted by a plethora of colorful horses, decorated with jewels and feathers, pulling flea-bitten, fragile old carts. This is the only means of transport on the Gilis. Cars and motorbikes have been banned and the odd adventurous explorer can hire a bicycle but the heat is off-putting. So a cart it is. We load up, ask the price to our hostel which turns out to be we imagine a reasonable $3, and are hot to trot. Within 20 seconds the driver has somehow managed to fling our luggage into a giant, filthy puddle of rainwater, mud and horse manure. 20 seconds later, we have reloaded the two bags, the unapologetic driver and a furious Russ. 20 seconds after that we are delivered to the hostel door. Yes, we'd actually travelled about 100 meters and had to pay $3 for the privilege of having our stuff ruined. We hand over the cash and spend the next few hours having to unpack our backpacks, rinse our belongings and hang them out to dry in the sun. Wow, this was real! I check in with Mr. Grumps to see how he likes *real* local life so far but he just keeps swearing under his breath, something about being taken for a ride.

Thankfully, our hostel is clean – apart from the by now ubiquitous blocked drain in the shower and waft of urine that permeates the bedroom. The bathroom is outside which isn't as romantic as it seems when your bungalow is in the middle of a mini forest and a quick pee means a few insect bites on the bum and a sprint inside before they follow you in. It also means that the people walking the busy path to the swimming pool past our abode could hear us taking a dump, something that further restricted my already difficult relationship with doing number twos. I mean, I might have to sit next to these people at breakfast, it was quite unbearable and the toilets seemed to be manufactured to give the most ear-shattering splash back if you were going to go for it.

The Gilis and its mother island of Lombok was, like most of Indonesia, a Muslim stronghold. So gone were the little baskets of fruits and flowers, daily – sometimes hourly – offerings to the kind gods and placations to the bad ones. I missed the colorful gifts. Even in the KFC at Denpasar they'd been little offerings of French fries, dandelions and apple slices laid along the counter. It struck a charming note of harmony. I also missed the stern looking statues, keeping a watchful eye over family compounds, temples and rice fields, wrapped in blankets and shaded under umbrellas. The Balinese believed in treating their Gods as they would their family, so if rain was expected, as of course it was in the rainy season when we chose to venture there, they honored their noble leaders with umbrellas and shawls to protect them from the elements. Therefore, Bali in February resembled Oxford Circus in April. Umbrellas could be seen in distracting clusters, vying for space above grey, stony heads. Stern and strong expressions looked outward, showing a sense of purpose and warning to the weather: *come and have a go if you think you're hard enough.* The Balinese caring was replaced with regular calls to worship from the one Mosque on the island and the promise of Halal water in the shops. Apart from that, it was all very similar.

Despite Indonesia's strict policy on drug trafficking – you'd risk a firing squad if they caught you – magic mushrooms were offered at every bar and food stall in the most carefree of ways. "Bloody fresh, bloody strong Magic Mushroom Milkshake! Drink it here!" urges one sign, obviously aimed at the British traveler. "Magic Mushrooms make you not worry, be happy, and buy now lots," persuades another. If it hadn't have been my Two Week Wait, I might have angled for a quick slurp. My drug resume was sadly short and lacking, free of anything more exciting than an occasional teenage spliff and a quarter of an 'E' I'd taken, aged 20, at a nightclub. It had made a sizeable clump of my hair fall out immediately and pushed me to spend the night hoovering my friend's apartment while he and our other friends danced till 6am, waving glo-sticks and talking about getting higher and higher. No, I wasn't a drug person, firmly believing that all you needed to have a good time was the right people and the right music. Mushrooms though, I'd always thought, seemed fun because they were just that: mushrooms. A good friend of mine had drunk a mushroom broth at Glastonbury a few years earlier, fallen asleep in a rain-sodden field and awoken late morning the next day, in surprisingly glorious sunshine, entirely cemented to the now sun-dried earth. That seemed as dangerous as mushrooms got.

The art of thinking slowly was not something that came easily to me. Physically slowly, yes. Unlike my wiry, nervous American friend in Bali, I was genetically disposed to sit on a comfy sofa with a good book and a cheese sandwich. I was a British woman after all. What were we without a day curling up in a corner with bread, cheese and Emily Bronte? I would pound a treadmill in a bid to divert major disasters from my bottom area but it wasn't something I sprung out of bed every morning, desperate to do. But thinking slowly had never sat right with me. From the age of nine, I was planning my career, writing short stories, running my own magazine (my brother was my only subscriber) and writing letters to publishers who kindly replied stating that although my little brother was lucky to have a sister who wrote him such sweet tales, I may not feel they represented my writing once I got older and to try again then. By the age of ten, English bookstores were unable to satisfy my rampant appetite for Sweet Valley High books so I spent every penny I had – pocket money, Christmas and birthday gifts, irregular offerings from my very distant and lacking real father – to join the Wakefield twins fan club in America, guaranteeing me the latest tome the minute it was published. Yes, as my Balinese medicine man picked up immediately, patience was not my strong point.

So perhaps, for the first time ever, the Gilis forced me to calm down. We'd learnt from our five weeks of solid one-on-one time to take our foot off the chit-chat pedal too. We could now sit and people watch, or drift in and out with the tide, without feeling the need to jump ahead and plan the next day's adventures, or the next few years' big decisions. If we didn't have anything nice to say, well, we didn't, a lesson our mothers had tried to teach us years ago.

A large portion of our time was taken up doing the simplest of things. Washing my hair, for instance, took over half an hour. The shower, situated outside in the open air, under a bamboo roof that seemed to house the island's quota of spiders, was a sea water shower. This was no good for my hair, which had resembled the mop of a screaming banshee since we left Chicago as it was. The combination of humidity, the drying effects of sea and sun and the lack of space in my backpack for a hairbrush, left me looking like I really hadn't just stepped out of a salon. More like a bush. Backwards. The sea water shower was however accompanied by a rusty, trickling tap at knee level, situated above a ceramic urn with a sign on it stating this was *'fresh water for rinsing – only!'* On top of the urn balanced half a cleaned out coconut shell to be used as the cup for delivering your rationed fresh water to whichever bit of your body needed it the most. When you have knotty, uncontrollable hair that flows way past your shoulders a coconut shell that sits in the palm of your hand can't do much. I could understand why all the other girls with long locks and backpacks I'd encountered on this trip seemed to have dreadlocks the size and texture of cigars. It may not have been a style decision. It may have been the fault of a coconut shell–shower situation.

It was tempting, of course, to spend day after day munching on fresh fruit while drinking jasmine tea, reading, sleeping, burning and whipping my mane into some kind of socially acceptable headpiece but the petiteness of the Gili Trawangan persuaded us to walk its perimeter one morning. We worked out the 6.5 kilometer would take us about three hours to plod around and that an early start was needed, before the crazy heat of the midday sun hit. So we set off at 9am, hired a snorkel (the man in the flipper hut took one look at me and said 'we have masks for big noses', which I thought was very rude but Russ found hilarious) and marched north. Copycat islands drift through our vision like lemon drops floating through Curacao waters. There was Gili Air, there was Gili Menor. We march on past dream destinations, normally only seen in holiday brochures on parents' coffee tables: Bali to the left, Lombok to the right.

***

Russ and I had become a stereotype: we were *has-been travelers*. Our marked characteristic? A wrist covered with every colored bead, bangle, wooden amulet, bit of plastic and cotton you can imagine.

Yes, not only did we whiff slightly but we had taken to cheap, local, craft jewelry like Morrissey to a bunch of gladiolas. Russ had even gone so far as to grow his hair with abandon (he was now sporting a style that was just slightly 80s mullet) and grow a beard.

That evening, we'd been sat on our mat (well, ancient moth-bitten eiderdown that looked like it had been stolen from my great, great Aunt Joyce's dusty attic) in a hookah bar for just a few seconds, looking out to the sea, about to order some sundowners when a tween stuck his head up from the beach wall and leapt onto our square of the bar.

'You need, you need, I make, I make,' he surreptitiously pulled out a bundle of friendship bracelets from his pocket. 'For you', (they always make it so personal) 'only 60,000 rupiah!' Now, this was about $6 per bracelet, which was steep. We'd been getting 2 for a dollar around the rest of Asia, and we could see – even by the fading sun and candlelight – that they weren't as good. 'Please help me, it took me all day to make them and I need to eat. My mother and father are dead and my grandfather beats me and I can't afford to go to school.'

Russ and I exchange glances that say 'do you believe it?', 'me neither', and we take up our bargaining positions. '2 for 300,000.'

He retorts that his parents are goners.

'2 for 400,000.'

He shakes his head and explains that his grandfather beats him.

'2 for 500,000, final offer.'

His eyes light up full beam and he puts out his hand to shake Russ's. '2 for 500,000 plus a Fanta, yes, thank you!'

A Fanta in Indonesia is 100,000 rupiah, so we're actually financially no nearer an acceptable price, but his English skills are impressive, his face cute and his ducking and diving skills winning. We order a mojito, a martini and a Fanta and pick out two more woven bangles. The doe-eyes go fast as the Fanta appears, he talks about his siblings and grandparents affectionately and explains that he's not looking forward to Ramadan, because he wouldn't be allowed to eat between sunrise and sunset and he loves his grandma's cooking.

We'd already assumed his sob stories were merely that, so forgiving the contradictions, we ask what it means to him to be a Muslim child in Indonesia. He told us he had to pray three times a day, and that was about it.

'What about you? You Hindu? You Christian? You Catholic?'

'No, we're nothing,' Russ says.

'Nothing!' he laughs manically. 'No, can't be! You Catholic? You Buddhist? You Christian?'

'No, really, we're nothing,' Russ confirms.

'Not even Buddha!' Everyone like Buddha! Not even Buddha?'

'Well, just a little bit of Buddha because he is a good guide,' I admit, 'but really, we are nothing.' Our new friend doesn't seem to like the heathen company he's keeping, so sucks down his drink, throws the can and straw on to the sand behind him and goes to leave.

'Pick up that can and put in on the table or in the rubbish,' Russ disciplines him.

Ali rolls his eyes, himself a teen stereotype, regardless of nationality or religious persuasion, and reluctantly bends down to the beach and retrieves it.

'Please, do not do that again,' Russ urges. 'If you do, the beaches will get ugly and dangerous and the tourists won't come.'

'I know, I know,' Ali nods slowly, flashing us a wide grin revealing rows of perfect white teeth, as if a thousand other would-be Western hippies had told him the same thing. 'OK. Bye Bye. See you later alligator.'

'In a while, crocodile,' I reply, but he's already gone to his next willing victims, easy to spot by their jangly arms.

***

'Do all boys have an obsession with Komodo dragons,' I ask Russ, as he's handing over a small fortune in backpacking budget terms, to a tour guide with a twinkle in his eye and an embroidered dragon on his back. 'Or is it just you. I mean, I'm sure I've heard of them before, I must have, but you're obsessed.' Since we'd been planning this Asian adventure, Russ had been counting down the days till we would get to Komodo Island, the home of the Komodo dragon – the nearest thing on planet earth to the dinosaur, a gigantic lizard who's bacterial spit could kill you, let alone its bite. Most grew to three meters long and they could run up to 16 kilometers per hour.

'I've always been aware of them and that the only place in the world you can see them is in their natural habitat, on their island, and I just thought seeing them would be the most amazing thing in the world.' Such a boy!

To get to Denpasar for 8am the following morning, we had to pack up quick and catch a boat back to Padangbai in Bali, then get a coach across the island to the surfers' paradise that is Kuta. This was the nearest tourist-friendly town with cheap hostels in to the airport. Kuta had been a town famous for its cheap love but that all changed in 2002, when the resort was destroyed by hatred. Islamic fundamentalists had set off a bomb in a packed nightclub, killing the Balinese and their Western visitors, and killing Kuta's tourism industry over night. Just when it started to recover in 2005, the fundamentalists struck again, setting off another bomb and killing more people and more hope for the town. The tourist enclave, once a place to venture if you were looking for a good time and some good loving, or an easy time and some easy loving, looked slightly down on its heels, as we pulled in to the main hostel district late afternoon. Rain clouds were coming in fast, so we rushed to the only hostel we could find. $15 per night with air conditioning? Bargain. Where do we sign?

Our hastiness was certainly not rewarded. Our bed was covered in a plastic sheet, and a yellowing (once white) sheet was thrown across it for us to cover up with. There were no towels, or toilet paper and apparently no flush. Electric cables and mystery wires mingled with cobwebs in corners while paint cracked lazily from the walls, falling in clusters on the muddy tiles. None of the locks worked.

As soon as we'd dropped our backpacks on the floor, a thunder clap crashed over head and the skies opened. It was the torrential rain rather that the nonrefundable $15 that kept us trapped in this Balinese hell hole. 'It's just for one night, it's just for one night,' we repeated while trying not to touch anything. As the downpour continued, the building site outside our door formed a moat, making it physically impossible for us to leave. For the rest of the evening, I read while trying to ignore the urge to pee (if you saw the toilet you'd know why, the lack of flush was the least of my worries), while Russ, who was convinced after taking a nap on the bed and waking up with an itchy crotch that he'd caught pubic lice, straddled the decrepit bath tub, shaving his nuts with the electric razor he no longer needed for his face due to the beard he was sporting. A quick wipe down with an antibacterial wipe, some antibiotic cream, a dab of moisturizer and a few hours of airing, and relief was his. Oh the joys of travelling.

'What have we learnt about each other during our journey around Asia?' I ask, desperate for some distraction in our grey-walled prison.

'Let me think... Well, all your little mannerisms have grown on me. Whether they're good things or bad, they stand out more now because we're together all the time, and it makes you even more unique and adorable to me,' he replies, as smooth as a Sade song. I lean in, lightly so as not to disturb the sleeping bed bugs, for a kiss. 'Oh. And you fart like a bloke.'

***

We arose early and checked out within five minutes (easy to do when you go to sleep fully clothed because it's more hygienic than placing your naked skin on the sheets), eager to escape to the almost mythical land of the Komodo dragon. Russ had dreamt of it for so long I was petrified he'd be let down. I mean, what were they really anyway? Giant lizards that look like alligators?

We walked as quickly as we could to the bus stop, me weighed down with a backpack now dangerously stuffed with sarongs for my friends back home, and Russ weighed down by a silly cowboy walk, the result of his genital self-flagellation the night before. What may have seemed like a good idea in the itching heat of the moment had rapidly progressed to a very bad one, his private parts stinging from a too close shave and the stubble rubbing his inner thighs. It actually made him walk like he was insanely well hung so I followed a few steps behind, giggling at the shocked glances from the petite local men on their way to work.

After a 30 minute ride to the airport, a bit of a delay, a two hour flight from Denpasar to Labuanbajo on the island of Flores, another bus ride to the harbor front and then a four hour slow boat ride... and we see our first dragon. Despite being pushed as one of the seven natural wonders of the world, Komodo National Park is very un-tourist friendly and rather chaotic. Despite being warned to never be alone without a guide, you have to face a 10 minute walk on your lonesome to get to the ranger's station. So, there it was, before we'd even met our protector, a dragon. Russ flinched, flushed and then begged for a photo shoot: posing smiling, posing frowning, posing with a shocked expression, crouched and standing. After a few minutes the dragon (a small one, hence our bravery) hissed, I screamed and ran (the two things, I later found out, that you are not supposed to do if one hisses at you), while Russ stayed calm and grabbed a stick (the two things you are, him having watched a series about them on the National Geographic channel), then we edged our way quickly to our waiting guard. The first thing he pointed out was the cafeteria – not in case we were hungry, but because it was the favorite lunchtime hangout of the hungry cold-blooded residents. And there they were: a pile of them, rolling on top of one another, heads lifted, claws outstretched as if doing a lizard version of a yogic Python pose.

'These are all female dragons. I can tell because they are small, with small tummies, and they love hanging out here the most,' Anto our guide explains. 'It's shady, they love the smell of the food being cooked upstairs and it's near where they've buried their eggs if they need to get back to check on the children.'

Komodos, we discover, are cannibalistic, by which I mean the large male dragons eat their babies. The female dragons spend a long time building decoy nests to throw their male counterparts off the scent. The eggs take 8-9 months to hatch, a long gestation period for any kind of animal and more similar to humans, and once born, the baby dragons know instinctively to run up the biggest tree and hide from the men folk. Up a tree is where they stay until they are two or three years old, feeding on the occasional gecko or snake. As we hike through the wildlife, I decide to turn baby dragon, and search out trees to scarper to if the need arises. Russ is calmer now he has a large stick to hold. Men must have sticks. They are kind of like barbecues and tool belts for making them feel secure in their sexuality. The guide has the bigger stick, obviously.

'If a dragon approaches, reach out and dig the stick into his neck, or place the double pronged end of the stick into his nostrils. Dragons can smell blood from 5kms away but block their nose and you throw them off the scent and they calm down,' Anto states.

166

When we'd booked the trip, the organizer told us two things: don't wear red, as the color is like a red flag to a bull, literally. And don't bleed.

'I'm sorry to say this to you, Sir', he apologized to Russ, 'but if your wife have her period, she has to stay on boat. If the dragons smell period, it is very dangerous.'

This was bothering me. Although I wasn't due until the following Monday, four days later, my body hadn't been doing anything I'd wanted it to do for the last year and my once regular periods had started to go a bit haywire, often starting early. I didn't want to upset Russ and his dream of us seeing these bloodthirsty beasts together, but I was getting the early 'period warning signs': boobs so sore I had to wear a bra in bed, slight constipation, an ugly spot on my chin and of course my hormonal moaning. So now, I was dreading my period arriving for two reasons. Not only did it mean another failed month of baby making but it would mean I could possibly be eaten by a dragon. I'd casually broached the subject with Russ the night before, as my stomach was being pulled in a slight cramp that could only mean one thing.

'We could try spraying you all over with our insect repellent', was all he suggested.

So here I was, nothing to protect me but two men with long sticks and citronella-sprayed nether-regions. There was no sign of my monthly joy yet but it could start once we were out in the bush and I was scared. The trek seemed to last forever, the heat not helping. Piles of dragon dung littered the ground.

'It's white because when the dragon eats anything, it swallows it whole, it's intestines then work through the calcium of the bones and hair. So it shits white,' our guard says with a chuckle, as if this is not the most gruesome thing. His giggles are even more shocking considering his good friend, a fellow guard, is currently in a critical condition in a Bali hospital after having his ankle chewed on a few days before. 'Oh he'll be alright, I'm sure. It was funny really! The dragon pounced as he was running up to his lodge, that is why the dragon only got his ankle – he got his nose caught between the steps.'

It didn't sound funny to me, so I continued to plan my nearest escape routes up trees and walked in a side shuffle, crab-like, with my legs crossed. Thankfully, the dragons, when we did spot them, seemed more interested in sleeping off lunch in the shade than chasing the tourists, our late arrival meaning we'd missed the most active part of their day. The true adventure was to come on our early morning trek the next day when they would be awake, alert, with rumbling tummies.

Due to the Komodo National Park's geographical isolation it is necessary to hire a live-aboard boat and stay in the vicinity for a few days if you want to really spend time looking and learning about the dragons. This is how we came to be booked on a dilapidated fishing boat with three Indonesian crew and two Spanish know-it-alls. I was the only girl in the party of seven and I quickly realized that I needed to become one of the boys: engaging in dragon talk, jumping off the side of the boat into the ocean to spot manta rays and eating too much. The only thing I couldn't do was piss off the side of the boat (it was like the Bellagio fountains after a few drinks), instead being forced to the back of the vessel, where behind a splintered piece of damp wood to protect my modesty, I could lean over a hole and wipe my bottom with disintegrating pieces of damp tissue, while my knees and my head could still be seen by all my other shipmates. It wasn't elegant, it wasn't pleasant and it damn well wasn't hygienic (the food was prepared on the ground next to the loo) but I kept repeating to myself, '*it's an adventure!*' and laughing at the absurdity of it all.

The bow of the ship was painted an exquisite Tiffany shade of blue but that splash of turquoise was the only classy thing about our vessel-home. Rusty nails and coarse rope stuck out of every panel, and if you sat anywhere for longer than five minutes, your thighs would take a layer of peeling paint with it as you got up. A washing line ran along the side of the ship which for some reason the Spanish duo decided to make good use of it and within a few hours the pegs were taken up with countless pairs of underpants and swimming trunks. I saw more bare arses on that first day than dragons. The average age on the boat was probably about 51, so that wasn't a good thing. But I didn't moan, even when a beautiful vista or watery sunset would be disturbed by the arrival of a pudgy Spanish man, blocking my view with a through-the-legs view of his testicles.

'You've really gone up in my estimation,' Russ admits, as our bedding is being pulled out from the engine room, an array of thin, damp mattresses, diesel-scented pillows and fish-stained sheets. 'Any other girl I could have brought here would have thrown a hissy fit and made my life hell,' he goes on, 'yet you're handling it better than me. I mean, if that old Spaniard bends over and sticks his ball bag in my face once more I might have to push him overboard. You're doing well though honey, I'm proud of you. You're a lot braver than I thought you were.'

'This isn't bravery,' I reply wistfully, thinking back to my days of luxury and thick, dry toilet paper at the Playboy Mansion and the Regent Beverly Wilshire, 'this is called being trapped on a boat with no escape and just having to get on with it.'

At 7pm it's getting dark and there is a rain storm brewing. Flying foxes swoop overhead, racing toward the lightening over the mountains. It's times to drop anchor for the night. As the first heavy drops of liquid fall from the sky the crew race around the boat, dropping tarpaulin sheets around the outside, securing it from the wind with fishing wire and determination. The storm whips up the waves and we are tossed from side to side as the heavens open and the little, old fishing boat takes a beating. The plastic sheets do the best they can, but water seeps in through cracks and holes. We hit the floor anyway, unable to see out and unable to stand up. We all lie down like sardines, me at one end guarded by Russ from the other five men. But the rain rushing in on to my face proved more of a menace than any wandering hands in the night. Russ and I held each other tight, soaking into each other as we got tossed left and right in the darkness, his smile occasionally becoming visible when a crash of lightening would flash about us. 'Thanks for doing this for me, Sweets,' he smiled. 'Thanks so much.'

The storm finally stopped, and the lashing wind and water was replaced with a stifling humidity that made our little plastic coated boat feel like a sauna – a sauna that stinks of petrol and rotting fish and six sweaty men. The Indonesians lay motionless, used to this life on ship, while Russ fidgeted, finding moments of peace in our restless melee, and the Spaniards snored loudly or, in other circumstances, comically, snorted and huffed, then abruptly stopped to release giant moans.

Finally, at 4.30am, the cries of prayer could be heard across the water, from the mosque on dry land, miles and miles away in the distance. I normally found the sound quite scary, but this morning it was my friend – a signal of time, a new day and of a distraction. Soon after, a ridiculously loud, long fart emerged from the Spaniards area of the floor, followed by a long sigh of relief.

And we were up.

The Indonesian crew emerges blinking from under their scratchy blankets, and burst into life, folding away the plastic sheets and pulling up the anchor. The Spaniards rose, seemingly refreshed and immediately pulled out their penises to wee over the side of the boat. I sat up, happy that the quicker things got moving, the quicker I could take a dip in the sea and feel somewhat fresh. Only Russ remained horizontal, muttering his dismay.

'They've kept me awake all fucking night with their snoring, then he farts and we all have to get up. I'm pissed off.'

I get a flashback to the fart, half giggle and half want to throw up, it certainly makes me feel sick enough to refuse the breakfast that is being offered round with dirty hands, a moist (and not in a good way) loaf of bread infused with some innocuous sugary substance.

***

'Is not good enough!' exclaims Papa Iglesias (his real name, not a Spanish stereotype), in his broken English. 'I want more dragons! More! Aye aye aye. Is crazy!' Apart from his snoring and farting, the elder Spaniard loved moaning and using the word crazy. Quite rightly so in most cases, after all he and his son had too paid $420 for this minus five star experience. But he wouldn't let anything go. He moaned the whole way through our trek about his lack of sleep (despite us having aural evidence to the contrary) and now the trek was over he was moaning about the lack of dragons, despite it being quite obvious that you couldn't control the whereabouts of these beasts in their natural habitat. And anyway, we'd seen a few very large ones – up to three meters long and hissing theatrically – chasing a herd of wild boar, so what else could he want?

'When I came to Komodo before, ten years ago…' Off he went again, talking about his last trip, rose-tinted and superior, while his son echoed his every word, quite sweetly in a child-like voice despite his own dotage. They were likeable, in a way, despite their noisy orifices and the fact Papa Iglesias looked like Saddam Hussein. Junior Iglesias looked like a less swarthy version of Javier Bardem, handsome in a frog-faced way. The father was retired and the son had just lost his job due to the bad economy in Spain, so they'd decided to take a trip around Asia together, to plan what to do next. Neither of them mentioned women, if they were present or missing from their lives, this was very much a father and son trip, man to man, to find some answers.

'I'd like to do that with my own son, one day, when I'm old like that,' Russ reveals, watching them together. 'I wish I'd done this with my dad.'

171

Throughout this trip, we'd been confronted with different dynamics – orphaned sons, abandoned teenage boys, and now a father and son with a dreamlike closeness and matching mannerisms – and Russ's reaction to them all had been heartbreaking to observe.

None of us could stand another night aboard the boat, so we decided to hit dry land that evening, rather than seek out another night under the stars, sweltering in plastic while risking the waves towering menace. We disembark on the collapsed pier of Labuanbajo with fond farewells but mostly sweet relief and head to the only hostel in town with rooms free at such late notice, a desolate place up the hill overlooking the harbor. Remove any romantic notions from your head. The harbor view could do nothing to disguise the danger zone of dirt and disarray. With no air conditioning but plenty of bugs, the beds seemed to dance with sand fairies who delivered grit to every corner of the pillows and gristle to the sheets. There was a sink on the wall but no one had bothered to attach it to a pipe or plumbing system. Instead of a flush, there was a bucket. And we seemed to be back to the Hong Kong days of showering over the toilet, too. It was as grim as the boat, and the wafer-thin walls didn't seem to promise much resistance to the snoring or exclamations of 'crazy' from the Iglesias brood, who had checked into the room next door. In fact, the walls seemed to have been hastily stuck together with plywood, cornering off an unused section of the main reception area. But at least we could escape by foot, as we did, immediately after dumping our backpacks. Russ, straight into the arms of a Nasi Goreng supper, while I surrendered to the smell of clean air and a toilet that had a door. There was no flush and there were too many geckos to feel I *wasn't* being watched, but at least it had a door.

And at that point, of course, I started to bleed. My body reminding me that although it hadn't done what I'd wanted it to this month – conceive – it wasn't a total bitch. It had waited till I was on dry land, safely away from human-devouring dragons, three Indonesians and two Spaniards, to put me through my bloody indignity.

When I get woken up, yet again, at 4.30am by the insistent crooning of a Muslim at a mosque with a microphone, I'm pretty upset. Not that I was in a blissful state of sleep. Our location in the foyer meant we were disturbed by every drunken, diving reveler returning to his bed, and the cock in the back garden seemed to want to cock-a-doodle-doo his heart out exceptionally early, starting at 2am for some reason. I was also in agony of course. My flow was strong and the cramps that always came along for the ride on the first day excruciating. Russ, with my permission, had given our painkillers, band aids, and energy booster sachets to some boat people we'd met on our journey from Rinca Island to Komodo Island when their need seemed greater than our own. Indeed, if they needed a pharmacy or a doctor, they had to travel four hours by boat to find one. I petulantly regretted our generosity now of course, curled up in a ball, desperately kneading my stomach.

***

Despite the pain, I was chilled. So chilled that when I found an ant in my Nasi Goreng that lunchtime I simply picked it out with a slice of cucumber, showed Russ, and carried on eating. 'Bloody hell, you've changed,' Russ remarked. 'An ant in your lunch would have caused a full body meltdown a few months ago. They'd have been tears, retching and a fair bit of moaning to the waitress. I'm proud of you, even more than yesterday.' It wasn't that I relished having an insect in my food – no fear, it still made me feel a little queasy and question the hygiene of the whole establishment obviously – but this trip had put small nuisances such as those into perspective. Has anyone ever died or got a broken heart from an ant in their rice dish? No. Well then, what's the problem?

***

Our travel guide described Sanur as 'Kuta in a cardigan', a supposedly off-putting term, meant to dissuade funky movers and shakers from setting a foot near the place. Yet this description was like manna from heaven to us and our sun-burnt, ringing ears. It had the wide, open, golden beaches of the nearby Kuta, but not the crowds. It had the nightlife... but of the gentle variety: live music while you ate your seafood buffet rather than all-you-can-drink happy hours while you snacked on a packet of crisps. The hostels were described as a bit pricey, the cheapest being $30 dollars a night rather than what we'd paid for our night in Kuta, $15, but we'd already decided to part with some cash so this wasn't a problem.

At Bali airport, we flagged down a taxi and stated our destination.

'You mean Seminyak,' our driver replies, as a statement, not as a question.

This was a flattering assumption to make, for those knowledgeable of the different scenes on the island, as Russ and I now were, knew that Seminyak was the destination for hipsters, those seeking DJ booths and sunset cocktails, or fusion food under imported chandeliers.

'No, no, we do mean Sanur,' I replied and our driver started our requested route East with a little chuckle.

At our bungalow – yes, we'd gone for a Balinese bungalow, which meant we got a tiny garden, filled with cats with short tails, and a straw roof – we began to unwind even more. Yes, there was a disgusting smell in the air, but at least it was the smell of ant killer rather than rotting fish. The bathroom wouldn't win any awards from *The World of Interiors* but it had a flush that worked, a sink that was plumbed to the wall and a shower that dispersed more than saltwater. Ah, such blessings.

'Shall we really push the boat out and pay the hostel to do our washing for us?' Russ suggests, marvelously, when he finds a leaflet about their services in a drawer. We were both incredibly stinky. Russ had taken to wearing his swimming trunks 24/7, even to dinner in the evening to keep from dirtying his boxers, and I'd actually turned my knickers inside out to get two wears out of them on more than one occasion. We'd been trying to keep up with our washing, scrubbing items with soap and rinsing them in the sink then leaving them out to dry in the sun, but we'd never achieved that fragrant, fresh feel that only a proper wash and dry could.

'Let's!' I agreed.

So while I dozed on and off, as much as my twisted cramps would allow me to, Russ counted my knickers and t shirts and ticked them off the itemized washing chart, only stopping to ask me 'what exactly are leggings?' That night, we ventured out smelling sweetly for the first time in weeks.

***

There was only one downside to our time in Snore – as Sanur is nicknamed by people who pass through on the way somewhere more exciting – and that was the amount of time it left Russ to get depressed again about is father's recent passing. He'd admitted himself that the busier he was, the better he was, that this tour and all its trappings had been a wonderfully restorative break from the inner grind and slog of his brain, and the workings out it had been doing since Peter's death. He'd been doing really well, talking frequently and fondly about his father and his idyllic childhood in Hertfordshire without getting maudlin or weighed down in the epic unfairness of it all. Our backpacks had definitely been weighed down by his understandable sadness when we'd left America and they were decidedly lighter now, as he'd seen and heard that his heartbreak wasn't his own, but a giant human burden to bear, shared by anyone who'd lost a parent, as invariably we all would – if things occurred in the *correct order* of life.

'I have so many questions left unanswered,' he admits, over yet more Nasi Goreng (I feared I'd wake up one morning and he'd have turned into a plate of this rice dish). 'Not painful questions such as *did he love me* and *did he love my mum* because I know that he did. Not just from his last words, which were very much about how much he loved his family, but from his actions throughout the whole of my life.' From all accounts, Peter had always been an exemplary father and husband – a loyal, fun and faithful man, a good friend and loved colleague. When he died, no one was in doubt of his devotion to them, even me who had only known him for just over a year. 'No, it's the other stuff he didn't tell me that haunts me,' Russ continues. 'He never cried, he never moaned. While the disease was killing him from the inside out, he never complained that it was unfair, or got angry at anyone. I want to know how he did that. How did he feel knowing he was going to die? Why didn't he tell me, or my mum, or my sister, let us help him with it?'

He'd been daydreaming of his dad all day long. They weren't nightmares – although he couldn't get the stench and fear of those last few minutes of his father's life out of his brain – but flashbacks and reenactments, painful reminders that these snapshots would not be added to, that there would be no more memories to be made of him and his dad: no more dressing up as Santa at Christmas, no more inappropriate mother-in-law jokes designed to offend Russ's Nan while everyone else laughed, no more lifts home from the pub when he'd had too much to drink with the lads and his dad was the safe bet replacement taxi service. So the daydreaming, my poor husband, assured me, wasn't nasty or painful as such, but just grey moments of the wonderful times he'd had with his father and the sad admission that it had now reached an end.

'The thing I don't understand is how death can still come as such a shock?' he says. 'I mean, we're all going to die. As the joke goes, that's the only thing we can be sure of apart from taxes. And yet, when it hits us personally, we don't know what to do. We fumble around in shock, dazed by the unfairness of it all. We don't ask questions, we don't reveal our inner thoughts. The whole death bed scenario you imagine when God becomes clear and the heavens open and the dying person comes out with something Jesus or

Obama would be proud of, it doesn't happen. I've been there. I've been inches away from it. And the angels don't come down in a golden light and play the harp. No, it just stinks, and there are horrible sounds, and you can hear your mother sobbing and your sister begging and you don't know what the fuck to do or say or think, because not one bastard can explain it to you. And then the person you love, who has been this massive presence in your life, just stops breathing and for a minute you stop breathing. And then you have to start arranging things. While my dad - my bloody amazing dad – is still lying there, in the special bed in the lounge the MacMillan nurses had brought him, warm and familiar, you have to start calling people and asking for advice, and referring to the person you love so much as *the body*, and trying to be efficient about it all. It sucks. It doesn't make any sense. We all have to go through it, not only ourselves at the end of our own lives, but watching our parents die or our siblings. As I sat and watched my mum clasp my dad's hand and tell him it was ok to go, that he should go, all I could think of was that would be *you* one day, clutching *my* hand with the same devotion and sadness. We all have to go through it. So why don't we talk about it? Why isn't death dealt with, like divorce and infidelity and bankruptcy? Why can't we all have an honest conversation about it?'

So our days were spent talking about Peter, unsure if he was somewhere else, or he truly was now just a pile of ashes, buried in the pretty churchyard a short walk from Russ's family home; remembered in a sunny spot by the front door of the chapel, where visitors couldn't fail to see that Peter had lived and was loved and would always be remembered. And that the wild flowers and the green grass and the abundant trees that decorated that little plot of land so prettily in the Spring would benefit from having his body interred there and nature itself would use him wisely to keep growing and prospering, as our memories would grow and prosper and help feed the next generation that were *surely* going to come along.

Russ had a miserable last few days in Bali. After the nasty nightmares and daydreams of death followed a wreck ball of food poisoning, that left him unable to stand up. As the sweats and chills took turns in playing havoc with his body temperature, he released an occasional groan as the pain gripped his stomach. Giving up on the idea of resting in bed, he soon just took refuge on the cold, tiled floor of the bathroom. Having suffered the same symptoms back in Cambodia, I knew the best I could do was offer silence and the odd offer of water or a cold flannel. The heavy, dank smell of illness clung to our bedroom like flock wallpaper.

'Honey, I feel bad I wasn't more sympathetic to you when you were ill last month now,' he apologized, limply, at my feet, 'I didn't realize it was this bad. I thought you were being a bit dramatic.'

'I didn't have the energy to be dramatic, you wally, I wanted to just lie down and fall into a coma,' I retorted, taking my standard position, near his head, for maximum hair stroking potential. 'But the good news is with food poisoning, it's normally all over in 24 hours. You'll wake up in the morning feeling like yourself again.'

He looked doubtful, but he climbed up into bed, and managed to get moments of rest between manic dashes to the loo.

I was wrong. Russ didn't wake feeling as good as new. He woke up with a crop of strange spots on his face, an urge to be sick and the same acidic feeling in his tummy that he'd had the previous day.

'It's Bali belly,' said a fellow English tourist I bumped into, on a quick trip out to grab a bag of crisps and some Coca-cola, the only nourishment either of us could be tempted to try. 'We've been coming here for the last 17 years and someone always ends up on a drip or in trouble!'

She relays how that very morning, when she'd ventured out for her morning walk, she'd spotted a frantic looking man, 'with one of those hurdy-gurdy European accents – he wasn't English', leaping into a taxi, barefoot and naked except for a towel wrapped round his waist, shrieking to be taken to the hospital. 'He'd had a misunderstanding with some bedbug powder apparently. He was supposed to put a few spoonfuls in his bath, but the itching was so bad he decided to rub it straight into the bites. Ouch!' She grimaces, shudders at the thought, and adds 'See, your husband's bum may be on fire but at least he's not getting his testicles iced by a male nurse in Denpasar right now!'

On our last night in Bali Russ felt well enough to go out. We decided to head to a bar called White Sands, where on the first night we'd met an old Liverpudlian couple who had been regulars there for the last 17 years. Al was an ex-professional footballer turned hotelier, who was now retired, thanks to a few major heart attacks knocking him off his feet and subsequently knocking him off his business path and towards an easier route of long holidays in the sun and family time. His elegant wife Jean was still a beauty at the age of 67 and a real firecracker. She'd just climbed Mount Snowdon with her church group, and spent her time in Bali visiting orphanages and villages, not just sitting on the beach drinking coconut water like the rest of the Blue Rinse Brigade.

After quite a long discussion on what Russ's stomach would be able to handle for dinner, which included the opinions of Jean and Al, plus the illegal Austrian chef Günter, his teen Indonesian wife Anna, an Australian couple who just happened to be walking past at the time and 'Jonny', the Balinese owner, we order fish and chips - which was considered by all to be safe thanks to its Britishness, despite it being Australian snapper, cooked by an Austrian in a restaurant in Bali - and settle down for our final few Bintangs. Jean had winkled out of me what I did for a living and Russ proudly revealed the true heady heights to which my career had risen, which impressed our new friends greatly.

'Well done, chuck,' Jean congratulates me. 'You must be dead proud of yourself.' Sensing my hesitation, she places a hand on my knee to chivvy me along. 'Well, you *should* be! Not many girls of your age could have done that! Moved to New York on your own, not knowing a soul, and launching a magazine! A weekly magazine at that! Well, good for you. That's girl power, that is!'

Instead of her desired effect, the combination of a conversation about my past glory and a few strong beers left me feeling a bit directionless. When she asked what was next I couldn't answer.

'I'm writing for a few travel websites, studying for a masters in English back in Kentucky, coming up with ideas for some new projects…'

It all sounded a bit loosey-goosey. I didn't sound like I was working hard for a living.

Jean had told me after ending up in an orphanage at the age of 12, getting married and divorced to a bully by the age of 19 and working hard to own her own house by the age of 22, she had decided to never rely on anyone else. She wouldn't ask anyone for help.

'Even God! People used to ask me if I prayed and I'd say "I don't bother anyone else for help, so why would I bother him. He's busy enough!" If I wanted something, *I'd* work until *I* got it!' She wasn't judging me. If anything, she saw me as a kindred spirit. Women who fought against tricky childhoods and unsuccessful first marriages to come out on top thanks to our own merit. I was judging myself.

'Your only job from now on,' jokes Russ, as we wave goodbye and walk back to our hostel a few hours later, 'is to be my sweetheart. A professional sweets!' Sensing this didn't help, he carried on.

'The way I see it, you've worked hard since you were – what - 14 years old? You got to the top, you were great at it and you moved on. It's an exciting time for you, honey. Look where we are right now? You'd never have been able to leave the magazine for this long. I mean, you used to take your Blackberry to the bathroom with you in case your boss emailed. Now, from this year on, you decide what's next – not your Blackberry, or your old boss, or your bank account. I have every faith that you will do something great again, so just lean on me during this time. Let me look after you, how you have looked after me. All you have to do is decide what it is you want to do?'

12

Stripped Down Self

'The fiery moments of a passionate experience are moments of wholeness and totality.'

Anais Nin

Tokyo was dazzling in its efficiency and sparkling cleanliness. It wasn't a place that had a list of *must-dos* to be ticked but everyone I knew that had visited had loved it's culture, its people and of course, its food. Within a minute of landing, and sailing seamlessly through customs with smiles and mutual respect for getting the job done, I felt at home. The constant pursuit of order and hygiene was far from boring or controlling, in fact after a couple of months in South East Asia, it was rather liberating and exciting. Oh, to have a meal without an insect in it or a trip to the toilet without witnessing something stomach-churning was bliss.

We were not as pretty as the city though. Embattled by the overnight flight and remnants of stomach flu (him) and menstrual drama (me, obviously), we were now coming down with colds and coughs, limbs heavy and heads blocked. Tokyo, and its lack of 101 top sights to see before you die, was a relief. The idea of hibernating in a hotel room, 50 stories high above the lights, traffic and noise of the city, was like a snatch of heaven. In the clouds of our white duvets, in the clouds hovering above Mount Fuji, we could nurse ourselves back to freshness. We weren't unhappy to be travelling, but sometimes the lack of the familiar (be it conversations with friends, a bed, a home-cooked meal) took its toll. People had warned us we'd get Backpacker's Beach Burnout but we went one step beyond: we had *everything* burnout.

Checking in to our beautiful hotel (gosh, what the concierge must have thought of us checking in amongst the melee of smart, Chanel-clad, Tod's-wearing businesspeople I dread to think), we waste no time dumping our clothes on the floor and jumping under the covers. Not with passion, with exhaustion. Despite the sexy air in this city, Russ and I were having none of it. Over the last few months anyway, sex for us had become less about lust and more about love – and my shameless pursuit of my new goal, motherhood. After a nap therefore, instead of reaching hopefully for a responsive part of my husband's body, I picked up a local magazine to check out if there was anything going on that we *had* to check out (other than the many wonderful sushi, tempura and noodle bars of course). The largest section of the magazine belonged to the personal ads. In my new somewhat sexless state, I found them shocking in their open, desperate need for varying degrees of intimacy. Some asked for sex sweetly (*'Honeymoon for life! Professional, handsome and financially secure man in 30s seeks partner to share the adventures of the world with!*); some asked for sex meekly (*Shy, sweet Japanese man looking for European lady for a serious relationship, hopefully leading to marriage*); some asked for sex straight-up (*British man looking for no-strings-attached sex on regular basis. Can't promise anything but a good time*); while some asked for sex on the side (*Good looking man trapped in loveless marriage would like to meet a slim, attractive woman 20-40 for regular hook-ups in afternoons. No evenings*).

My favorite ones were the total out and out perverts, who needed a rare fetish fulfilled and clearly had to throw the net wide open to catch someone with a similarly weird desire. There were people advertising with requests for every kind of nationality, plus huge breasts, no breasts, big bottoms, women with men's bodies (hmm, you can theorize on what's really going on there!), virgins, people to take their virginity, stocking-wearing older ladies, dangerously young girls… and then real peculiarities, such as a gay man looking for a non-gay man to have a physical relationship with and couples looking for attractive people to move in to their marital home on a permanent *swinging* basis. There were sad ads too, one from a '*French student, 23, unable to pay bills/rent, looking for financial sponsor. I'll know how to thank you, with conversation, massages or in bed. Accompanying you to functions as 'your partner' any time or any day.*' One from a man in a wheelchair asking if someone would take pity on him and give him a hand job. At the other end of the scale were the cocky regulars, full of themselves and just looking for a good time. These were the ones with the funny email addresses, such as istoptraffic@gmail.com, and uptothenuts@yahoo.co.uk. One scan of this Tokyo magazine left an imprint of absolute debauchery, absolute loneliness and absolute confusion on my whole view of the city.

It's amazing when you hit your 30s sex becomes something so different to when you first discover it in your teens and twenties. When I was younger, I used it to fulfill something much more than a physical need. It made me feel wanted, attractive and worthy. Then, when I was single, I didn't need sex. Bizarrely, this time in my life – just before I met Russ – I was perfectly fulfilled, and felt attractive and worthy – without a wet patch. I lusted after warm pajamas and a new magazine to read more than a night of passion with a random. Now, again, sex had become something I needed to feel worthy, but on a different level: not worthy as a girl, but worthy as a woman, a bundle of emotions and processes I felt I needed to be more of a woman, which was *I needed sex to become a mother*. Or not to become more of a woman but to elevate my experience as a woman. I didn't want to miss out on this fundamental part of being a female. I thought that pregnancy and motherhood would put me onto another plain perhaps, a higher plain of greater compassion, understanding and purpose.

This was a totally ridiculous notion of course – I'd estimate that over half of woman I most admired in the world were childless, through choice or otherwise – but I couldn't help how I'd started to feel over the last few months. I was disgusted with myself but I felt a lesser member of my sex. I remember, just a few years ago, getting angry that women were congratulated and admired for getting pregnant, while I would be less honored for launching a magazine, or getting a book published. 'All they did was have unprotected sex and they get all this kudos, I actually had to do something that took some skill,' was my old argument, shared only with my mother.

***

Sometimes you get out of bed on the wrong side and everything is wrong. Really, it would be sensible just to climb back under the covers and ride it out but no one ever thinks to do that, do they? They get up, look at their weary face in the bathroom mirror and attach a mask of jolliness over their grim visage. Russ and I had both got out of bed the wrong side this morning, and there weren't enough masks for the both of us. Within seconds of arising, a jostle over who could go for a pee first, highlighted to us that this day would not go well.

'You have something in your teeth,' I alert Russ in a disgusted manner at our breakfast table in the rather fancy hotel bistro. 'And something round your mouth.' He sorts himself out without thanks for the heads up. 'Gross,' I say, under my breath.

'Your spots are coming back. Wow, yes there's a big one there.' Russ scrutinizes my pores, as the waiter brings up our hot dishes. Meanness makes Russ hungry, so clearly famished he orders a'la carte *and* the all-you-can-eat buffet. Shaking his head, 'It's probably all the shit you've been eating' he decides.

We munch through our eggs and smoothies in silence, air between us so tense you'd need a chainsaw to cut it.

'I'm going to read a book about carpentry when I get home to get some ideas and new skills. *I've* decided what *I'm* going to do with the bar in the basement.' This was meant to annoy me, and it did. He was good. I was always asking him to think 'we' not 'me'; that we were a team who made big decisions — like what to do in our house — together.

'Really? You're going to read a book, are you? Good luck Russell, dearest!'

'What's that supposed to mean?'

'Well, you've only read three books in your life, so I'm sure that won't happen.'

In calmer moments, Russ admitted this with pride — he's read three sports autobiographies in all his years, passing his English exams by watching film adaptations. A few months earlier, an ex colleague of mine, hearing this, had turned to me in disdain and snootily retorted, 'how on *earth* did you two get together? I mean, Sarah, you *write* books and you're with someone who can't even *read* them.' At that time, our togetherness bolstered by her rudeness, I answered truthfully that 'I read my own books. I don't need someone to do it for me. And it wasn't his reading skills that attracted me to him in the first place.' Indeed, in kinder moments, I would find Russ's rebellion against sitting and reading one of the sexiest things about him.

He got it from his mother, who had phoned us before our trip with an update on her new life as a widow, and told us she's joined a book club. She read through the list of titles she had to read and discuss over the following weeks and I was quite envious. Brideshead Revisited, Rebecca — many of my teen favorites. When I expressed my envy, she replied, 'I was hoping you'd say that, because I have no plans to read them, I'm just going to get out of the house and have some company. So you can fill me in on what I need to know.'

This was how Russ had been raised. As a child, while I was sitting with my nose in someone else's story, he was learning to play the guitar, winning swimming competitions and scoring goals for his football club, all skills he still has today. We were chalk and cheese and I actually liked that. I liked that he thought I was exhaustingly clever for knowing so much about art and culture and was so proud of everything I did from a published article to an A grade at university, while I was constantly floored by his athleticism and get up and go.

'You're just being rude now. I'm going to the buffet.'

'Can you bring me back a croissant?'

'Get yourself one.'

'I haven't paid for the buffet, only you have. Please. Just sneak me one.'

Russ comes back a few moments later with a plate piled high with everything one could wish for in the morning, except a croissant. He plonks an apricot Danish in front of me.

'What's that?'

'Your croissant.'

'That's not a croissant Russell,' I snarl.

'Well, how am I supposed to know what a fucking croissant is?'

'Well, because I know that you *do* know what a croissant is. And there's a massive mountain of them right in the middle of the buffet. And well, I don't like apricot Danishes,' I pushed it away, back onto his half of the table.

'Why can't you just say thank you and eat it?'

'Because it's not a croissant.'

'Well just pretend it is to be pleasant.'

'You want me to pretend this fruit pastry thing is a croissant, rather than you just going and getting me a croissant?'

He stands up from the table, leaving his food, grabbing our room key and leaving me in the dining room, with my apricot Danish, and a swell of embarrassment as the waiters hover about, refolding his napkin and asking if 'Sir would like any more tea on his return.'

I stayed a few long minutes, pretending to be finishing my own tea, not giving them any obvious reason that my husband had just marched out in fury, and then made my own exit. Russ answers the door after a few seconds. 'I think we should give each other space today. I don't like you very much at the moment.'

This wasn't up for debate, it was a command. But I hadn't finished playing with his head yet, so I stropped and moped around the room for a good hour until he eventually agreed to accompany me to the nearest shrine, an ancient structure set in a park full of cherry blossoms only a short walk away. Of course, it was a terrible idea. Walking, more shrines, trees. After bringing the wrong map and getting lost in some Japanese, directionless bird sanctuary, my sarcastic comments are out of control ('I thought men were supposed to be good with maps', 'You couldn't organize a piss-up in a brewery', 'Oh, just let me sort everything out again'), he snaps.

'I'm not sure what is wrong with you today, but this wallowing in self-pity is pathetic. Either tell me why you're being such a bitch, or shut up.' The truth was I didn't know why. I just felt sad, and confused and fed up and unloved. 'Because you are really starting to piss me off and I'm not in the mood. Either tell me what I can do, or just stop with this sniping.' I cry until my face is blotchy.

'I mean it now', Russ says determinedly when we finally get back to our hotel room after a super-expensive, short, stressed cab ride, 'I don't want to talk to you and you clearly don't want to talk to me either. So let's just ignore each other, okay?' I nod. 'You've probably forgotten, but it would have been my dad's 62nd birthday tomorrow.

It's going to be hard for me. It's hard for me now just thinking about the call I have to make to my mum tomorrow. It's hard for me just to think about the fact he's not here and that my mum has to wake up tomorrow in their big, cold bed and instead of bringing a cake with candles in, she has to walk round to the church and take flowers. My dad wasn't a flowers kind of guy, but what else can she do? She can't exactly leave him an M&S jumper, can she?'

***

No one tells you that perhaps the most shocking thing about Japan isn't the price of beer, or the noodle bars that only offer eel-based products, but the plethora of large, menacing crows that gather in dark corners and dive-bomb passersby from great heights. Their call is eerie, making the hairs on your arms stand straight on end, and loud, seriously rising above the constant hum of the ever-present traffic. These great oil slicks of the sky give the city a dark air; our beautiful hotel which rises through the clouds up to 51 floors, is circled as a witch's castle would be in a terrifying tale. The crows make Tokyo seem like a place where 'bad things happen', despite its efficiency and cleanliness and modernity. I loved the city – mostly, I admit, for its lack of anything to do except eat and watch people go about their business – but it had a miserable edge to it.

The day was of course awful because of everything that was missing from it. First, of course, Pete. For 61 years – while he was alive – this had been *his* day, and it still was. But there were no birthday phone calls to be made, or surprise parties to be thrown, or restaurant reservations to be kept. Russ was dreading was the call he had to make to his mother, back in Hertfordshire, alone and widowed, with her only son thousands of miles away. Her shattered sentences couldn't hide her devastation. She'd been 'getting better,' as she called it, by her own admission, but today was a set-back. An expected set-back (she too had been dreading it all week, like her son) because Pete had always loved parties and being the centre of attention. His birthday therefore was a big deal – for him and everyone else. He made sure of it! My admiration for my mother-in-law grew even more speaking to her. Her daughter had offered to cancel her planned day (she had a close friend's wedding but would have rather have been at the family home with her mum) but my mother-in-law was determined there was no point just hanging around, moping, doing nothing. 'Your father would have hated that', was a phrase well used. So her daughter got her blessing to carry on with her life, and determined to keep busy, my mother in law had decided to redecorate her bedroom – a cathartic act, not only for new beginnings but a challenge. She'd never put up wallpaper before, and today was the day she's decided. 'Well, I'm good at ironing and it's got to be the same thing, just vertical.'

So as she papered, we decided to finally, in the evening, get out and do something too that would have made Pete proud. He'd never been to Japan but we knew he'd have loved their obsession with karaoke bars. He'd been a DJ and loved pop music.

'I don't know if I'm up for this. I won't sing,' announces Russ. I agree to his demands, but say we should pay up and go into a room for an hour anyway, for this really is *the* one thing we'd been told to do by friends who had visited the city before us. We order a couple of Sapporos to our day-glow den, and flick through the all-encompassing song book. I work my way through a few David Bowie numbers, and a George Michael tune. I'm a terrible singer and my pitchy renditions as least brought a giggle to Russ's lips. I don't know whether he'd truly cheered up or was just desperate to silence his whiney wife, but he warms up, demands the song book, and plugs in a number.

'This is for my dad,' he announces to an imaginary audience. 'He loved this song.' The first beats of Queen's *You're My Best Friend* blast out through the amplifiers. 'Stand up, stand up,' he reaches for me. 'He'd have wanted you to sing too!' The lovely lines about being there for one another, for being there come rain or shine, for being a reason to live, swirl through the air of our little chanteuse' cabin. 'This is for you Dad, Happy Birthday,' Russ announces in the style of a Vegas showman during a gap in the lyrics.

This was all quite jolly. Respectful, reflective and fitting for Pete; the man; the father. But this was also the song that the family had chosen to play after the funeral, as the curtains started to be electronically pulled around his coffin for the cremation to begin. This song was playing as Russ – who had been a remarkable strength to his mother and sister throughout this whole excruciating period – broke down for the first time, weeping into the pew and finally pushing past me and the vicar and out into the open air to breathe again. I remember everything moving in slow motion; aware of Freddie Mercury's voice; aware of Pete's aged father, across the aisle, crying into his handkerchief; aware of how beautifully kept the crematorium was. And then being aware, that even though he'd run away to escape the moment, my husband needed me. So I ran too, out through the same fire exit door, leaving the path and running in high heels down a grassy hill towards my inconsolable beloved. His convulsions rocked me, as I tried to gather him in, whispering meaningless words of comfort into his hair. His exit had caused quite a worry and soon we were joined by the close family members invited to the crematorium.

'Is it done? Is it over? Has he gone?' Russ looked around, asking his uncle.

A grim nod told him it was, and so he wiped his tears away and started walking towards the car, his gaggle of worried, grieving, tear-stained, empty, heart-broken, angry, black-clothed family behind him. He later told me that that moment- letting go of his father's body for the very last time – had been worse than the few minutes after Pete had just died, ten days before the funeral, when he'd helped the nice man from the funeral parlor wrap *the body* in a bag and slug it out to the ambulance. His mother had been distraught by his father lying there in the lounge you see, growing colder and colder by the minute. So rather than waiting for more men to arrive to help, he'd done the job himself. He'd wrapped up his hero in plastic, put him over his shoulder, and put him in a car, while his mother racked with grief, cried into his sister's shoulder. But this moment, in a peaceful, well-maintained crematorium in Essex – the last goodbye – was worse. And that song would mean so much to my husband for that very reason. It was one of his dad's favorites when he was alive, and it was the one he said goodbye to the world with.

***

An Englishwoman, an American girl and a Japanese lady walk into a spa. The Englishwoman (me) doesn't waste any time asking what the rules are so I can follow them correctly without upsetting anyone. No horseplay in the swimming pool, no problem. No dive bombing either, no worries. I can 100% commit to not displaying any aggressive or offensive acts in the spa area in general (because I am British and don't like rocking the boat after centuries of rocking everyone's boats – then stealing whatever was on the boat while flying a Union Jack from the mast). The American checking in next to me is loudly complaining that the rules are ridiculous and she can judge for herself what is appropriate. She continues to test the sound barrier in the changing room, gossiping on her mobile phone (despite them being banned) while bizarrely putting on *more* makeup for her dip in the pool. The Japanese woman is quiet and focused.

When I emerge upstairs to the pool deck, a plethora of worried face in white outfits make a run for me. 'No jewelry', one prim and petite employee announces, eyeing my armful of bracelets ruefully. 'You must wear your hair in a swimming hat, it is not enough to tie it up into a bun (as I had done) and I need to make sure you have no tattoos. We do not allow tattoos into the spa in case they cause offense to other bathers.' Wow, that's a new one. I'm not a fan of any tattoos and so obviously did not have one but many of my friends did, who would seemingly be barred from Japanese bathhouses. 'We consider them not only ugly but quite aggressive and vulgar and we do not people think people should be made to look at them while they are trying to relax.' Well, ok. I don my harsh, tight swimming cap until my cone headedness is greeted with a semi-smile of approval, then submerge myself into the cool water

192

like an egg in a saucepan, swim 30 laps, then head to the relaxation area.

In this bathhouse was a united nations of private parts, a living guide to female forms. Some of the Americans had groaningly large boobs, taut and round like helium balloons, nipples facing skyward as if launching to the moon. They must have cost a small fortune (I'm sure they considered them an investment) and meant a lifetime of sleeping on their backs. These fine Yankee women had no-hair down-there, a nod to their 12 year old selves. The Japanese ladies unanimously sported tiny boobies with enormous nipples the size of light switches… and big, full, beards over their nether regions. I was sort of in the middle, as us Brits tend to be so often these days when we have a superpower either side of us: I had big boobs but they were natural, which meant they nestled into my armpits at night, and my lady garden was trimmed into a generous landing strip, apart from in the Winter, when all hell broke loose. We were, however, all bonded by issues with cellulite, or tummy flab, or varicose veins, or crinkly flesh.

***

We only had a few days left in Japan and despite the fact we were both still feeling ropey and felt a fandango with the flu was on the cards, while finding each other toe-curlingly irritating, we agreed we should get out and see more of the country. The legendary bullet train would take us to Kyoto in two and a half hours, killing two birds with one stone: the boy could have an adventure on a fast moving vehicle *and* it provided the chance to see more temples for a sentimental-sometime-spiritual old broad like me who needed some good luck.

Leaving luxury behind, we check into a cheap (by Japanese standards of course, in reality *everything* is extortionate) Roikan, a traditional Japanese boarding house. A sort of hotel, sort of hotel, sort of family home that provided a touch of the local to wide-eyed explorers such as us. Greeted with a hot pot of green tea, we are ushered up to our cubicle of a room, where we were shown how to use the futon. There was a large space where we could put our backpacks behind the futon, except we couldn't put our backpacks there because that was a sacred space – every room has one! – that had to be left empty at all times.

We were awfully miserable by this point. All four of our nostrils were blocked; we had two tickly throats, eight aching limbs and two poisonous tongues. Still not exactly being the love bugs we'd been during our tougher trials on Komodo Island, we decided to just make our futon (it involved pulling stuff out of a back wall and lying down essentially), have a bath and sleep. We took it in turns to sit, knees up to our chins, in the bath that would really only have fitted a toddler comfortably, dry off, and get wrapped up in the charming traditional kimonos that had been left, neatly folded under the towels, for us to sleep in. We both looked ridiculous – pale, gigantic, husky-voiced Westerners, wrapped in printed fabric bound tightly with decorative sashes. But we loved it and went to bed a bit lighter than we had the previous night. It's hard to keep a straight face when you are lying on the floor, feet pressed against the wall, head touching the opposite one, with your husband in Japanese drag beside you.

***

We decided this would be the last day of the trip when we'd go searching for old buildings filled with monks, golden Buddhas or burning incense. They were all beautiful and lovely of course but they were all melting into one another in our traveler's brains. If you've seen one sitting, standing, lying, praying, life size, gigantic, gold, silver, emerald, wooden, marble, terracotta Buddha... well you've probably seen enough.

Jishu Shrine, a postcard-pretty place from the 1300s, was our destination. I didn't tell Russ that is was also known as Kyoto's love Mecca, Cupid's abode in Japan, for fear he'd run a mile and insist we headed to the more sensible tombs of war etc. Eventually, after a few missteps with the local buses and a long walk up a hill, we made it. Russ was immediately surrounded by young school girls, who handed me camera after camera so they could pose with my husband. I didn't quite understand why they were so keen to be snapped with him and not me, but they made me laugh and all the attention cheered Russ up considerably so I didn't mind and turned tricks as a photographer while they made peace signs and giggled.

The shrine was a colorful Easter egg of distractions, charms and shrieking worshippers. For over 600 years, the love den on the hill had been considered the dwelling place of the god of love and matchmaking. There were bells to ring (to call on your future lover), incense to be lit (to pray for your future lover) and coins to be tossed (to bring luck for your future lover). Despite his current grumpiness, I had the only love I ever wanted, but decided to ring, light and toss anyway, thinking about making the love I had calmer and happier instead of wanting a new one. According to tradition, coupled up adults pray for the happy love lives of their children rather than their own, but needleless to say, being childless, it was all about me. Instead of begging or praying, I instead offered up a truism, a thought that I'd come to realize across the countries, time zones and days of our trip together: I would rather be childless with Russ than have had a child with anyone else. The more I mumbled it under my breath, the more I felt it vibrate through my whole being, the more I looked over at Russ, a few steps away being assaulted by more Harajuku girls in mini-kilts, the more I knew it was true. This was where I stood: I *would* rather be childless with Russ than have a child with anyone else. He was my future and even if no one else came along, between my own life and the life I had built with him, I'd be happy. I insisted on it.

Unable to leave anywhere such as this without a new acquisition, I buy a charm to reflect my mood. There are stalls upon stalls offering up baubles of positivity, promising a good marriage, a good life, good health, good friends, good family, lots of money, lots of children, and also the more specific: a safe delivery of a child, a good grade in an exam, a new job. In the end though I decide on the one that I found the prettiest – a sweetly rainbow-woven thread from which a pink and silver globe covered in tiny ornate flowers dangled. Its meaning? It was just a general charm – it promised good luck. And this is what I needed, I suppose. My future was wide open and without a clear path so why commit my Yen to a narrowly defined cause?

'You love all this shit,' Russ, shook his head as I paid over the money. 'You are nuts. But there is something sweet about it too.' As we descended the hill, through the white faces of Geishas, the tea houses offering cream puffs and the shops splaying fans like peacocks in every color, he continued to look at me, but there was a smile playing on his lips. My fingers clasped on to my new charm in the pocket of my hoody.

***

Russ's hair, which he'd been haphazardly growing for a few months now, was starting to look utterly ridiculous. It *had* gone through good stages on the trip, when the salt water and sea air had given it a textured, tousled look that suited his tan and beachy wardrobe but without the waves and wash of our shoreline excursions, his hair was now resting offensively on his head in the style of a mullet. Yes, my handsome beau now resembled a 1980s footballer. He just needed a diamond stud earring and a *Foreigner* album to be the cheesiest man in Asia.

Yet this unfortunate hairdo, this crowning carnival of chaviness, was the making of us. For it was so ridiculous, I couldn't help laughing at him. And he couldn't help laughing at me laughing at him (and his own reflection, obviously). A week of Japanese shampoo had made it all come to shocking head, excuse the pun, and cheerfully, and with a great relief, it allowed us to re-bond, re-love and re-friend each other on the way back to Tokyo on the bullet train, then on the way to the airport on the Narita Express, and then through customs and on to our plane, headed for Honolulu.

13

America the Beautiful

'The future belongs to those who believe in the beauty of their dreams.'

Eleanor Roosevelt

During our first dip in the huge waves of Waikiki, Russ loses two friendship bracelets. 'It's symbolic. It's happening; the holiday is coming to an end. Our tour is almost over.'

I tell him this is a good thing. We can't travel forever, especially when perhaps our adventures are an excuse to not grow up, make definite plans about the future and accept certain truths. Now, in Hawaii, we stood facing the immense momentum of the Pacific and knew we could move with the flow, together, without drowning.

We'd booked this stage of the trip carefully. It was to be the half way house, to gently ease ourselves back into American life and the brash speediness with which we'd have to do everything. Even in the South, there were expectations that things needed to happen pretty God damn quickly. Here, life was half-American and half-tropical. There were torches lit at sunset every evening instead of lamps being turned on; women wore flowers behind their ear – left if they were taken, right if they were single; men could be spotted along the coast aboard paddleboards; and of course there were people on the street earning money by playing the ukulele or hula dancing. It all felt a little fake though, like we'd entered Polynesian Land at the Epcot Centre. The island desperately needed dollars and the islanders knew tourists paid many dollars to feel like they were somewhere exotic, not actually just holidaying in the 50th state. In reality, it was like Chicago-on-Sea. A city like any other - just with more bikinis.

This isn't to say we didn't instantly fall in love with the place. After our time living on noodles, ant-rice and dodgy water, we were relieved to be back to hygiene and familiar brands. I gorged on US television and newspapers for the first 24 hours, amazed at what I'd missed. Russ was happy to see Club sandwiches on menus again, so gorged on those. Yes, this was what we'd hoped it would be: a sort of middle ground. So while the bucket loads of mainland American tourists felt like they were visiting somewhere tropical and unique, and the handful of Japanese tourists felt like they were visiting somewhere that was, well, American, we had the unique position of seeing it was neither of these things but a thoughtfully contrived mixture of the two.

We laid our backpacks down and decided we'd stay here for a couple of weeks. We could finally unpack! We could live leisurely without rushing to catch a plane, train or bus! So on our second night there, while listening to the ocean, watching the sun drop into the sea and the sky turn into a canvas of pink and lavender strokes, we decided to give ourselves daily questions and discussions, to tie up the loose ends, make new rules and consign unhealthy, negative fears or insecurities to a trash bin.

The easiest thing to tackle first was our relationship. We'd got on well – except for a few mishaps with sunsets in Bali and breakfast goods in Tokyo – and we'd had the 24/7 togetherness to allow us, two relatively newlyweds, to work out the habits we'd formed to take into the future, and the ones not to. So we made a list, a very simple list, of basic rules to keep us on track.

1. Never have a television in the bedroom
2. See our friends more (when Russ was depressed, he hadn't wanted to leave the house, but not seeing his friends had made him even more depressed)
3. Don't publicly berate each other. If one of us does something the other doesn't like, take it up at home, not in front of a crowd.

4. Pay more compliments to each other. We feel all these lovely things but often feel too busy to say them.
5. Ban chocolate and crisps from the house.
6. Cook together after work and eat together. No television. Use more herbs.
7. Work to our individual strengths. We each prefer to do certain things, so split the chores to suit our skills.
8. Never sleep on an argument. It will ruin the next day as well.
9. Appreciate that we are two people *not* two halves making one. Therefore we won't always want to do the same things. That's cool. We have other people to be with us for different aspects of our lives.
10. Love isn't easy but we both committed to this so we should make it work. That sometimes involves saying sorry first, swallowing pride, not doing what you want, making sacrifices and having to share a house with someone you'd love to slap.

Deciding a few days later to construct our Hawaiian Plan for the Future Part II, we head out for huge, steaming cups of hot chocolates, topped off with whipped cream and caramel sauce. The combined deliciousness and sugar spike should have sorted us out. But just as the creamy goodness started working its way into our brain, a smartly dressed woman about my age marched in, clutching a huge coffee table sized book in her hands. The book had the Dalai Lama on the cover, his big face smiling out serenely from under her arm. She was here to protest. Against what no one quite knew but she seemed to be having a lovely time, screaming in people's faces, calling them idiots, pulling out the cords of their laptops and generally turning the typical quiet coffee shop atmosphere rigid with bizarre terror. As her screaming got louder and more personal, two servers from behind the counter stepped forward and politely and firmly asked her to leave. She just got louder. They asked again. She got hysterical and insulting. One of them went to get a security guard. The two of them returned and as the security guard backed her out, towards the door without touching her, the Dalai Lama came crashing down on his head with such force it made an enormous thwack sound ring around the cafe. And then the barista got a pummeling from the grinning Buddhist leader. Russ and I were just stuck in the spot. Pathetically scared, for ourselves and each other, wishing we could crawl into our recycled paper cups. A few more hits and she's out the door. Everyone is ok, just shaken, and then people turn back to their laptops without making a comment. It was a wakeup call. This place was fun, it was pretty, but it wasn't paradise. It was America with a suntan. It struck me as odd that of all the places we'd been to, where pain and unfairness and poverty had been so palpable it got stuck in your throat as you breathed, it was here, in the relative wealth and comfort of USA's utopian ideal, that people were so violently and openly unhappy and disturbed.

'Should we move on?' I asked. 'We can change our tickets, go somewhere else, or go home early?'

But Russ was defiant. 'No, 'we're just tired and shocked that this place isn't exactly like the islands we've inhabited for the last few months. We'll get used to it. We need to! It's more real, in a way. You'll be fine, Sweets, you've got me and nothing will happen to you while you're with me.'

Russ's grandfather was determined we should go to Pearl Harbor while we were in Hawaii. As a 14 year old, he had just avoided fighting in the Second World War but had witnessed the Blitz ravage London from his home in Tottenham and he was thrilled his grandson was getting the chance to pay his respects.

Despite the polished entrance, café and shiny new visitors centre, it was still a haunted, dark place. The USS Arizona was still there at the bottom of the water, entombed in a fishy grave, pieces of its engine poking through the surface as if making a dying bid to be saved, to be remembered. There were two million gallons of oil stored on the battleship when she was sunk in 1941 by the Japanese air force. The liquid is slowly, gallon by gallon, making its way to the surface, marking the water with rainbows, 'the black tears of the mother ship,' a US Veteran mumbled as he stood and mourned for his fallen brothers.

At the far end of the memorial, an open, white structure built over the top of the wreckage and only accessible by boat, is a huge marble slab listing the names of the dead. 23 pairs of brothers were killed that morning. A father and son were lost too. The average age of the murdered American was 19.

As the years went on, many of the survivors had gone back to pay their respects, to pray for the men below, trapped in their watery resting place. Now, as they too were starting to die, at the acceptable ages of 80 and 90, not 18 and 19, they were asking for their ashes to be interred with their shipmates in their sea graves. A special internment wall had been designed and special services were held, when their urns would be plunged into the oily blackness. As one of the rangers who worked there told me, 'the families want them reunited with their ship and their shipmates. They always tell me, "When he was alive, not a day went past when he didn't speak of what happened at Pearl Harbor and about the good friends he lost. He belongs with them. That is right." So we return these old men to sea, to be with the young men they missed so much.'

The saddest story for me was of a young shipmate who was a loving husband and devoted father. In 1937, his wife had given birth to twin girls, Mary and Nancy. Nancy died a few days after birth, while Mary had been healthy enough to leave hospital with her mother after a few weeks of careful observation. The heartbroken father returned on leave to comfort his wife and to take Nancy's ashes off to sea, where he wished to scatter them. He had done this with another daughter's ashes, when she had died a few years earlier and he found it comforting that she was out there, free and at sea, like him. So he took the urn and returned to his ship. He was a religious man and wanted there to be a little ceremony, for Nancy, performed by a chaplain. He waited and waited for a religious man to come aboard. He waited for months, keeping the urn safe in his locker.

Finally, on the afternoon of December 7th 1941, a chaplain was to come to live upon his boat and a ceremony could be held to put his baby girl to rest. But we all know what happened on the morning of December 7th. And this kind, devoted father was killed that morning, while his daughter's ashes were still in his locker. Neither his body nor her urn could be retrieved, so together they still are. Under the sea. Every Thanksgiving since she has been an adult, without fail, Mary returns to Pearl Harbor, to remember the father and twin sister she never knew.

'At least if we can't have children there'll be fewer people to hurt when we die,' Russ concludes after our visit. 'At least, we won't be leaving behind children who will be devastated by our deaths like me and my sister has been over my dad. It will be easier in a way.' It's a strange logic, but I know what he means. Like those people who don't want to fall in love because they'll only get their heart broken. The people who live on an emotional island, cut off from people they could possibly care for. It's just so strange how the unfortunate timing of trying to start a life while another one is ending has thrown up all these painful realizations.

***

Today was the first day of our next attempt, an attempt Russ was *convinced* would work. This would be our month! We did the deed, planted the seed, and my sensible husband wedged a pillow under my hips and made me stay there until my feet went numb.

With extra time on my hands, I picked up a pen and paper to work through some dilemmas in my head: I wanted to work through the dungeons and dragons of my mind to understand this mental block I had that I could *never, ever* get pregnant. I was starting to think that perhaps my problems conceiving were linked to my mental attitude and not just my physical problems. Yes, I had a cyst on my left ovary and yes, I had too much fluid in my womb (nope, I still don't know what that means either) and yes, I was turning 35 in a few months, but come on… I needed to start thinking positive surely. All my life, well since my teens when I'd fainted in a general studies class when the teacher had talked about giving birth, I'd had a deep-seated belief that I would never get pregnant. Not that I'd never be a mum, but that I'd never get pregnant. Perhaps it was the psychology of my uterus I needed to address rather than the diagnosed, visible issues. It turned out my gynecological parts had more issues than *Vogue*.

The first pregnancy I was aware of was my mother's, when I was six. We were all so excited when James arrived, he was a beautiful baby, but around the same time my father – who I had adored, quite wrongfully, often wearing 'Daddy's Girl' t shirts that he'd carefully picked out to spite my mother – left home. I didn't understand why or how back then, I just remember the swap: my mum had a big belly and a baby arrived, but my dad had to leave to make room for him. It was years later, when pushed, my mum told me my father had been having affairs and stealing money from her, as well as mentally abusing her, throughout her pregnancy, and with a new baby to protect she finally knew that enough was enough.

The second pregnancy I was aware of was my mother's again, and this time my cheeky younger brother William joined the family. My mother had got married 11 months before to Keith, a brilliant man who has been a true father – the *only* father – to me and James, and because of her age (she was 38, eek!) she had to get a move on. Again, she has since told me that she'd have loved to have given me and James more time to adjust to our new father before a new brother was introduced, but she just didn't have the *biological* time for such niceties. So within a year, I had a new father, new brother, new surname, new house, new school, new extended family, and new friends. I remember sitting on my bed one day, while my mother's bump was growing bigger and bigger and thinking, 'Mum will be busy with her new husband and her new baby from now on. I have to look after myself. She'll be too busy to worry about me.' And I grew up over night. I mean not totally, and my parents would argue I still haven't grown up now. But I became more independent, more self-contained. So much so that when I started my period, aged 12, I didn't tell my mother for about six months, until she found evidence and confronted me. When it was just me, mum and James in our old house, we'd had a chat about periods and she'd even bought me some brightly-colored, exciting looking sanitary pads on standby. But now, she wasn't just *mine* anymore, and there was a man in the house who I'd only known for a year, and this was too personal to become public knowledge. So that was it: I was ashamed of my period, and I blamed much of my self-imposed distance from my mother on her quick pregnancy and the subsequent arrival of this mischievous little blond brother.

It wasn't until I was reaching the end of my school years that pregnancy became relevant again. This time, it was the sordid matter of classmates mysteriously leaving History class and never coming back. The girl would be spotted a few years later, trudging up and down the local high street, yanking a toddler behind her, often pushing another in a pram. She'd look tired and older than she should, and harder, as if life had taught her a difficult lesson and stamped the results on her shoulders. The boys of course, would get a pat on the back from their rugby teammates and often carry on, like the good girls, to university. The other option was just as stigmatized: the girls would stay in school but the whispers of abortion followed them down the chlorinated corridors and they became easy targets for the boys who wanted a good time; the termination of their pregnancy seeming to show a willingness to have a good time and deal with the consequences on their own. These girls, some of whom were my friends, were left so rocked and insecure by the abortion that they often numbed the pain with the unhealthy attention of bad boys, before going home and crying themselves to sleep.

Then pregnancy disappeared from my mind as I soared into the most freeing, educational and fun years of my life, and living away from home for the first time, at university. And then once my degree certificate was safely framed and displayed in my parents' lounge, I was too busy climbing the slippery media ladder to even think about babies. Even during my first marriage, my being pregnant would have been ridiculous.

And that is how I got here: nearly 35, desperately hoping to get pregnant but unconvinced that my body or mind would ever let me. I thought back to these episodes, tried to look on them with calmness and understanding, and wished them away. I closed my eyes and held my stomach in a tender hug and said to myself, '*there will be a child in here one day.*' And I tried to believe it.

***

Mother's Day! After a phone call to both of our lovely mums back in England, Russ decides to try his hand at boogie boarding while I decide to spend the day contemplating what kind of mother I'd be. Although I hadn't been able to imagine myself pregnant before, I'd always seen myself with a mess of kids around my ankles, a few balancing on each hip – kind of like that first photo of Princess Diana when she was still Lady Di, in the garden of the nursery where she worked, in the see-through skirt. Since I was about 14, I'd kept a list of my favorite boys and girls names in my diary for when the need arose, and since meeting Russ I'd often wondered what kind of child our combined genes would produce: I hoped for his nose and mathematical ability but my fondness for fruit and love of literature.

I hoped I'd be a fair mother. I have no aspirations to be my child's best friend – hopefully I'd raise them to be able to go out into the big, wide world and make friends of their own – but I wanted to be a mother that they knew was fair, that they could trust to make the right decisions for them, no matter what. I wanted to be a mother who could still laugh. I'd seen too many women so bogged down by the daily grind of feeding, washing, cleaning that they forgot – quite understandably – why they'd had these creatures in the first place. I wanted to laugh at my children's mishaps and moments, to have fun with them, not to find anything they did that was not expected or planned an inconvenience or hassle. I wanted to be an encouraging mother. Not a *stage mom* or some pushy monster who forced exams for children years older down the neck of her tiny tot, but a mother who recognized potential and nurtured interests, and would allow her child to explore the world not just with financial backing but with positivity too. I wanted my heart to burst at the first smile, first steps, or the first song. I wanted to tuck a mini me up in bed with a story and a kiss. I wanted to have someone run to me as if I was the only person in the world. I wanted to watch my child sleep as expressions danced across their face. I wanted to get splashed at bath time. I wanted to watch as they chased after their older, braver cousins in the garden on a summer's day. I wanted to curl up on the sofa in the evening with my husband, our house finally a home, knowing that we were all safe and warm and together, and that no one else could disturb us until morning.

What kind of a father would Russ be? 'I'd be present. I haven't waited till my mid-thirties to have a child to just disappear, I want to witness everything. I want to go to football games obviously, take them up to White Hart Lane whenever we can, and to teach them to play football in our back garden. I'll teach them to swim too, as young as possible, so when we go on beach holidays we'll be able to all go in the sea together and snorkel. You'll have to be the firm one if we have a little girl. I have no doubt I will fall madly, deeply in love the minute I see her and she will be able to wrap me totally around her little finger. I'll be a coward in her presence. She'll be able to get exactly what she wants, especially if she looks like you!'

Russ's commitment to being a good father was like manna from heaven. I had bagfuls of father issues, obviously. I had a bad real father, then I had no father, and then I had a step-father who was (*is!*) marvelous and became my dad... but I was always aware this made me different to all of my friends. My mother was the beacon of security throughout my whole childhood, my stabilizer. Single-parent families weren't so common in the early 1980s but she fought against the stereotypes, got a good job as a chef yet still picked me up from school every day. The neighbors gossiped and good friends suddenly disappeared as they feared my mother would be after their husbands, but, despite the inevitable distress, I look back on our five years without a full-time father with fondness.

Because I had the help of my grandmother and various aunts, in time I realized that not coming from a conventional family didn't matter, although I was envious of other girls my age and their conventional family lives. I was aware that Dad not living at home made me different, somehow less fortunate and freakish. My mother was careful not to poison us against our father and the lawyers granted him weekend access. Every Saturday, my baby brother James and I would sit by the front door waiting for his arrival with great anticipation. He bought me a Care Bear every time he let me down. I soon had the whole Care Bear collection.

On the few times he did turn up, the promised visits to the zoo or to a football match never materialized. Instead, we'd be taken to the homes of various new girlfriends and plonked in front of a television. I would be told to keep an eye on James while they disappeared to the bedroom. I felt crushed by his lack of interest. I was convinced I must be irritating, boring or ugly. After all, men are supposed to adore their daughters, as Russ warned me he would adore any daughter we produced. But my real father showed no interest in me and my life. However simple my chatter may have seemed between the ages of six and 10, my heart would break a little every time he ignored me.

My mother, unsurprisingly, wasn't very interested in finding romance after her marriage ended. Between looking after us, running a home and working every day, she didn't have the time or the energy to pursue a relationship. Various men asked her out, and

I remember one exciting Valentine's Day when 50 orchids were delivered to our house from an admirer. As an adult, I can understand she didn't want to introduce a stream of different men to her young children just to improve her self-confidence or social life. Then one day, when I was 10 and James was five, she sat us down and said that a man who came into the restaurant where she worked had asked her out and that she had accepted. This seemed fine to me, rather exciting, in fact, as men were rare visitors to our home. Date night soon arrived and I danced about the lounge trying to get his attention while James, who didn't appreciate the prospect of another man vying for his mother's affection, sulked and threw plastic dinosaurs at him. I decided I liked him for childlike reasons: he had a black car like the one in Knight Rider and he, too, supported Tottenham Hotspur. What else could matter to a 10-year-old?

Their dates became more frequent and, as my natural father's interest in me hit an all-time low - I would go without seeing him for six weeks at a time - Keith became a more positive influence in my life. He paid us the attention we craved and, most important, he did things to make my mum happier than I had ever seen her. The only time I can remember being upset was when I called him Uncle Keith and he told me not to. Growing up as I did, surrounded by aunts, I was just doing what I thought was polite. I didn't realize that a few days later he was going to propose to my mother and that he loved her so much he wanted to take her children as his own. He didn't want to be our uncle - he wanted to be our father.

When my mother told me she was going to marry Keith, I took it as a compliment. In my 10-year-old head, I thought that, for him, getting a beautiful wife and two well-behaved children was a blessing. I didn't realize back then the stigma he had to take on and the unnecessary comments he received from those around him about us being a charity case. Despite this, they were married within a year, and I sat proudly in the front row of a London register office as a bridesmaid, with a beautiful bouquet and vintage velvet frock coat.

Once my new brother William arrived, Keith decided to look into legally adopting us, in an effort to make James and me feel more secure and to protect and equalize our financial futures. Hours and hours of meetings with social workers followed, which made me feel even more different from the new, fabulous friends I'd fought to make in my new town. Deep down, I assumed the thought of having his children adopted would kick my real father into reality. He'd rebel and fight to keep us and the trips to the football would resume. But a social worker told me quite harshly that once he'd established that signing his rights away would mean he wouldn't have any financial responsibilities to us, he practically begged her for the pen.

I have seen my natural father once since. I was about 19 and shopping with a friend when I heard a voice I recognized. I knew it was him and turned round to see what his reaction would be. He carried on his conversation, looked me up and down and turned back again with no flicker of recognition. I felt a wave of nausea and stumbled away before bursting into tears. My friend followed me in horror and couldn't understand my mad ramblings. I'd been so embarrassed about my unconventional double life that I had told no one. Later, I felt relieved he didn't know me, that he had never been a major influence on my life. And Keith has become a wonderful father – and grandfather to James's children – so that no obvious father-shaped holes are left in our hearts. No obvious ones, although this constant white noise in my head about becoming a parent had brought back many of my early fears and insecurities.

That night, in Hawaii, though, Russ said something quite out of the blue that made me appreciate just what a great second chance James and I had been given, and just how lucky we were. Over a cool beer, after a good few minutes of quiet musing looking out at the ocean, he turned to me with a plan. 'Do you think Keith would adopt me?'

My eyebrows knitted, confused. 'It's just that I don't have a father anymore, and I miss that. I want a father figure to talk to and get advice from,' he explains. 'Keith is a rare, great man. To take on somebody's else's children and to love them as his own must be a difficult thing for a guy to do. I don't know if I could do it. But he has this amazing capacity. So can you ask your mum for me? Ask if Keith wouldn't mind if I called him every now and again, like I used to call my dad, to talk about football or to get career advice. Just to be there, really.'

I assured him that my dad considered him to be like a son already, and that he should add his mobile number to his speed dial.

***

'I haven't had my hair cut since my father died, and I think it's time. I think I should chop it off today, I feel ready.' Russ's hair had been a comedic worry for some time, but I was aware of the Samsonite strength he seemed to get from it and had not urged him to do anything about it. He'd shaved his head completely bare in comradeship with his father when he'd lost his to chemo, and now it was down to his neck and over his ears, a physical symbol of the time that had passed. 'Yes, I need to get it cut, its time. A new haircut will represent a fresh start. It will remind me every time I look in the mirror that I have moved on.'

I started to cry with relief. The last few months had been so horrible. There is nothing more terrifying than watching the person you love most in the world crying and depressed when there is nothing you can do about it. 'My father has moved on and so should I. Our tour has made that clear to me. I'm ready for the world.'

With this great news, I started searching for hairdressers in Honolulu. A fresh start couldn't come quick enough.

We decided to leave Hawaii early, probably an unfathomable move to the outside world, but we felt that we'd worked through a lot of stuff here, were exhausted by it, and kind of wanted to get away. We booked flights to Seattle, a city we'd always fancied going to but never had any reason, as a suitable and convenient stop on our way back to Kentucky. Russ fancied climbing the Space Needle, I fancied rebelling against my non-java diet and ducking into one of the city's many famous coffee shops, and we both fancied walking around a new city with a new lease of life.

***

Our first must-see, after we spent a day in bed (yes, doing *that,* this was going to be *the* month, you see) was Pike Place, the famous, old market that had been feeding and watering the city for decades. There was an air of freedom and health to the place that was really quite inspiring. The by-now iconic Obama *HOPE* posters were framed in all the bean houses and diners, and juice bars and flower stalls battled for space amongst the fishmongers and cheese makers. There should be a Pike Place in every city in the world, and that's a fact. The crowd was thinner and quieter than the American Mid-Westerners we'd encountered in Hawaii. And there were lots of pregnant women. Everywhere. There were big bumps, little bumps, tight bumps on stick thin legs, Rubenesque bumps on voluptuous bodies. Rather than quickly and consciously diverting my eyes before they started to mist over with tears, I found I could look at the women and smile if they caught me staring. They all looked beautiful; although I'm sure they didn't feel it: swollen and heavy climbing the many hills of Seattle. For the first time in my life I could imagine the kind of pregnant woman I would be. I'd be appreciative, that's for certain. That was the word my mum used, when she rang me from England as I was in the midst of my depression a few months earlier. 'But Sarah, when you do finally get pregnant imagine how much you'll appreciate it. Imagine just how much you'll love that longed for baby!' I'd certainly be honest. I wouldn't be one of those glib pregnant women who pretend conception is always easy. 'My husband only has to look at me and I'm up the duff!' one woman, on her fourth child, had told me a few months earlier, 'I mean getting pregnant isn't rocket science is it!' That is what I'd always thought... before I'd tried. Now I knew about suffering; of monthly heartbreak; of constantly worrying about bursting into tears when you saw someone pushing a newborn in a pram or acting jealous of a friend if she tells you her good news.

We walked the market, navigated the sculpture park, ate fish and chips and gawped at the Space Needle. Our legs were tired and the rain Seattle is famous for was starting to drizzle down our necks. A cinema ahead looks like the perfect place to take refuge. It was mysteriously quiet for a Saturday afternoon.

'Can I help you?' a smiley, helpful woman rushed over to ask.

'Er, what films are you showing?' I asked, feeling stupid asking such a question in a cinema.

'You're not here for the Seattle International Jewish Film Festival are you?' she shook her head, 'You were expecting Shutter Island.'

We nodded.

'Sorry, the cinema is shut for the Jewish Festival but you are more than welcome to buy a ticket to one of their selected films. We have an interesting one starting in 30 minutes about a woman who loses her boyfriend to a suicide bomber but finds happiness again through her faith.'

We thanked her, contemplated it for a few seconds, before heading out into the rain again. It sounded interesting but another thing we'd worked out on this tour was Russ and I weren't much into the organized religion or faiths of everyone else, we just needed to have faith in ourselves and each other.

14

Blue in the Bluegrass

*'There can be no transforming of darkness into light and of apathy into
movement without emotion.'*

Carl Jung

Two weeks after our return, when our tans were slowly fading and
our backpacks were stowed away in the attic, I gave Russ an offer he
could not refuse.

'You can look first,' I said to him, the minute I'd pulled up my
knickers and emerged from our en-suite bathroom. After all, it was
he who - after our 12 plus fruitless months of trying to conceive –
had the feeling we'd hit the jackpot this month; he who had cycled
as fast as his legs would take him to pick up a couple of pregnancy
tests the minute I giddily admitted that not only was I two days late
but that I was also tired with sore boobs which suddenly weighed
the same as a couple of bags of sugar. When he emerged from the
bathroom, clutching sticks with plus signs, I thought his smile would
explode and take over the universe.

'Really? Really?' I screamed, clinging to him in delighted shock. We'd
done it. We were finally, joyfully, thankfully pregnant. We both
collapsed onto our bed in maniacal giggles and snotty tears, kissing
our mutual wetness and linking fingers. We couldn't believe it, so we
just stared at the plus signs, kissed some more, and returned out
gaze to the plus signs. Parents! We had to tell our parents. In joyful
speaker-phone announcements to England we first told my parents
and then Russ's mum about the fabulous baby we were making.
More than a simple happiness or excitement, a sense of relief

washed over us from all those miles away. The three of them had been more worried for us than they'd ever let on.

Our new expectant life acquired sacred, private rituals immediately. Every Sunday evening in bed, I'd cuddle up into his chest as Russ would read a week-by-week baby book to me in bed, preparing us for what was going to happen to the baby and me over the next seven days, paying careful attention to the *Dad Tip* printed in its own special box on each page, which I encouraged for it seemed to require lots of massages, kisses and general treating of your good lady like a goddess. He'd bring me grapefruit and chips at midnight when the thought of anything else turned my stomach – and even allow me to steal his food after I'd repeatedly told him that I could not eat anything so he shouldn't cook for me. And we spent hours discussing names and laughing about how unfortunate our child would be if it inherited my mathematics skills and his way with words. We agreed on one thing: this much-wanted, already-adored little baby was going to break his dad's heart.

'You'll have to be the disciplinarian,' Russ warned me around eight weeks, when I was at the peak of my projectile vomiting and hormonal weeping to Country music ballads phase. 'I won't be able to keep a straight face or refuse anything Little Sweets wants.' His pet name for me had always been Sweets and now there were two of us he needed to distinguish us. So he'd kiss my tummy – and Little Sweets – goodbye every morning before he went to work, then peck me on the lips – his Big Sweets - and tell me to take care of us both. I had no option. I had to take care of us both: I had to eat small meals every few hours or risk pebble-dashing the bathroom, I could never be more than a short sprint from a toilet. I had to avoid all my favorite foods (imported cheeses, gummy bears and eggs Benedict) and wave goodbye to the wine evenings my girlfriends and I had every week. A good night's sleep was also a thing of the past: my bladder would allow me two hours of uninterrupted snooze if I was lucky. I was up and down like one of Gordon Ramsey's mood swings. But it was all worth it. I adored being so sick and tired from it all because it meant it was real. Russ adored looking after me while I was sick and tired because it meant he could be useful in a process in which he, otherwise, felt redundant.

At ten weeks, we went to the doctors for a check-up and to hear the heartbeat. Russ recorded our baby's rapid heart on his iPhone and emailed it to our parents and siblings back home in England. The messages came rushing back. My mum had cried on hearing it. My mother-in-law couldn't stop replaying it. Both my sisters-in-law wrote back that they couldn't wait for their children to have a little cousin. At this point we hadn't told the whole world our amazing news. There is an enforced secrecy in pregnancy today, a rule that states you can't tell everyone until you've hit the 'safe' 12 week mark when the likelihood of miscarriage has dramatically reduced from 25% before 6 weeks to 0.6%. This state of first-time motherhood is so blissful and exciting– despite the exhaustion and sickness – that I was in a quiet denial that anything could go wrong, I felt too powerfully ghastly to think this was a risk for me though. The baby had taken over my body. I was purely its vessel now, and it wasn't going anywhere.

When we did hit the 12 week mark, we celebrated by telling the world and its mother. I happily told the waitress in my most-regularly haunted restaurant why I could no longer enjoy their blue cheese salads while Russ's football team took him out for beers after their game to prematurely wet the baby's head. Everyone was so happy for us – especially those who had shared our infertility fears. At last my sudden and bizarre abhorrence of coffee, fast food, late nights and margaritas was explained. At this point I was halfway through my summer term, studying for a Masters in Literature, and was thrilled to be taking a course on the 'cult of motherhood'. I could at last understand everything the female writers from the 19th century felt: I was part of their gang.

Because of my apparent dotage (I would be 35 years old when the baby arrived), my pregnancy was deemed high risk for genetic disorders so along with our first scan at 12 weeks and 2 days, the doctors performed a Nuchal Translucency procedure on me to test for Down's and other such issues. As the faces of the medical staff turned ashen around me, I knew something was wrong especially when the ultrasound technician left the room, returning immediately with my doctor and a nurse.

'The baby has increased fluid behinds its neck,' our usually jolly doctor informed us flatly.

'Is that a good thing?' Russ was still willing the best but I remembered from his reading a few Sundays previously that this meant the very worst.

'I'm afraid not. The fetus has cystic hygroma, a genetic abnormality which greatly increases chances of Down's and Turner's Syndrome and other fatal defects. You need to see a specialist immediately,' was her reply. 'And start thinking about your options: abortion and learning about what it means to have a Down's child.' At this point, she was hinting that perhaps - if we were blessed with being the luckiest people on earth, the baby could survive but she implied the best thing that could happen to me now was to miscarry naturally, for my own physical and mental health, rather than because she didn't think I could cope with a Down's baby, I'm sure. Pathetically, I swooned on the hospital bed - my belly still exposed and covered in ultrasound gel - and had to be fed juice while being cooled with a flannel. Russ swore under his breath and shook his head, while asking any medical person he could find what they thought - was this as serious as the doctor was making out, could she be wrong....? He then drove home in silence while I sat weeping beside him, clutching my tummy, willing with every part of my being that we'd have good news – it had been a mistake! – at our appointment with a fetal specialist three days later.

Our doctor had told us we could look up cystic hygromas on the internet to get more information. 'But be careful and don't believe everything you read,' she'd warned us. Russell who that evening had logged on was quite vehement in his belief that I should not look at anything at all. 'I've seen things, things I will never forget. And I don't think it will help you to think of our baby that way. Please promise me you won't look', he urged me. But what is a distraught pregnant woman with a few days of nothingness ahead of her to do except look for any sign of hope or change? And so I spent the next 72 hours at my computer, trying to understand our chances of this being a viable pregnancy. I learnt that cystic hygromas were a chromosomal defect that resulted in lymphatic malfunction and, in serious cases where the pockets of fluid had spread across the body and were thicker than 6mm, there was a 99% mortality rate. Along with the scientific facts, were horrific images of tiny, dead babies, distorted grotesquely by their misfortune? Sometimes a photo would pop up on screen and I would cry so loudly that I deafened myself, or read such sad stories written by desperate pregnant women like me that I'd hyperventilate in agony. Yet still, during this awful waiting game, I stayed on my organic healthy diet, avoiding anything that could harm my baby. I'd whisper to my belly, 'come on Little Sweets! Get better and prove the doctors wrong'. Russ would come home from work and find me slumped in my home office, computer screen glaring while I lay, head on my desk, surrounded by used tissues and piles of papers and little fluorescent sticky notes with statistics, and phone numbers, and definitions on them.

After 72 agonizing hours of waiting and weeping, the specialist provided us with a frankness and kindness that I will always be thankful for. 'This fetus has zero chance of survival,' he said, explaining why he advised against even going through with the amniocentesis or CVS test that would provide us with extra information. 'The fetus has some of the largest cystic hygromas I have ever seen, and not just around its neck and brain but around its chest and stomach too. And the heart is deformed. This fetus will die inside you within weeks or months, and for your health and future fertility I recommend you eliminate it immediately.'

An abortion? My only options were to abort this loved little baby or to have it die inside me? I have always been pro-choice so the idea of abortion didn't appall me morally but I didn't feel I was being given a choice. This wasn't the black and white scenario the pro-choice and pro-life activists like to imagine when they're deciding who to terrorize that day. I had always felt strongly that women had the right to decide what to do with their own body but had carefully avoided a situation where I had gotten pregnant and not wanted to keep the child.

As soon as the news sank in, Russ and I knew an abortion was the only way I could cope – how could I function as a rational, sane woman knowing my baby could die inside me at any moment? I was petrified of leaving it too late for a D and C and being forced to deliver a dead baby, a nightmare a dear friend from university had been through a few years earlier and was still tormented by till this day. 'If there is no hope for the baby, allow them to take care of it as quickly as they can,' she pleaded with me over the phone from her home in England. 'Waiting for the baby to die and then having to deliver it was the worst experience of my life. But I already had two healthy girls. Please don't let this be your first experience of childbirth. You may never recover.' We cried on the phone together for an hour, weeping for each other and the two lost babies who we would never have in our lives. *I hope no one I love ever has to go through this,* I thought at the time, *but I'm so blessed to have my friend's wisdom with me now. Without her, I would be even more alone and confused.*

I remained strong in our decision until the next day, when I was dressed in my pale blue hospital gown and told to lie down on the gurney. The anesthetist was struggling to get the IV into my arm because I was crying so much, the tears soaking my cheeks and neck. I could hear my husband, just outside the curtain, on the phone to my devastated mother in London, assuring her that I would be ok, his voice cracking as he struggled to keep his own pain hidden so not to upset her even more.

'We really wanted this baby,' I felt the need to explain to the nurse. 'We'd been trying to get pregnant for a while. My father-in-law has just died from cancer and we really thought this baby was a positive sign that our lives were improving; that my husband could be truly happy again.'

'Are all your family in England? That must be hard,' she replied, as she started to administer some drugs to calm me down. I was near on hysterical at this point, trembling with fear and grief, shaking from a coldness that I had never felt before. An icy freeze that had sunk into my bones.

'They are but by some good luck my mother-in-law, who I adore, and my good friend Hayley are coming to visit over the next few weeks. And we are lucky to have really great people around us here in Kentucky, new friends who have been supportive and sweet and who I already know I can rely on even though I've only lived her for 18 months. And my husband', I looked under my cubicle curtain, to where I could see his feet. I could hear him quietly weeping; 'he is the most amazing person in the world. I'm just happy to have him.'

She shook her head. 'But are you religious?'

'No.' If our 3 month trip around Asia had taught me anything it was that peace and salvation – for me – came from within and from the people around me, not by some wonderful hope in faith or invisible guidance by an unknown entity.

'But you believe in God?' she assumed, and I just nodded wearily, unable to argue in my current state. If God was the name for the love shared between family and friends, perhaps I believed in it. If God was the force that made flowers bloom and rainbows appear, then perhaps I believed in it. God in the conventional sense – the sense the nurse meant, a man in the cloud who decided what we could or could not do – not so much. But she was a middle-aged lady in Kentucky and a theological discussion could get me nowhere and would prove little to either of us at this moment, so I just gave her another nod.

'Good. Because you may think your husband, your family or your friends can help you now, but the only person that can help you after this is God.' As the drugs started to take effect and my breathing slowed, she bent over and whispered, 'so you'd better start praying for your soul.'

Although the nurse did her best to preach her truth and save my soul (from the goodness of her heart, I honestly believe), I knew *my* truth. I just remember thinking how unthinkably cruel she was to undermine my support network at a time when I needed it most.

I'm not sure living in Kentucky was the perfect place to be while going through this experience. I was forced to drive by giant billboards with photographs of fetuses on them and pull up behind cars with "Pray to End Abortion" bumper stickers. I wouldn't have had to endure these spiteful reminders in London, or in New York, the crazy city I was once desperate to escape. Not everyone in trh South has fundamental views of course, but those that do seem to scream the loudest. A friend of mine in Georgia had been to an abortion clinic a few months before and been abused by protesters outside. She was devastated, on the eve of her 40th birthday, that impossible circumstances meant she had to end perhaps her last chance of having a baby. Her boyfriend has told her that unless she aborted their baby he would kill himself. She felt she had no choice. Did she really deserve to be told she would burn in hell? Thankfully, because I had good health insurance and medical approval, I could avoid that scenario and go to a local hospital. In my fragile state, I don't know how I would have coped.

Our baby was to be due on Christmas day. I doubted that once joyous day could ever feel the same after this loss, there will always be a shadow of 'what ifs'. Our families were quick to hope that we will get over it; especially if and when we do conceive and go on to have a healthy child. We knew already that if we did, we would value it even more than we would have done before. We thought our struggle to conceive had taught us something about the meaning of life, and patience, and being strong, but this whole living nightmare had raised our pain threshold to another level. We felt more than ever before than a healthy baby is life's biggest blessing, and we had sadly learnt that an unhealthy one is its biggest curse. If I had learnt anything from this whole experience, other than what it *actually* feels like to be driven insane with grief, it is that women need to support each other, talk openly about this secret topic and have faith in whichever support network will get them through this personal decision, be it family, friends and inner strength, or a God who listens to their prayers.

The weeks following my abortion passed in a blur of emptiness. I was mentally *and* physically empty. My swollen breasts and belly slowly deflated but the pain remained as prominent. My husband no longer kissed my tummy as he left for work each morning. I feared seeing newborn babies in the street in case I burst into tears. Pregnant women seemed to pop up everywhere but I was no longer part of their gang. My heart felt like it was too heavy to carry on beating. I couldn't concentrate at school anymore; in fact, I'd deliberately think of other less painful things while the students around me discussed the mother as a literary heroine. I had to sit through one seminar where my fellow students philosophized about how the frequency of stillborn babies affected feminism in the 19th century in a very cold manner that I found impossible. My cheeks flushed a deep fuchsia as I pulled my hair out from my ponytail, to cover my teary eyes from the class. I'd told my professor loosely what had gone on – that I'd lost a baby at 13 weeks – because I'd had to miss two classes. I was amazed she let the pointless discussion take place. But it was also one of my first insights into how women that have not been through any pregnancy trauma can sometimes be completely unaware of the devastation and gaping hole a lost, unknown baby can cause. Some friends were sympathetic for a few weeks and then I'm sure they assumed I was over it. After all, I never actually *knew* my baby. I'd never held it, or named it, or nursed it. I didn't want to explain why it had mattered so much and their unintentional cruelty was just that: unintentional.

Russ and I clung on to each other even tighter than normal during my recovery time, shell-shocked by the strange unfairness of it all and the physical changes I was going through. For two months after the operation, we could not make love – not that either of us felt inclined to anyway – and I had to follow a list of other strange no-nos: I couldn't take a bath, lift heavy weights, run up stairs, or drink too much. All that was left of our little baby was a collection of memorabilia hidden away in the bottom drawer of Russell's beside cabinet (our positive pregnancy tests, the blue crosses still visible; the baby books he used to read to me from every Sunday night; a CD of the baby's heartbeat at 10 weeks and an ultrasound photo) and this bizarre list of things I couldn't do. Our baby hopes, ripped-up hearts and dreams for a sweeter future were shut in that same bottom drawer too, until we could start trying to conceive again.

Eight weeks after the traumatic removal of Little Sweets, our kind and honest doctor told us that everything had recovered nicely, that my uterus and womb looked perfect and that we could start trying for another child whenever we wanted to. For another month after that, we were too numb to even think about another baby, let alone have sex. My body had become something painful to us both. The love-making that had once filled us with hope (and sometimes impatient frustration) was now a reminder of horrifying pain. We wanted a child so badly but we had to remove the psychological barricades before we could attempt to make a second little baby.

My mentality, when faced with a struggle, was to run away. To escape. Russ's had been the same. So it was no surprise that after a dreary summer of bleached-out sunshine and too long days, he came up with an idea that he thought could help us both. This time we wouldn't run – we would drive away. Our ancient, decrepit Volkswagen Jetta had broken down for good so we'd bought a new car: a white pepper Mini Cooper, a car so sweet we both smiled whenever we looked out of our front door and saw it waiting for us on the driveway. It reminded us of England, a little symbol of Blighty in Kentucky.

'Let's go off somewhere. Let's see some new cities. Forget about the last few months by making new stories and planning new things,' he suggested one Thursday evening. 'We have no plans, we can go tomorrow.' We'd been low-key and anti-social since we'd lost the baby, so we weren't expected anywhere by anyone or to do anything in particular. 'Let's drive to Memphis. I've always wanted to see Graceland, and listen to some Blues on Beale Street. Then we can stop off in Nashville and get some BBQ and go Honky Tonking. We could even make our way down to Chattanooga and sleep on the Choo-choo. It's a hotel now. And from there we could go to Atlanta, visit some friends, and eat some peaches. Let's reclaim this summer before autumn arrives. It won't make us forget, but it will make us smile again. I'm convinced.'

So we packed up and headed off the next day, armed with two cowboy hats and a travel bag full of hope. After a five hour drive South-west from Louisville, we got to The Peabody Hotel in downtown Memphis – an old grand palace of a place, complete with famous ducks who swim in the lobby fountain and a man who plays Noel Coward songs on a piano by the cocktail bar. We already felt better. Our Asian trip had got us into an amiable companion state, where we actually worked well together while lost, confused, or stuck in traffic. We dumped our bags and headed out on to the street. First stop: Rendezvous for some Memphis ribs and coleslaw and a few glasses of wine. It was the first time I'd had a drink for a long time, and my head instantly whooshed into a relaxed and happy state. Russ looked more carefree than I had seen him for months as he munched on a pulled pork sandwich, handsome and strong in a way he hadn't looked since he'd had had to watch me go through the abortion.

'Your carriage awaits, m'lady,' Russ ushered me from the BBQ joint into a fairy-lit Cinderella coach, which was over-priced and completely tacky but adorable all at the same time. We took our horse-drawn ride to Beale Street, kissing in the back seat below a canapé covered in embroidered hearts and fake flowers, and emerged onto the Soul-effused street to a cacophony of trombones and deep voices, fighting for attention from the different bars. We stopped in a few places, for a few drinks and a listen, admiring the various women who were inebriated enough to dance at the front on their own or sing along with the professionals. We then took the short walk back to The Peabody, hand in hand and ready for a good night's sleep. We dozed off listening to the BBC World Service, a new trick we'd engaged for the last months, when dark thoughts kept us awake into the early hours of the morning. We preferred to hear about global problems than the domestic ones we were having at home. Our bodies sank into the crisp sheets, the black-out curtains shielding us from the lights of Memphis.

In the morning, I am awoken with a distant, lovely feeling: Russ had huddled over to my side of the bed, pressing his naked self against me and stroking my hair. With light kisses, he makes sure I'm awake and turns me towards him with a smile.

'I love you, honey. So much. I don't know what I'd do without you.' As he pushed his face into my arms and wrapped his around my torso, I felt that we were making progress. With him, I would be okay. If no one else ever came along, I would survive as long as I had him. I wiped away a few tears, tears of happiness rather than sadness for the first time in a long time: we'd made it through the dire path of losing a pregnancy and had emerged even more in love for it. We kissed and held each other tight for the longest time and as the hustle and bustle of the hotel started to make it known to us, in our tiny, darkened hotel room, we made love. And it was lovely. And it was just for that reason alone: to make love.

***

We dressed and went to Graceland, to gawp at Elvis's carpet-covered Jungle Room and rhinestone stage outfits; then journeyed to Nashville to party with newly-engaged friends on Honky-Tonk Alley, slow dancing to Country bands and stealing kisses next to the Dolly Parton display case in the Country Music Hall of Fame. We made the journey directly south to the Chattanooga Choo-choo, where we were presented with crystal champagne flutes to commemorate the train's 100th anniversary and drunkenly bought fridge magnets of all fifty states in the ubiquitous souvenir shop. Then our final stop in our Mini adventure was to Atlanta, to visit my old wonderful deputy Katie from my OK! Magazine days in New York, who now worked at CNN and gave us a backstage tour of the studios, then took us to sample about 100 fizzy drinks at the Coco-cola world headquarters. We drove back tired, happy and more in love than ever. I always used to try and persuade myself that *what doesn't kill you makes you stronger* and three months after the most upsetting experience of my life, during a time when I was at my happiest; I was starting to realize that could be true.

***

Two weeks later, I instantly recognize the sweeping exhaustion and sore boobs that I'd felt that one time before, over six months earlier. This time, we go to the chemist together, not quite believing what we could be about to discover.

'This would be unreal if we were pregnant,' Russ enthused, grinning and practically hopping up and down as I peed on the stick in front of him. 'This would mean it was meant to be. After all the planning and hoping and worrying we went through trying to conceive before, and then the heartbreak of losing Little Sweets, I feel we deserve this. It feels right.'

The test shows positive. Rather than jumping around and kissing as we had with our first baby, we both sit on the bed, humbly.

'I feel so lucky,' I turned to my teary husband and snaked my fingers through his on my lap. 'I feel shocked, and weird, but I feel so lucky.'

'Oh Sweets,' he says as we both burst into tears and he bends down and kisses my tummy.

Being pregnant after such a traumatic experience isn't all hearts, bells and flowers. It's stressful; terrifying. We were unable to celebrate as we had done the first time, and we resisted the comforting little rituals that we'd performed before. We didn't want to tempt fate. So the baby books stayed hidden in Russ's beside drawer and I resisted any cravings I might have otherwise indulged. We didn't tell anyone except our parents and siblings, who also exercised nervous caution rather than the overwhelming outflow of excitement that they had with our first baby.

'It can't happen again, honey. The doctors said what happened before was one in 500,000. We were just very, very unlucky. This will make the baby – this lovely little baby – all the more special.'

Russ was right. The value we placed on my expanding tummy was immeasurable. We would have loved it anyway, of course, but now, we took every twinge and tingle with a deep gratitude. I loved projectile vomiting and not getting a good night's sleep and not many people can say that. Mingled in with this promise of new life and grief for losing the little life we had loved before, was an immense sense of togetherness. Undoubtedly, Russ and I were more in love than we'd ever been. Going through something so painful had brought us closer. I respected his kindness towards me, he admired my strength. And together we were able to admit that we'd learned yet more lessons about what matters in the world, what one's life should really be about. We would not have wished the pain of losing a baby on anyone.

'We took one for the team,' Russ would say when we reflected on my previous pregnancy. 'Hopefully our bad luck means that another couple who wouldn't cope so well won't have to. The universe knew we could cope.'

The 12 week scan was horrific. I felt mildly envious of the other women, waiting in line with me, who were able to smile and plan and get excited without knowing how such a joyous event could break your heart.

'Ah, I remember you two,' the ultrasound technician greeted us as we walked into the darkened room. 'What happened before? Did the baby have Down's?' She flipped through my files to look for the answer, while tears started to drip down my cheeks.

'Yes,' I replied.

'Well, yes and no, not really,' Russ added. 'We didn't get as far as learning too much about the Down's. There was a heart problem and other things...'

'Ah, right. Well at least you're pregnant again now,' she continued brusquely, her throw away comment being once we'd heard echoed around a lot the previous week. People seemed to assume that this new pregnancy meant we could forget about our last baby. On the contrary, despite the immense blessing of our quick conception, we were still heartbroken and we discussed on an almost daily basis the guilt we felt at our hurry to move on.

Seconds later our new baby was up on screen, wriggling and spinning on its head. I felt my first glimpse of being the parent of a naughty child.

'I can't take the measurements or get a clear image until it keeps still,' the technician said, asking me to lean forward, lean back, cough, walk around, anything to get this active little tyke to keep still. I loved seeing it, the baby's break dancing. Our last baby hadn't moved in the ultrasounds, it just lay in my womb motionless. After half an hour, the baby decided to cooperate and all the crucial measurements were made. Everything looked perfect. That was my doctor's word later, 'perfect.' A week later, the Nuchal Translucency blood test results came back and that word was repeated down the phone line. Perfect.

Feeling our shoulders unclench, we told our wider circle at 14 weeks. The outpouring of support was lovely and made the baby's life more real to us. We were still scared, but I was getting the feeling that a good parent feels this worry for their offspring every day until they die. I had a reason to be overly nervous, but this feeling of wanting to protect your child was natural for everyone.

As the day of our first baby's due date got nearer, which coincided with the 18 week scan of my current pregnancy, I had a setback and spent a few days in tears – grief for my lost pregnancy and fears for my new one overwhelmed me and I was unable to sleep. Once again, I leaned on a friend who had been through the same trauma, in an email:

I feel like I'm going mad, because everything should be so fun now but two things - please tell me if you felt the same – but two things have just hit me really hard. We have our 18 week scan on Wednesday when we should find out the sex, but we're both so scared. We're so nervous. We're not looking forward to it at all really, though we're pretending to. We thought having the good 12 week scan would make it better but it hasn't. Did you and Steve feel that? Secondly, our first baby was due in 10 days time. It could have healthily been with us by now if everything had been ok. And I'm so sad. I'm so grateful we got pregnant again quickly and I'm nearly half way along, but I just hurt so much knowing that this date is looming. Did you feel that? I feel like I'm ungrateful, or miserable. I just need to know I'm not going mad? That this is normal. Love you lots. Sorry for this outburst.

My dear, old friend replied immediately:

Oh bird, it's all so totally normal. I remember being terrified of the 18 week scan, terrified even during labor, in case something had been missed. Having a baby is a really scary, terrifying time anyway, there's so much that can go wrong, but after losing a baby all those fears are far worse. Plus, all your hormones and maternal instincts for the baby are growing inside you, it's all so new. I really feel for you my darling, but these are totally normal feelings my love. Statistically, if something was wrong, you would have seen it on the first scan, but it still won't stop you worrying, it is so, so normal. And of course you're going to think about the first baby's due date. It's the most natural thing to do in the world. I thought about our baby's due date, and then his first birthday, then his second birthday, etc. It was only a couple of weeks ago that he would have been four years old and

I thought about it lots and felt so, so sad. I don't think about him all the time like I did after it first happened, but there are days like the termination date that bring it all back hard. I think you've held it all together amazingly well, considering all you've been through. You've always been such a strong, brave person, but you need to accept these are normal feelings and if you want to feel sad, be sad. Don't try and ignore it, or feel bad because you're carrying another baby... you still need time to mourn the first and then you'll be able to be happy again and look forward. Think positive.

It felt great to be understood and to know I was normal. Pepped up by these feelings of shared grief and love, a slow, creeping sense of excitement about the 18 week scan started to warm up my heart.

***

'Do you want to know what it is?' The high risk specialist our normal doctor had sent us to asked us as soon as our baby burst onto the screen, 'because I don't think this one wants to hide it!'

'It's a boy,' Russ and I squeal in unison. It was obvious.

'He's built just like his father,' Russ laughed, making the joke countless fathers of little boys have made up and down the land since time began.

'He's an active little thing too,' the doctor added. 'He does not want to keep still this one. He's going to be trouble.'

'Again, like his father,' I joked, unable to cry for once – my first experience of not doing so in one of these ultrasound moments.

'Well, even if he's a handful, he's a perfect handful,' the doctor added, measuring everything from his blood flow to his heart beat. 'He's the average weight but he's a little taller than average. But looking at you two that's hardly a surprise.' She printed out a dozen black and white screen grabs and wiped my tummy clean of the sticky, cool jelly. 'See you soon. But don't worry. Everything looks wonderful and your baby is beautiful.'

She leaves us in the room alone to gather our hearts and things, and we cuddle and grin at each other.

'A boy feels right,' Russ says, laying a hand gently on my tummy. 'I lost my father but now I get to be a father to a son, and like my dad, I'll look after and take him up the Spurs and teach him how to play football and tell him to look after his mum. I feel like the circle is complete now. I feel like my father's name is going to live on. I'm going to give everything I have to you and our little boy.'

He gently leads me to our Mini in the car park, grinning all the way, and seats me carefully in the passenger side, before calling his mum to tell her the great news about our much-hoped for, much-imagined, little Master Moffett, the product of every positive thought we'd ever had. Our Ameri-karma baby. The boy we couldn't wait to meet.

***

William George Peterson Moffett arrived on a warm afternoon in May, the perfect 60th present for my mother-in-law, who shares the same birthday. Our little Kentuckian has the biggest, most beautiful blue eyes in the world.

Printed in Great Britain
by Amazon.co.uk, Ltd.,
Marston Gate.